Rhetoric and Compositic

An Introduction

Rhetoric and composition is an academic discipline that informs all other fields in teaching students how to communicate their ideas and construct their arguments. It has grown dramatically to become a cornerstone of many undergraduate courses and curricula, and it is a particularly dynamic field for scholarly research. This book offers an accessible introduction to teaching and studying rhetoric and composition. By combining the history of rhetoric, explorations of its underlying theories, and a survey of current research (with practical examples and advice), Steven Lynn offers a solid foundation for further study in the field. Readers will find useful information on how students have been taught to invent and organize materials, to express themselves correctly and effectively, and how the ancient study of memory and delivery illuminates discourse and pedagogy today. This concise book thus provides a starting point for learning about the discipline that engages writing, thinking, and argument.

Steven Lynn is Louise Fry Scudder Professor and Senior Associate Dean of the College of Arts and Sciences, University of South Carolina.

Rylan Nguyen

Rhetoric and Composition

An Introduction

Steven Lynn
University of South Carolina

CAMBRIDGE
UNIVERSITY PRESS

CAMBRIDGE
UNIVERSITY PRESS

University Printing House, Cambridge CB2 8BS, United Kingdom

One Liberty Plaza, 20th Floor, New York, NY 10006, USA

477 Williamstown Road, Port Melbourne, VIC 3207, Australia

314-321, 3rd Floor, Plot 3, Splendor Forum, Jasola District Centre, New Delhi - 110025, India

79 Anson Road, #06-04/06, Singapore 079906

Cambridge University Press is part of the University of Cambridge.

It furthers the University's mission by disseminating knowledge in the pursuit of education, learning and research at the highest international levels of excellence.

www.cambridge.org
Information on this title: www.cambridge.org/9780521527941

First published 2010

A catalogue record for this publication is available from the British Library

Library of Congress Cataloging in Publication data
Lynn, Steven, 1952–
  Rhetoric and composition : an introduction / Steven Lynn.
    p. cm.
  Includes bibliographical references and index.
  ISBN 978-0-521-82111-7 (hardback)
    1. English language–Rhetoric–Study and teaching.   2. Report writing–Study and teaching.   3. Critical thinking–Study and teaching.   I. Title.
  PE1404.L96 2010
  808'.042071–dc22
  2010033342

ISBN 978-0-521-82111-7 Hardback
ISBN 978-0-521-52794-1 Paperback

For Annette and Anna

Contents

List of illustrations

Acknowledgments

Some years ago I proposed a collection of essays on rhetoric and composition to Ray Ryan at Cambridge, thinking that it would be easy enough and fun to renew some relationships, initiate others, and gather a useful introduction to the field. Dr. Ryan was interested instead, he said, in a single-author introduction to the field. Having crossed over to the dark side of administration, and spread myself more thinly by dabbling in science fiction, nanotechnology, eighteenth-century rhetoric, Samuel Johnson's eyesight, and science and religion (not to mention table tennis and bluegrass fiddling), I doubted I could write such a book – but I knew that several of my colleagues could, including especially Christy Friend. So Christy agreed to "help me" (meaning in my mind that I would hitch a ride on her intellect), and she participated in the early crucial stages in conceiving and planning this book. All the problems here however, as the author's standard disclaimer goes, are my own, as Christy became trapped in the timewarp forcefield that is directing a large first-year English program (not to mention two daughters and a dashing husband). A more reasonable person would have given up this project – there is, I discovered, a very good explanation why there hasn't been a book quite like this one previously, despite the obvious need – but I was driven to write this book by Dr. Ryan's fiendishly clever manipulations, by my own experiences of the absence of such an introduction, by the encouragement and exasperation of my exceedingly patient and wonderful wife and daughter, and by the need to focus on something more constructive than my father's declining health. This book has been a good friend to me in various hospital and hospice rooms, through some very long nights and gloomy sunrises. I say this not to court any forgiveness or lowered expectations, but simply as a way of acknowledging that my father's elegant courage and pervasive desire to be useful inspired me to press on. And that this book, although it gave me fits, has been very good for me, and I sincerely hope that it is useful for others.

In addition to Ray, Christy, Anna, Annette, and Benjamin, I am also indebted to my colleagues in the English department. I've learned much from reading and talking with the Davids (Cowart, Miller, and Shields), Nina Levine, John Muckelbauer, William Rivers, Chris Holcombe, Susan Courtney, Rebecca Stern, and many others. I'm also deeply appreciative to Dean Mary Anne Fitzpatrick for her superb guidance and leadership. My fellow academic deans, Tim Mousseau and Roger Sawyer, kept me out of some trouble and provided good cheer. My staff assistant, Latasha Middleton, and my research assistant, Pang Li, were industrious and imaginative in their efforts to help me. Lisa Meloncon at the University of Cincinnati and Philip Sipiora at the University of South Florida provided excellent responses to drafts of the manuscript, as did the anonymous reviewers for Cambridge University Press. I deeply appreciate Lynn T. Aitchison's careful copy-editing. My graduate-school colleagues at the University of Texas – Thomas Miller, Cynthia Selfe, Philip Sipiora, Brooks Landon – have inspired and educated me in various ways over the years. We were all privileged to study with James L. Kinneavy, and even though this book is a very pale reflection of his erudition, I continue to be inspired by his example. At Texas, Kinneavy, along with Maxine Hairston, Steve Witte, Lester Faigley, John Trimble, John Rusckiewicz, and John Walter, helped to lay the foundation for the emergence of Rhetoric and Composition as an academic field, convincing generations of graduate students that the history and pedagogy of writing and argument ought to be widely understood and studied. There was a twinkle that would come into Kinneavy's eyes whenever he was about to make some

mind-boggling connection, between say medieval grammarians and
Gilligan's Island, that reminded me of the look in my dad's eyes
when he would realize that a few innovative holes bored here and
there would render the instructions-for-assembly unnecessary.

Jan Steen, "Rhetoricians at the Window," The Philadelphia Museum.

1 The open hand: Meet Rhetoric and Composition

> Why was it necessary to imagine freshman English as separate –
> as different enough from the other English, or the other Englishes
> represented in the curriculum, to require a separate professional
> organization?
>
> David Bartholomae, Chair's Address to the 1988
> CCCC Convention (172)

> So we must keep trying anything and everything, improvising, bor-
> rowing from others, developing from others, dialectically using one
> text as comment upon another, schematizing; using the incentive to
> new wanderings, returning from these excursions to schematize again,
> being oversubtle when the straining seems to promise some further
> glimpse, and making amends by reduction to very simple anecdotes.
>
> Kenneth Burke, *A Rhetoric of Motives* (265)

This book is an introduction to a field, an emerging (although over
2,500 years old) and especially exciting (although often technical
and service-oriented) academic discipline. Although not everyone
would agree that "Rhetoric and Composition" is the best name for
this field, it is in some sense situated (most people would agree)
at the intersection of the art of persuasion (or "rhetoric") and the
process of writing (or "composition"). Narrowly conceived, this is
a field that is predominantly North American, focused mostly on
higher education, arising in the latter half of the twentieth century.
More expansively, this is a field that extends into every aspect of
communication, from the beginnings of learning to the end of life,
worldwide, throughout history, perhaps extending even beyond the
human species.[1] On the one hand, a surprisingly small proportion
of people outside of this field seem to be aware of even the most
fundamental research in it – as much of what passes for instruction
in "Language Arts" or "English" or "Communication" appears to

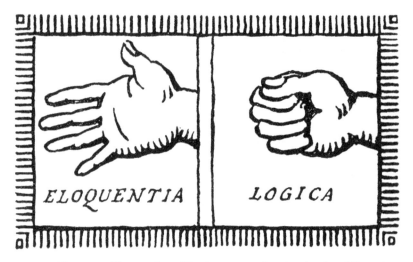

Figure 1.1 Eloquentia and Logica, an open hand and a closed fist, taken from a Renaissance rhetoric text.

be relatively uninformed: Curricular administrators, school boards, and teachers, as we shall see, continue to do many of the very things that decades of research and the consensus of experts have declared to be ineffective and sometimes even possibly injurious. On the other hand, knowledgeable teachers and scholars, from the elementary grades into post-graduate training, have been celebrating for over thirty years a radical transformation in writing pedagogy, not only within the language arts but also across the curriculum.[2] It is, in other words, an especially interesting and vital academic field.

Thus, all sorts of readers are imagined for this book, but most immediately I am thinking of people who want to know more about this discipline because they are entering it, or considering doing so, or even find themselves within it, willingly perhaps, or not. My audience certainly includes graduate students primarily in Literature or Rhetoric and Composition programs, but also in Film, Rhetoric, Theory, Speech, Communication, and other fields that provide teachers for college writing courses. You may in fact be reading this book because you are taking a teacher-training course in a composition program, preparing to teach writing for the first time, or perhaps even teaching writing as you are learning how to do it. (That, as you might suspect, will in fact always be the case, and it's one of many charms and delights of this field – that even the people who are most informed and adept are constantly learning their craft, discovering new and stimulating things, often from their students, and sometimes from other experts.) But I am also thinking of teachers in any field who might be interested in helping their students communicate more effectively. This part of the audience thus includes not only people who will call themselves writing teachers, but historians, third-grade social studies teachers, biologists, legal theorists, and others. Indeed, given the foundational nature of this field, I would hope this book will appeal to almost anyone with intellectual curiosity.

Both "rhetoric" and "composition," taken separately, are terms with complex, shifting, contested meanings. These terms and their meanings are part of an ongoing struggle to define and determine what the field is and ought to be, and this multiplicity and resistance to closure is in fact another aspect of what makes this field so interesting and alive. Before putting the two terms together in the chapters that follow, let's consider briefly the sense of each apart – a task that will lead directly to a brief explanation of what's in the rest of this book.

THE RHETORIC OF "RHETORIC"

Rhetoric's beginning supposedly occurred in Syracuse, Sicily, around 467–466 BCE when someone named Corax began teaching the art of persuasive argument to paying customers. Many Syracusans had lost their property and wealth under a succession of tyrants, and a new government and judicial system, requiring citizens to represent themselves, offered the opportunity to set things right. Here at the origins of rhetoric we can see its great potential to do good, its inspiring relationship to justice, free speech, and democratic institutions – and at the same time we can also easily see rhetoric's dark side, for what if your clever neighbor can argue more convincingly that your olive trees belong to him? Indeed, legend has it that Tisias, Corax's student, refused to pay for his instruction, and so Corax sued him, arguing, "You must pay if you win the case, thus proving the value of my lessons; and you must pay if you lose, since the court will force you." But Tisias countered, "I will pay nothing, because losing would prove your teaching was worthless, and winning would absolve me from paying."

At a glance, this story seems to support the popular idea that "rhetoric" is just a bag of verbal tricks. When politicians accuse one another of engaging in "rhetoric," they aren't referring to carefully reasoned and persuasive arguments. And rhetorical training in this story seems only to have given Corax and Tisias the skill to be irritating, as the case was thrown out by the judge, who said, legend has it, "From a bad crow, a bad egg." The judge is playing on "Corax," which means "crow," and some scholars, thinking that these names and the story itself are a bit too clever, have wondered if these guys really existed (see Cole), while others doubt at least the accuracy of the fifth-century date (see Schiappa). Rhetoric's big bang, like cosmology's, is in fact based on indirect evidence and conjecture, yet even if Corax refined and adapted pre-existing ideas, or a group of later teachers invented him, perhaps to give their own ideas more credibility, it seems clear that some sort of formal teaching of argumentation, especially in a judicial setting, was emerging in and around fifth-century Greece.[3] Where there is teaching, can textbooks be far behind? And so within decades a substantial number of authorities had come forward, mostly it seems with advice on the structure of a speech (how many parts, what goes in each part), or with examples of the various parts to be emulated or perhaps even memorized.[4]

At some point, training in argument and persuasion was included in Plato's famous Academy, which was founded in 387 BCE. The Greek term *rhētorikē* may have been coined by Plato, adapting the word *rhētōr*, a legal term that designated among other things a person who addressed a public body (from the ancient Greek *erō*, "to speak"). But Plato's writings indicate that his attitude toward *rhêtorikê*, as he encountered it, was at best ambiguous and arguably quite negative. The Academy was remarkable not for its persuasive lectures and speeches, but for its innovative reliance on Socratic questioning (and also for its innovative admission of women – an orientation arguably not unrelated to learning by conversational inquiry). In Plato's *Gorgias*, rhetoric is defined as the training and practice that produce an art of public speaking, which sounds innocent enough unless you mistrust language and the public – which Plato certainly did. But Plato's problems with rhetoric can be seen most clearly in his *Phaedrus*, the work that deals most extensively with rhetoric, where such training is referred to as the "art of enchanting the soul" or "the art of winning the soul by discourse" (576). Plato does not believe that the people who are doing all this training – in particular those who were called "the sophists" – have any clue about the nature of the soul or the dangers of enchanting it, and he also worries that the focus on winning an argument is dangerously foolish. Someone who is entirely ignorant of the truth but has memorized dazzling phrases and strategies, who has learned tricks of logic and verbal manipulation (that is, from Plato's point of view, someone who has studied with the sophists), can be more compelling than someone else who is actually a knowledgeable expert. Plato does not simply dismiss rhetoric (as is sometimes suggested), for he does observe in the *Phaedrus* how an art of rhetoric based on an understanding of the soul and an inquiry into truth might be possible. But he is deeply troubled by the sophists' approach to rhetoric, which is based on what seems probable and plausible and moving to most people. This is the aspect of rhetoric that would lead John Locke some 2,000 years later, in his monumental *Essay Concerning Human Understanding* (1690), to call rhetoric "that powerful instrument of error and deceit" (508), and it is the usual meaning of "rhetoric" in modern-day politics, used as a dismissive insult, often preceded by "just" or "merely."[5]

Western civilization might have veered away from rhetoric altogether, if we really thoroughly despised it, and toward something like the Vulcan civilization in the *Star Trek* universe, in which all sorts of persuasive appeals and verbal manipulation are shunned in favor of logic and truth. Plato did after all famously ban the poets from his utopian *Republic* and put the philosophers in charge (having no knowledge of Vulcan science officers).[6] But Aristotle changed everything, altering intellectual history in virtually every discipline, and (most importantly for our interests here) rescuing rhetoric in particular.

Aristotle came to teach at Plato's Academy, and the classes he offered included the school's first lectures on rhetoric – apparently as an afternoon elective or special interest course – during two different periods, from 367 to 347, and 335 to 323 BCE. So many textbooks on rhetoric had already appeared at that point, apparently, that Aristotle thought it would be useful to produce a summary of them all, the *Synagōgē tekhnōn* ("A Collection of Arts").[7] All of the rhetorical handbooks that Aristotle might have included have now disappeared, perhaps because his guide rendered them unnecessary; and Aristotle's synthesis itself has also been lost, perhaps because his own later work, *On Rhetoric*, which appears to be based on his lectures, so thoroughly eclipsed both these handbooks and his summary.[8] Aristotle's opening sentences seem designed to address the worries – articulated by Plato among others – that rhetoric is merely a formulaic means to an end, equally susceptible to good and evil applications, and perhaps even more attractive to unscrupulous people: "Rhetoric," Aristotle begins, "is an *antistrophos* [counterpart, or correlative, or coordinate, or converse, or mirror-image] to dialectic ...." (28), an assertion that assumes of course that Aristotle's audience knew what he meant by "dialectic," which was apparently so familiar that in his textbook on dialectic, the *Topics*, Aristotle never feels the need to define explicitly his subject.[9] We can gather easily enough, however, from various sources that "dialectic" for Aristotle is the art that is concerned with a certain kind of logical argument. Aristotle's students engaged in this philosophical disputation often, and this practice became an essential part of education through the Middle Ages and beyond.

In a dialectical exercise, one student would adopt a thesis – say, "Old teachers are better than young ones" – and another student would be assigned to oppose this position. But instead of simply arguing with each other, one student would ask questions that could be answered "yes" or "no," and the other student would have to respond and explain, following certain logical rules. The questioner's goal would be to force the respondent, by a chain of reasoning, either to accept the thesis or to contradict himself. If for instance the questioner could get the respondent to agree that "Energy and enthusiasm are the most important attributes of effective teachers," then the questioner might be able to force the respondent, based on this premise, to agree that youthful teachers may be better, despite their inexperience. The respondent's job, in other words, was to resist the questioner's efforts and thereby maintain the thesis in this verbal chess match.

If rhetoric deals with one person persuading others in an extended speech, and dialectic deals with two people engaged in a particular kind of debate, then how in the world are they mirror images or counterparts for Aristotle? Why does he say this? Although Athenian citizens, if they could afford it, might hire someone else to compose their arguments, they had by law to represent themselves in court. For someone who might be listening to (or reading) Aristotle's lectures in hopes of finding some practical advice, this opening is certainly not very promising. "I want to know how to represent myself more effectively in court next Thursday," we can imagine someone responding, "and this guy Aristotle is on some philosophical quest to define his subject!" But Aristotle has his purposes, as we shall see, when he notes that dialectic and rhetoric are counterparts in that they both deal with common opinions and probable knowledge, not with specialized expertise and scientific certainty. There is no particular field of knowledge to draw from in a dialectical dispute or a rhetorical performance: dialectic and rhetoric apply to everything.

Dialectic proceeds according to logical rules, which Aristotle claims elsewhere to have discovered and presents in a series of works that came to be known as the *Organon*, or "The Tool."[10] Rhetoric employs similar kinds of logical progressions, taking an audience from some established or assumed propositions to their logical conclusions, but rhetoric adheres less rigorously to logical rules (you don't have to spell out all of your supporting assumptions, for instance), and rhetoric also makes use of how the speaker is perceived, the style of what is said, and how the audience is reacting emotionally. An ancient comparison likens dialectic to a closed fist, and rhetoric to an open hand – an odd comparison, perhaps, but we might think of dialectic as a karate match, featuring contestants competing according to strict rules of procedure and scoring, whereas rhetoric is a politician shaking hands, patting backs, holding babies, reaching out and touching people to create feelings of relationship and common interest.[11]

Also, Aristotle says, rhetoric and its counterpart dialectic are alike in that both are endeavors undertaken by all people "to a certain extent," as they "try both to test and maintain an argument [as in dialectic] and to defend themselves and attack [others, as in rhetoric]" (29).[12] While some people argue and persuade without much skill ("randomly" Aristotle says), other people have "an ability acquired by habit," and it is "possible to observe the cause why some succeed by habit and others accidentally." And "such observation" is precisely what Aristotle will proceed to offer us, which "is the activity of an art [tekhnē]" (29). For students or parents or teachers over the ages who might have wondered why some kind of rhetorical study has been required of students in medieval monasteries and in twenty-first century vocational schools, in the grammar schools of Shakespeare's England and the most elite modern research universities, Aristotle has captured here one driving idea: every human being who is capable of thought and articulation is going to argue with other human beings, inevitably and necessarily, and it is possible to learn how to argue more effectively: there is an art beyond luck or trial-and-error. It is an important and ultimately ethical art, Aristotle asserts, "because the true and the just are by nature stronger than their opposites" (34). We just need everyone to be able to argue effectively in order to arrive at the true and the just.

Had Lady Rhetoric (the academic subjects were tradition-ally depicted as women) wanted to hire a high-powered advertising agency to do a makeover for her, dispelling the idea that she was available to serve evil and goodness alike, and that her charms often made the truth more difficult to discern, clouding perception with emotion and flash, it is hard to imagine how she could have done better than Aristotle, Inc. Rhetoric may not have been a core subject when Aristotle began lecturing on it, but it would soon for many centuries become essential to the foundations of learning, form-ing along with Dialectic and Grammar what came to be known as "the Trivium," the three basic subjects of human discourse (see Wagner).

And this elevating association – rhetoric, a distinctive and essential art, is dialectic's partner – sets the stage for Aristotle's more explicit and influential definition at the beginning of his second chapter:

> Let rhetoric be [defined as] an ability, in each [particular] case,
> to see the available means of persuasion. This is the function of
> no other art; for each of the others is instructive and persuasive
> about its own subject: for example, medicine about health and
> disease[,] and geometry about the properties of magnitudes[,]
> and arithmetic about numbers[,] and similarly in the case of the
> other arts and sciences. But rhetoric seems to be able to observe
> the persuasive about "the given," so to speak. That, too, is why
> we say it does not include technical knowledge of any particular,
> defined genus [of subjects]. (Kennedy, trans. 36–7)[13]

Aristotle aims to establish that rhetoric is a separate academic domain, comparable to medicine, geometry, and arithmetic as well as dialectic – as if subjects might be known by the company they

C | RHETORICA · XXIII | Z3

Figure 1.2 This image of Rhetorica is from a set of fifty engraved prints depicting various entities, including the seven liberal arts. Although the engraved cards are usually called the Mantegna Tarot, they are actually not Tarot cards, nor are they most likely by Mantegna. The unknown artist is generally agreed to be Italian, and the engravings were created about 1465. Many of the surviving cards are in poor condition.

keep. Rhetoric however, unlike medicine or geometry (but like dialectic), is not confined to a particular body of technical knowledge, but rather is applicable to whatever topic is under discussion – "the given." With this range and importance, rhetoric in Aristotle's definition here seems surprisingly intellectual and passive, directing our attention away from what it might do or perform in the world, and toward the internal knowledge and insight it offers. Rhetoric is "an ability," not even an action or performance, allowing one "to see" what strategies might be used to persuade, but not necessarily to use them. Compare Aristotle's philosophical stance, for instance, to Gerard Hauser's definition of rhetoric in his *Introduction to Rhetorical Theory* as "an *instrumental* use of language," in which "One person engages another person in an exchange of symbols to accomplish some goal." Rhetoric, Hauser asserts, "is not communication for communication's sake" (3); it's persuasion, aimed at getting something done.

Many other definitions are similarly goal-oriented, and they foreground the "available means of persuasion" that are beyond logic. Francis Bacon's sixteenth-century definition, for instance, describes rhetoric as "the application of reason to imagination for the better moving of the will" (177), and George Campbell in the eighteenth century defines rhetoric as "that art or talent by which discourse is adapted to its end," identifying the four possible ends as enlightening an audience's understanding, pleasing their imaginations, moving their passions, and influencing their wills (1). For Bacon and Campbell, reason is part of rhetoric, but so are the imagination and the passions. Although he expresses a variety of views in his *Rhetoric*, Aristotle is clearly uncomfortable, especially here at the outset, with the idea of rhetoric as simply a means to an end. Thus Aristotle says in his opening paragraphs that "it is wrong to warp the jury by leading them into anger or envy or pity: that is the same as if someone made a straight edge crooked before using it" (30), but this elevated sentiment falls away as the treatise unfolds. Realistically, Aristotle has to acknowledge the effectiveness of playing to an audience's emotions, and he will go on to devote much of his work to understanding the different kinds of people and the different appeals that will work.

The "Aristotelian theory of rhetoric," as Sharon Crowley says in her *Ancient Rhetorics for Contemporary Students*, reflecting a consensus view, is "usually what is meant when a modern scholar or teacher refers to classical rhetoric" (24). And yet, strangely enough, for centuries Aristotle's *Rhetoric* was neglected or read as a work on ethics, politics, and psychology, receiving in the twentieth century "more scholarly attention ... than it did during all the rest of its long history." As Thomas Conley says, "For all the ingenuity – indeed genius – shown in it, the *Rhetoric* failed to exercise much influence in the centuries after Aristotle's death" (17) and was widely disregarded as a rhetorical achievement well into the nineteenth century. We'll return to Aristotle's influence and his historical place in Chapter 5 below, but for now it is easy enough to imagine how the range of meanings of "rhetoric" in his work might undermine his popularity. At one end of the spectrum, Aristotle envisions a rhetoric that is paired with dialectic: essentially logical, an established academic discipline, useful to everyone. From this vantage point, rhetoric is not defined by what is successful, for its "function is not to persuade but to see the available means of persuasion in each case, as is true in all the other arts": in medicine for example, Aristotle says, it is possible "to treat well those who cannot recover health" (35). One might make a wonderful speech and lose the case, but still be successful in rhetorical terms. Indeed, Aristotle, who is not known for any speech he wrote or delivered, who is said to have been called "the Reader" by Plato, and who is in fact reported to have had a speech impediment, crafts a definition that defines rhetorical success not in terms of accomplishing a particular goal, or even in terms of making a persuasive speech, but rather in terms of *seeing* how one might make an effective speech. At the other end of the spectrum, away from this theoretical or philosophical rhetoric, is "rhetoric" for the real world, which Aristotle pragmatically comes to embrace. We need to know how to present ourselves, how to size up our audiences and say what will spark their imaginations and move their emotions. Theory is nice, but if your olive trees are on the line, then winning is what counts, at least from this other end of the rhetorical spectrum.

Rhetoricians may well wish that we had some other term for rhetoric's dark side, when persuasion crosses over to manipulation ("bloviation" is a good candidate, I think), but the single term can remind us, if we have only "rhetoric," that there is no "pure" communication or any unbiased persuasion: what one person thinks of as "rhetoric" in Quintilian's sense, "a good man speaking well" (*vir bonus dicendi peritus*), from a different point of view is "mere rhetoric." So, relatively speaking, is every assertion an instance of "rhetoric"? Are human beings always making use of "the available means of persuasion," or adapting any discourse "to its end"? If I say "Good morning," for instance, am I engaging in rhetoric? It may be difficult to think of this as "rhetorical," but I'm not saying "Howdy" or "Cheers," which send different messages, or "Guten Tag" or "What's shakin' dudes?" or "Dear God, where's the coffee?" I am making a choice when I fashion a greeting (even if the choice is to mumble the same thing everyone else is saying, the most innocuous and nondefining greeting), and I am shaping language toward some goal.

Rhetoric, as Aristotle said, is about particular situations, and you can imagine the different rhetorical effects of using "Guten Tag" to begin a breakfast meeting of the German club (I'm friendly and I at least know how to say "good day" in German, but perhaps not "Guten Morgen"), or the French club (I'm either dumb, or trying to be amusing, or at the wrong meeting, or something), or the Parents and Teachers Association (maybe I've just been to Germany and I'm showing off, or we are going to discuss starting a German language course?). If a greeting is rhetorical, then perhaps all language is rhetoric – and this notion, as you can imagine, is intoxicating to some. "We are twenty-five-hundred years old," Victor Vitanza says, and "We inform all the other disciplines." "We're in control," Susan Jarratt says, "we're the master discipline over these other disciplines."[14] Some scholars even include images, architecture, music, and more under the purview of rhetoric, and George Kennedy even suggests that animals use symbol systems rhetorically: "Rhetoric in the most general sense may perhaps be identified with the energy inherent in communication: the emotional energy that impels the speaker to speak, the physical energy expended in the utterance, the energy level coded in the message, and the energy experienced by the recipient in decoding the message" ("A Hoot in the Dark" 2).

So "rhetoric" resides somewhere between (a) "professional training for making a legal argument" and (b) "the energy inherent in all communication." In light of the preceding overview, where should we place "rhetoric" for the purposes of this book – as in "Rhetoric and Composition"? Here's a framework to get us started:

(1)   "Rhetoric" refers to practical instruction in how to make an argument and persuade others more effectively. Such instruction, which goes back to ancient times, originally focused on oral arguments, but those apparently were often written down or composed in writing to be memorized, and the line between teaching oral and written rhetoric is a fuzzy one at best.

(2)   "Rhetoric" also refers to the strategies that people use in shaping discourse for particular purposes. These strategies might be the result of (1) above, or the product of observing people persuading, or trial and error. The strategies might be elegant or crude, motivated by noble and lofty aims or the most disgusting cowardice or greed.

(3)   "Rhetoric" also refers to the study of (1) and (2). Such study is thus limited in theory to everything there is to know about human beings (to understand how they generate and receive persuasion), and everything there is to know about language (although it is possible to talk meaningfully about the rhetoric of music, or architecture, or wrestling, for purposes of expediency we've got to draw the line somewhere!). Some interests, to

be sure, seem more directly related to rhetoric than others: the study of morals and ethics, for instance, seems immediately useful for the light it might shed on how people are persuaded to make decisions and choices; the study of literature also seems closely related because of its interest in carefully weighing language and intention and effect.

THE COMPOSITION OF "COMPOSITION"

As a school subject, for much of its long history, "rhetoric" has been at the heart of education. It was essential to the "rounded education," the *enkyklios paideia*, that evolved throughout the Hellenistic world. The Roman and Western medieval world continued this tradition as the *artes liberales*, which we still call "the liberal arts" – liberal, historically, in the sense of "free": those disciplines suitable for anyone who is free to study them, who does not have to study for a particular vocation, who is not an unskilled laborer, or a slave. As we just noted, rhetoric, logic, and grammar formed the three discourse arts, the trivium.

Rhetoric flourished with the Renaissance's enthusiasm for eloquence, its celebration of human wit and ornament, its passion for ancient learning. Although the body of theory and practice that comprised the long tradition of rhetoric certainly changed over its history, there is a clearly identifiable rhetorical tradition that would be familiar to Aristotle, Cicero, Quintilian, Augustine, Boethius, Martianus Capella, Chaucer, Shakespeare, Dryden, Pope, Swift, Johnson, and many others, well into the nineteenth century. With the Enlightenment, however, as the explanatory power of science grew, the fortunes of rhetoric declined. Faith in numbers, experiment, and observation expanded; concerns deepened about the slipperiness and delusiveness of words. Until fairly recently, it appeared to most scholars that rhetoric for all practical purposes expired sometime in the nineteenth century, "that there *was* no nineteenth-century rhetoric," as Robert Connors puts it (*Composition-Rhetoric*, 2). The obituaries were premature however because the historians of rhetoric were in

Figure 1.3 This image, from Gregorius Reisch's *Margarita philosoph-ica*, printed in 1583 (by Sebastian Henricpetri in Basle), illustrates how the student (lower left corner) can only get into the castle of know-ledge by means of Grammar (the Lady with the tablet). The two most famous grammarians prior to 1583, Donatus and Priscian, occupy the bottom floors. Above them, different figures represent each field of knowledge: Aristotle for Logic; Cicero, Rhetoric; Boethius, Mathematics; Pythagoras, Music; Euclid, Geometry; Ptolemy, Astro-nomy; Plato for Physics; Seneca, Ethics; and at the top, Peter Lombard for Theology.

Speech or Communication (or Speech Communication) departments; looking for oral rhetoric, Connors says, they failed to see that "written rhetoric ... is the great contribution of the nineteenth century" (2). Advances in technology no doubt played some role in the increasing importance of writing in nineteenth-century education, and especially in American colleges: the development of inexpensive and durable paper, the invention of the mechanical pencil in 1822, the fountain pen in 1850, the attached eraser in 1858, and the typewriter in 1868, for example, all helped to make a classroom emphasis on writing more practicable. Debating societies and oratorical exercises were popular student activities on nineteenth-century campuses. But for their classes, students regularly wrote essays, and professors commented on them in brief conferences.[15] This relationship between students writing and professors conferring and coaching was transformed by various developments, including the Morrill Act of 1862, which established the Agricultural and Mechanical Colleges and helped to inaugurate, after 1865, after the US Civil War, the age of the modern universities, with undergraduate and graduate programs, faculty ranks, various specialized departments, and most importantly larger and larger numbers of students. Professors found themselves better able to comment on a piece of writing than to observe and critique students debating (most teachers can read a speech much faster than a student can deliver it; we can scribble comments in a margin faster than we can have a conversation about a performance).

Writing was also crucial to the ongoing emergence of the modern disciplines and modern scholarship. Whereas the medieval doctoral candidate needed to be able to think on his feet, to defend his thesis orally in public against anyone who might want to argue, the modern scholar published his (and eventually her) findings. Scientific truth was not going to be discovered by debate, but by experiment and observation, and conveyed best by plain and simple language, not rhetorical display – in writing. The most influential rhetoric textbook during this emerging modern period emphasized writing: Hugh Blair's *Lectures on Rhetoric and Belles Lettres* had a stunning 130 editions between 1783 and 1911, making it arguably the most popular textbook ever printed. Blair assumed that students would improve their writing most effectively by studying good writing, and he therefore emphasized the importance of cultivating good taste in students, who should read and analyze the greatest literature, the *belles lettres*.

This turn toward the study of writing, using literature both as a model and a subject for students, marks a dramatic departure from the rhetorical tradition's focus on the process of creating and delivering a persuasive argument for specific occasions. Blair's view of invention – of how writers think of things to say – was especially significant, for he assumed that it was "beyond the power of art to give any real assistance" in this endeavor (399). The writer must rely on "a thorough knowledge of the subject, and profound meditation upon it," he said, which sounds reasonable enough, but not very helpful. If discovery occurs outside the realm of rhetoric, and if rhetoric is concerned with written not spoken texts, then rhetoric as it was understood for many centuries is in effect reduced to organization and style. Thus, Blair's strikingly popular lectures radically diminished the significance of traditional rhetoric, valorized style and taste, and elevated the analysis and appreciation of literature. A number of textbooks by American imitators of Blair further expanded his influence and began to put "rhetoric" and "composition" together, linking an emphasis on writing to the ancient tradition of persuasion: George Quackenbos's *Advanced Course of Composition and Rhetoric* (1855), James Boyd's *Elements of Rhetoric and Literary Composition* (1844), and John Hart's *A Manual of Composition and Rhetoric* (1870), for example.[16]

The familiar history of the Boylston Professor of Rhetoric at Harvard is the story of how "rhetoric" connected to or morphed into "composition" in higher education:[17] In 1806, the first holder of the Boylston Chair, John Quincy Adams, United States Senator and future President, vowed to inspire his students with the precepts of "ancient oratory," and Adams taught classical rhetoric's art of persuasion as a foundation of democratic engagement. The next Boylston Chair, Joseph McKean, a minister, turned away from the richness of classical rhetoric, preferring instead the ecclesiastical simplicity of the Puritans, teaching students to write and speak clearly and correctly. The next Boylston Professor of Rhetoric, Edward Channing in 1819, revealed a similar disdain for the rhetorical tradition, noting in a remarkable sentence in his inaugural lecture, "We have now many other and more quiet ways of forming and expressing public sentiment, than public discussion in popular assemblies" (qtd. Heinrichs 40). Channing believed it was important (and "more quiet") to teach writing, to show students how to communicate clearly, and if the ancient principles of rhetoric were ever needed, then "It [rhetoric] would awake from the sleep of two thousand years without the aid of the rhetorician."

Channing, known affectionately as "Potty," was so uninterested in awakening the sleeping rhetoric that he himself, as the Boylston Professor of Rhetoric, did not teach rhetoric, but assigned it to an assistant (his "bland, superior look,/ cold as a moonbeam on a frozen brook," as his famous student, Oliver Wendell Holmes put it). But Channing did teach writing to Ralph Waldo Emerson, Henry David Thoreau, and many others over his popular thirty-two year career, while the next Boylston Chair, Francis James Child, abandoned rhetoric entirely to focus on appreciating literature. "I feel only little interest in what is called declamation," Child wrote to his employer, Harvard's president, "and would much rather be a teacher of dancing" (qtd. Heinrichs 42). Child truthfully changed the title of his course from "Rhetoric and Criticism" to "English Language and Literature." With Child's successor, Adams Sherman Hill, "the high priest of correctness" as Harvard historian Samuel Eliot Morison called him, the foundation for the modern split in English Departments was clearly laid: serious scholars (in the more spacious offices) study literature and language; service-oriented teachers (usually sharing smaller offices) instill good grammar into students (who should have already learned it). Subsequent holders of the Boylston Chair in Rhetoric – poets and literary critics – have tended blissfully to ignore rhetoric.

But if one had to point to one event, one turning point at which the implications of Blair and many followers come to fruition, at which the oral-rhetorical tradition tipped decisively toward written composition and the modern Rhetoric and Composition course, a candidate would certainly be the institution of a written entrance exam at Harvard in 1874. Such an exam, necessarily subjective, must either confirm that things are fine (and no action needs to be taken) or that there is a problem (in which case, money needs to be spent, and people given power). It is not therefore surprising that the exam revealed a problem, but it is still nonetheless startling to learn that over half the students admitted to Harvard failed this initial exam, sparking the first national crisis regarding the poor writing skills of American boys. Harvard immediately charged the secondary schools to do a better job preparing their students – not by any means the last instance of buck-passing with regard to writing skills. But Harvard then soon created in the 1880s English A – "the prototype for the required freshman course in composition that within fifteen years would be standard at almost every college in America," as Robert Connors puts it (*Composition-Rhetoric* 11).

Thus, the specialized focus on the teaching of writing in higher education originates in the United States as a remedial endeavor. Other colleges and universities quickly followed Harvard's lead in this urgent effort, and in some other universe the most experienced and accomplished teachers and professors might have taken on this difficult challenge, but women, adjuncts, and graduate students have typically been assigned to teach composition in our world, as Richard Miller and many others have noted.[18] To be sure, the sheer scale of this undertaking also seemed to preclude the extensive use of regular faculty in composition: In 1894 for instance, at the University of Michigan, four English teachers and two graduate assistants faced 1,198 students; even at Harvard, twenty teachers were responsible for 2,000 students. Thus, it has often been noted that "Rhetoric and Composition" emerged as a teaching field unlike any other: whereas other disciplines coalesced out of a critical mass of knowledge and methods (like Biology or Physics or Psychology) or in response to vocational training (like Nursing or Accounting or Law), the teaching of writing addressed a basic skill, preparatory to other disciplines, but not a true field of scholarship itself.

In the nineteenth and early twentieth centuries, some brilliant and prominent scholars and teachers were seriously interested in rhetoric in the richest sense and devoted to teaching writing as more than grammatical correctness and structural clarity – Barrett Wendell, Fred Newton Scott, Gertrude Buck, and others. But these were exceptions, and composition was for the most part consigned to the academic basement, figuratively if not literally. Another turning point occurred in the fortunes of "composition," however, in 1949 when the Conference on College Composition and Communication was founded; or 1958, when the Basic Issues Conference drew national attention to writing instruction; or 1963, when Braddock, Lloyd-Jones, and Schoer published *Research in Written Composition*; or 1966, when British and American educators gathered at Dartmouth to advocate interactive and expressive writing pedagogy; or 1971, when Janet Emig published *The Composing Processes of Twelfth Graders* and James Kinneavy published *A Theory of Discourse*; or perhaps 1978, when Mina Shaughnessy published *Errors and Expectations*; or at all these moments and more as a cluster of key ideas – writing as a mode of discovery, teach process not product, the teacher as a researcher, the intelligent logic of errors and dialects, to pick a few of the most obvious – helped to promote the ideas that rhetoric and composition ought to be taken seriously as a field; that smart people could devote themselves to it; that one could make an academic career with such a focus.

Today, the "Composition" part of the field's name casts a wide and arguably porous net: it would certainly include anyone who is assigned to teach writing in a required college or university course, which might include "Writing" in its title, or "Rhetoric" or "Composition" or both, in any order (informally abbreviated Comp-Rhet, Rhet-Comp, Comp). It would also arguably include anyone who is teaching a high school or preparatory school course in the "language arts." And it would also seem to include people in any number of other educational settings, since the teaching of writing can certainly reach beyond courses with "composition" or "writing" in their titles. Composition is thus unusual in its potential interdisciplinarity: Most people would think it odd if a biologist or engineer argued that every class ought to include biology or engineering, but many people think it sounds quite reasonable to say that writing should be part of every subject – that writing is a powerful catalyst to learning, whether the subject is literary studies, anthropology, or even mathematics.

When an enlightened professor in the Anthropology or Maths department substantially includes writing as part of the coursework, and even assumes responsibility for improving students' writing skills, should we say then that these teachers have (bravely) moved into Rhetoric and Composition, or vice-versa? The "writing across the curriculum" (or WAC) movement, which dates back to the 1970s, tends to think of this symbiotic relationship in terms of writing specialists sharing their expertise with faculty in other fields, enabling students to "write to learn" in every subject. The "writing in the disciplines" (or WID) movement theorizes that there are distinctive discursive practices in different fields: learning to write as a biologist is not the same thing as learning to write as an anthropologist, and therefore the composition specialist cannot provide all the necessary writing expertise for writing in every discipline – at least not without entering into that discipline in some sense.[19] Whether one emphasizes writing to learn (across the curriculum) or learning to write (within disciplines), WAC and WID implicitly draw attention to a pivotal issue in the teaching of writing – the question of expertise, of professionalization. If a biologist can teach writing, in what sense is composition an academic specialization? This disciplinary uncertainty, combined with the second-class citizenship of writing teachers, has led to considerable anxiety and, yes, rhetoric about the reality and place of the field. In fact, according to Louise Wetherbee Phelps, "From the 1960s to the present, much of the content of composition scholarship can be assimilated to the metagoal of rationally defining a discipline and legitimizing its intellectual work (and its practitioners) within the academy" (125).

In one very practical sense, "Rhetoric and Composition" is without question a specialization because about a quarter of the academic jobs advertised in the Modern Language Association's *Job Information List*, the "Help Wanted" pages for North American universities, have recently been in Rhetoric and Composition and related fields. Since nothing like a quarter of the doctoral graduates in English have taken their degrees in Rhetoric and Composition, it is indeed a particularly appealing specialization for those who would like a job. It is also a specialization, one could say, because more than seventy programs are granting PhDs in Rhetoric and Composition.[20] These graduate programs are relatively new, in academic terms at least, with the two oldest dating back to the 1960s, and seven others established in the 1970s. For many other jobs not "in" Rhetoric and Composition per se, some training and willingness in the teaching of writing are especially valued. Further, most English departments in research universities in the United States have faculty who list "Rhetoric and Composition" or "Composition" as their specialization, and some institutions even have separate departments.

Another measure of the vitality of "Rhetoric and Composition" as an academic endeavor would be the thirty-one or so journals currently publishing work related to the teaching of writing, or the various thriving organizations focusing on rhetoric and composition, with their increasingly popular annual meetings. One way to learn about this field would be simply to read the current issue of several journals and look at the annual programs of a few meetings: most of the journals are available in a major library or online (ask a reference librarian if you have trouble). You won't understand everything you're reading, and in some cases you may not understand a great deal – you're entering a conversation that has been going on for several decades. But this kind of immersion, as with a language, allows you to learn a great deal quickly if you can tolerate the sure-to-decrease confusion.

Some Journals in Rhetoric and Composition

College English and *College Composition and Communication* are arguably the most significant general venues for composition studies, and both are usually accessible and interesting.

JAC: A Journal of Composition Theory (formerly the *Journal of Advanced Composition*), *Rhetoric Review*, *Rhetorica*, and *Pre-Text* cater especially to historical and theoretical issues.

English Journal focuses on writing before college.

Research in the Teaching of English features quantitative and empirical concerns.

Computers and Composition, *Journal of Basic Writing*, and, *Teaching English in the Two-Year College* reveal their particular interests in their titles.

Some organizations

CCCC   (the Conference on College Composition and Communication), sometimes called "the 4Cs," started in 1949 with the stated purpose of supporting and promoting "the teaching and study of college composition and communication."

ISHR   (the International Society for the History of Rhetoric), organized in 1977, aims to "promote the study of both the theory and practice of rhetoric in all periods and languages and the relationship of rhetoric to poetics, literary theory and criticism, philosophy, politics, religion, law and other aspects of the cultural context." Its biennial conference assembles "several hundred specialists in the history of rhetoric from around thirty countries."

MLA   (the Modern Language Association), which originated in 1883, is the umbrella organization for faculty in English and "foreign" languages, and it includes allied and affiliated associations related to rhetoric and composition, including the Association of Writers and Writing Programs, the Association for Documentary Editing, the Association of Teachers of Technical Writing.

NCA   (the National Communication Association), adopted its current name in 1997, but its inception can be traced back to the establishment of the National Association of Academic Teachers of Public Speaking in 1914, when Speech teachers separated from English teachers. As a scholarly society, the NCA "works to enhance the research and teaching on topics of both intellectual and social significance, representing the academic discipline of communication in those national efforts."

NCTE   (the National Council of Teachers of English), established in 1911, is dedicated to improving the teaching of "English" at all levels. NCTE therefore promotes research in the language arts, and strives to nurture teachers' professional careers.

ARS   (the Alliance of Rhetoric Society), started in 2001 to bring together scholars who study rhetoric and are dispersed in various disciplines, including communication studies, English, composition, rhetoric, and writing studies.

In other words, Rhetoric and Composition is a specialization, one could say, because it is perceived as such in academia. But such recognition has not come suddenly or easily. In 1984, in the opening sentence of their *Bedford Bibliography for Teachers of Writing*, Patricia Bizzell and Bruce Herzberg declared, "The study of composition is well established as a specialization in English, a serious discipline worthy of advanced graduate work." But the insistence here suggests an insecurity: not just "established," "discipline," and

"graduate work," but "well established," "serious discipline," and
"advanced graduate work." In fact, as Bizzell and Herzberg (joined
by Nedra Reynolds) acknowledge in the opening of their sixth edition, published in 2004, the earlier claim was "a statement of confidence and hope rather than a clear fact" – but now, they assert, "the
study of composition seems unequivocally well established" (vii).
And it is, to be sure, recognized as a field by the National Research
Council's forthcoming assessment of US doctoral programs – the
golden standard for ranking academic programs. However, "Rhetoric,
Composition, and Technical Writing" was not listed in previous
NRC rankings, in 1995 and 1983; in fact it was not listed in the initial version of the 2007 taxonomy, and it was added late, after some
lobbying, only as an "Emerging Field" – along with "Film Studies,"
"Feminist, Gender, and Sexuality Studies," and "Race, Ethnicity,
and Post-Colonial Studies," which are without question exciting
and increasingly important fields, but which (again) generate only
a fraction of the jobs that are advertised and filled in Rhetoric and
Composition. Some disciplinary anxiety, in other words, would seem
to be understandable.

In his important and influential 1987 history, *Professing
Literature*, it seemed to Gerald Graff that he could best tell the story
of English studies without including the thousands of teachers and
millions of students involved in writing pedagogy:

> I will deal only in passing with the teaching of composition,
> though the pioneer work of William Riley Parker, Wallace
> Douglas, and Richard Ohmann has shown that without that
> enterprise the teaching of literature could never have achieved
> its central status, and none of the issues I discuss would matter
> very much. (2)

Graff arguably does not fairly represent the position of William Riley
Parker, whose classic essay "Where Do English Departments Come
From?" does not exactly celebrate the teaching of composition,
which he referred to as "the dismal, unflowering desert, freshman

theme-writing" (349). Richard Ohmann likewise exposed the troubling gap between the subject that the profession had chosen to study – literature, and the subject that created the funding for the profession – composition (94). Why did Graff make composition peripheral, even while acknowledging that literary study "could never have achieved its central status" without it, citing ambiguous testaments to its importance? In the same way, we might speculate, that a history of agriculture might "deal only in passing" with the workers in the fields. The real story concerns the literary class and "its central status," as Graff puts it, not the menial laborers.[21]

Of course, my comparison is arguably insensitive to those who risk life and limb to do the most unappealing jobs: teaching writing, while difficult, is not picking artichokes or carrying bricks. There is no evidence that teaching writing will, as one scholar has suggested, turn your brain into wet tissue paper. But this comparison between menial laborers and writing teachers is in fact a surprisingly recurrent theme in the field of Rhetoric and Composition. In 1992, for instance, surveying the development of composition from 1963, Donald McQuade noted that "metaphors from the work of such manual laborers as gardeners and janitors surfaced frequently" in discussions of the field. "More recently," McQuade continued, "composition instructors have been given the even more marginal identity of migrant workers – undocumented aliens, border crossers hired to cultivate, pick, and prepare the best in each year's new crop for delivery to more privileged people" (494–5). To some extent, the comparison works, as the undocumented (that is, untenured), migrant (that is, part-time, adjunct), and disadvantaged (that is, women, junior, service-oriented) teachers take on the jobs that the more privileged faculty shun.

It is however increasingly difficult in many respects for those who are specialists in Rhetoric and Composition to complain about the status of their field or their treatment. Simply because of supply and demand, salaries have often climbed higher for new faculty in Rhetoric and Composition than in other fields. Only the most backward English departments do not accept the idea that the teaching of writing is a specialty, just like the teaching of Shakespeare, and that some of their faculty should have this expertise if they are going to offer those courses. In many research universities, it is true that graduate students generally do the bulk if not all of the teaching in Rhetoric and Composition courses, but this practice requires the employment of faculty who are trained to train those graduate students. The idea that anyone can teach writing effectively, without any preparation or expertise, is perhaps held only by the Flat Earth Society and a few other allied organizations. The struggle to establish Rhetoric and Composition as a distinct field in other words, has been won, to the extent that in some institutions Rhetoric and Composition faculty have been empowered to form their own independent departments, sometimes in alliance with Speech Communication faculty, joining together over the bridge of rhetoric.

Not everyone, however, as we noted at the beginning of this chapter, agrees with this marriage of Rhetoric and Composition (not to mention Speech). In the Modern Language Association's most recent edition of their *Introduction to Scholarship in Modern Languages and Literatures*, a prestigious and authoritative landmark, both Susan Jarratt, who wrote the chapter on "Rhetoric," and David Bartholomae, who wrote on "Composition," celebrate the assigning of separate chapters to these two terms. The case for separation has been made by Elizabeth Flynn, among others, who says that "rhetoric is the parent discipline of composition studies, but the latter is an identifiable field with its own institutional structure and purposes," and "serious problems arise if we conflate the two" (138–9). I would suggest, however, that more serious problems and missed opportunities arise if we do not connect the two. To be sure, one could argue that we need to distinguish, for instance, rhetoric's orality from composition's textuality – although the rhetorical tradition, including its speeches, has come down to us in writing, and composition's best practice depends upon conversations between and among students and teachers. Similarly, we would not want to lose sight of the contrast between rhetoric's long sweep through history, compared with composition's recent flowering in academia. Student enrollment today in narrowly-defined "Rhetoric" courses is tiny compared to the vast armies of students who populate broadly-inclusive "Composition" courses. "Composition" as a term and as an educational requirement is a relatively new invention, whereas "Rhetoric" has lived through the centuries in the courtroom, the assembly, the memorial gathering. Composition's home is in the classroom, emerging in the nineteenth century. We can see this coming out, for example, by comparing Edgar Allan Poe's "The Principle of Composition," published in 1846, which deals only with creative writing, to Alexander Bain's *English Composition and Rhetoric: A Manual*, published in 1866, which is concerned with our subject here. These contrasts could easily be extended: the two terms are indeed distinct and different.

But the argument for calling this field "Rhetoric and Composition" insists, in fact, that the terms are, as Andrea Lunsford says, "not synonymous." Joining them is not conflating them, although I would note with Lunsford that they are "closely allied, often overlapping" (80). "Rhetoric," Lunsford says, "is interested in building and testing theories of persuasion primarily through the symbol system of language," and "composition is concerned with the way written texts come to be and the way they are used in the home, school, workplace, and public worlds we all inhabit" (46). This distinction sounds a bit like "theory" (rhetoric) plus "application" (composition), which reinforces the idea that composition is the lower status, or "applied" member of this binary. People in "rhetoric," this way of thinking might go, are scholars of history, philosophy, critical theory, classics, languages (the International Society for the History of Rhetoric impressively recognizes as its official languages English, French, German, Italian, Spanish, and Latin), and more. People in "composition" – well, it is possible to think that they "just" teach writing. They mark papers and deal with students.

In his landmark study in 1987, *The Making of Knowledge in Composition: Portrait of an Emerging Field*, Stephen North addresses this issue of the status (real and perceived) of faculty in Composition by dividing them into Researchers, Scholars, and Practitioners (that is, teachers). Composition teachers, North observes, are the "lowliest members of the English academic community," "second-class academic citizens," inhabiting an "academic ghetto" (14). But North argues that the knowledge of teachers, or practitioners, ought to be given more value, even though this knowledge is private and is not generated by reliable empirical methods (28). North explains that he does not mean to be condescending when he refers to the knowledge of teachers as "lore"; but in terms of prestige and power, "lore" is an alternate form of knowledge that simply cannot compete with the normative knowledge of researchers and scholars. The politics of separating "Rhetoric" and "Composition" no doubt involve the effort to evade a secondary, applied, practical status for "Composition."

Separating the two terms may in fact tend to move each of them away from the practical and applied, and toward the theoretical and speculative. If the name of the field is not "Composition," Rhetoric's former partner, or sidekick, but rather "Composition Studies," a move that is getting some traction, then the field is arguably moved more securely out of the shadow of "Rhetoric." As early as 1983, Robert Connors was considering how "Composition Studies" aspired to the prestige of the sciences, and a variety of research projects informed by linguistics and empirical research sought to establish a firm scientific footing for writing pedagogy. Composition teachers, Connors noted, "have had an institutional inferiority complex, and we looked beyond our own discipline for something that would validate what we do" ("The Politics of Historiography" 30). This scientific quest has yielded some interesting results, but it has not produced a science of writing or teaching writing, and it has arguably generated more opposition and skepticism than science-like prestige. Composition's more immediate competitor for prestige, however, has always been literary studies, and many considerations of the relationship between literary studies and the teaching of writing have been undertaken – are they partners, antagonists, what?[22]

Susan Miller's *Textual Carnivals* has offered one of the most compelling new narratives displacing the "denigrating tale" that makes literary studies "high" and composition "low," but one cannot say that scholars outside Rhetoric and Composition have widely been persuaded by Miller's arguments. One of the most revealing assertions regarding the relative merits of Composition versus Literature has been made by John Schilb, who argues that Composition Studies "can analyze broad social questions better than literary studies can" (176). This assertion of superiority leads Schilb to look forward to the day when composition is "not a plodding servant of other disciplines but a key force in the diagnosis of the contemporary world" (188). It's an interesting strategy: If Composition Studies loses status as an applied subject, perhaps it can move beyond the manual labor of writing pedagogy by focusing on the analysis of "broad social questions" and "the diagnosis of the contemporary world."

But at this point the field has morphed into something other than its traditional mission of teaching students how to argue and write more effectively. As Louise Wetherbee Phelps says, "An emphasis on 'practice' is probably the single most distinctive feature of composition studies; the discipline's sense of moral purpose in teaching has pointedly shaped its intellectual curiosity and provided a reality check for its discourse and knowledge-making" (132). Social and cultural analysis are not off-limits in Rhetoric and Composition, but they should be at the service of teaching students how to work with language, as a commitment to teaching students how to express themselves more effectively, how to persuade others, how to use language adroitly, seems essential to the field. "Rhetoric and Composition" captures the richness of this commitment better than "Rhetoric," or "Composition," or "Composition Studies," or "Writing," I think.

So, "Composition" in the name of this field, like "Rhetoric," refers to three layers of attention:

(1)   "Composition" refers to practical instruction in writing skills.

(2)   It also refers to the study of how people write and learn to write.

(3)   It can also refer to the consideration of (1) and (2), the kind of
meta-analysis that characterizes "theory" in literary study.

What isn't included in "composition"? Creative writing?
Usually not, although it is hard to argue that all writing isn't creative in some sense, but poets and fiction writers and dramatists
generally do not believe they are teaching composition. Technical
and scientific writing? Journalism? Advanced non-fiction or expository writing? These are all usually considered to be related to composition, and people who are interested in those areas usually pay
attention to work in composition (and sometimes vice-versa) – but
those interests are typically thought to be distinct from composition. What about the understanding of how children learn to write
and develop? What about writing disabilities? Again, these interests
demarcate the borders of this field, where theory and research are
certainly related to composition, and may in fact be perceived to
be crossing its borders. The same could be said of many interdisci-
plinary kinds of projects: the history of the invention of writing, the
history of how children have been taught to write, the functioning
of the brain in the act of writing, eye movements while writing, the
effects of listening to music while writing, the effects of anxiety
levels on writing, the impact of computers on writing. Someone who
says he or she is working in "composition" might engage in any of
these projects, which are arguably "in" composition to the extent
that they deal with the teaching and learning of writing in a general educational sense. Testing molecules that may hold the cure for
cancer isn't in "composition" – but the effects of writing on health,
psychological and physical, and how to use writing to affect your
health – yes, those can be in, I think. The manufacture of devices and
materials on the nanoscale – not in there; but the study of the composing processes of scientists who are writing about nanoscience –
yes, come on in.

Like other fields with two names (Biochemistry, Humanities
Computing, Industrial Mathematics), Rhetoric and Composition does

involve some fruitful overlap and even tension, as theory and practice, past and present, speaking and writing, public and academic,
work out different ways of engaging with human communication.

RHETORIC "AND" COMPOSITION

This introduction to the field of Rhetoric and Composition is
organized in terms of one of its most enduring and influential concepts: it's called the "offices" of rhetoric, or the "canon," and it follows an idealized process of developing and giving a speech: invent
ideas, arrange them, articulate them with style, memorize what to
say, and then deliver it. There is actually some evidence, both historical and cognitive, that speakers and writers may actually begin
with structure, with a notion of how their material is going to be
arranged, even prior to content. By the same token, we might think
of "style" as something that one adds to ideas that have already been
invented and arranged, but more ideas may well occur to the writer
or speaker in the act of articulating, and the arrangement also may
be altered as the style and everything else unfolds. In this sequence,
delivery comes after invention, arrangement, style, and memory,
but it is easy to imagine how delivery might actually in some sense
precede the other activities: you wouldn't invent the same speech
for Kenneth Branagh (eloquent Shakespearean actor) and George
W. Bush (oratorically-challenged former US president) to deliver.
Memory obviously comes after invention, arrangement, and style –
what is there to memorize until the speech is done? And yet how
can one invent without materials already held in the mind? In some
sense, aren't the pieces of what one wants to say already somewhere
in the mind, waiting to be put together? In other words, although it's
easy enough to challenge these offices as a sequence, this durable
structure remains nonetheless a very useful construct for organizing this field.

Chapter 2, "Invention," talks about how writers get ideas –
or rather, about how theorists and researchers and teachers have
imagined that speakers and writers get ideas, and what different

pedagogies have developed from those assumptions. I explore here the intriguing relationship between originality and imitation, and how invention might illuminate (and extinguish) plagiarism. Chapter 3, "Arrangement," deals with what writers might learn or already know about structure. What are the parts of an essay? Does it make sense to think in terms of a template for a piece of writing? Is it liberating or constricting to follow a set form? This chapter evaluates what we know about structure and teaching structure in writing. "Style," Chapter 4, covers everything from the fixation on grammar and error, to the celebration of fluency and eloquence. Is style an outgrowth of who one is, or is a style a kind of verbal costume, assumed and adjusted in order to create a certain effect? What can we do to influence or expand our students' selves or wardrobes? Should we in fact infringe on such personal choices? Some strategies for enlarging a writer's stylistic performance are presented, along with some consideration of the more elusive question of how style constructs a person.

The fourth activity, taught for many centuries, is "Memory." Although Chapter 5, dealing with memory, does cover briefly the methods students have learned in order to recall their speeches, the focus in this chapter is on another kind of memory. Specifically, the chapter provides a brief historical overview – not by any means "the" history, but an attempt to bring together disparate facts and observations and speculations, not only orienting you but also enabling you to question very soon the too-neat order that has been imposed on a rich and diverse past. The final office, and the final chapter, is concerned with "Delivery." Again, the chapter considers briefly how students were taught to deliver speeches, and what teaching "delivery" might mean in a print culture, but my emphasis here is on delivering Rhetoric and Composition to the student: the craft of teaching. The teacher invents, arranges, and styles a course of study; there is certainly a rhetoric of teaching. My intrepid discussion ranges from the most mundane (Does it matter what a writing teacher wears? How does one initiate and sustain discussion?) to the most philosophical (why are you teaching writing in the first place? Is writing instruction related to democracy?).

Here's an open hand: Welcome to the great adventure of Rhetoric and Composition.

The Problem: The blank paper or screen just sits there. It won't tell the writer what to say. No little voice is going to whisper in anyone's ear, "Here's a great idea...." Trying even harder to think of something to say will only make it more difficult. And doesn't the writer need a cup of coffee, was that the phone ringing upstairs, have the bills been paid this month, what was the name of that friendly soccer player last night...?

Oh, but when the ideas are flowing, when you are almost watching yourself putting down words as quickly as you can, even surprising yourself with your insight and creativity, then writing is about as much fun as anything else on the planet. If you haven't experienced this kind of writing groove, it's as if you've never eaten chocolate. You have a treat in store. If only there were some reliable way to get those ideas to flow....

2 Invention

What is the process we should teach? It is the process of discovery through language. It is the process of exploration of what we know and what we feel about what we know through language.... The writer, as he writes, is making ethical decisions. He doesn't test his words by a rule book, but by life. He uses language to reveal the truth to himself so that he can tell it to others. It is an exciting, eventful, evolving process.

Donald Murray, *Learning by Teaching* (15)

The invention of speech or argument is not properly an invention: for to invent is to discover that we know not, and not to recover or resummon that which we already know; and the use of this invention is not other but *out of the knowledge whereof our mind is already possessed, to draw forth or call before us that which may be pertinent to the purpose which we take into our consideration....* Nevertheless, because we do account it a Chase as well of deer in an inclosed park as in a forest at large, and that it hath already obtained the name, let it be called invention: so as it be perceived and discerned, that the scope and end of this invention is readiness and present use of our knowledge, and not addition or amplification thereof.

Sir Francis Bacon, *Advancement of Learning* (VI, 268–9)

In the sixth century, sometime before 523, one of the most remarkable scholars of all time, Anicius Manlius Severinus Boethius, declared that he had found "the paths of discovery" – the means, he said, whereby "abundant and bountiful matter for discourse must arise" (*De topicis*, trans. and ed. Stump 42, 41). Just imagine how such a rhetorical philosopher's stone, transforming ordinary thought into rich material for writing and speaking, would enable students to compose out of plentitude – rather than struggling to think of something to say, guiltily wondering if those new write-for-hire websites can deliver (and if those new plagiarism-detection programs really work). So why hasn't everyone heard about Boethius's "paths of discovery"? Why isn't every student cheerfully brimming over with "abundant and bountiful matter for discourse"?

This chapter not only reveals the discovery of Boethius and what happened to it (and why Boethius is a particularly illuminating case), but also considers the whole spectrum of how people have been taught to generate material for speaking and writing. The goal here is not an exhaustive history of "*inventio*," but rather an overview of this art that is sufficiently rich and historically grounded to give you some sense of what's possible, of how teachers have intervened in the composing processes of their students in the past. For any given writer, in any given situation, there are probably many effective ways to approach the discovery of material. There are even times when and writers for whom the material presents itself, or at least seems to do so. But teachers and students will have the best chances for success, will approach the empty spaces of composing with the most confidence, if they have some sense of the diversity – historically, philosophically, theoretically – of resources and approaches. If one strategy doesn't work, then another one will.

The stakes here are substantial. Writing teachers today generally expect students to think for themselves, not to recycle someone else's ideas. Writing *is* invention, as Donald Murray's epigraph above suggests: the student should be viewed as a writer, and "the writer" pursues, as Murray sees it, nothing less than a revelation of "the truth," made possible by "the process of discovery through language." It is however very hard to be original. It is in fact impossible to be entirely original and be understood, as we all depend on the resources of language and culture that we inherit. Even those students who appear to be most determined to reject the status quo and to express their individual difference so often seem to fall into entirely predictable imitation, whether we are talking body piercings or positions on nuclear disarmament. But in a culture that prizes so highly individuality and innovation, the most heinous academic crime is of course invention's antithesis, the absence of originality, plagiarism, which somehow has seemed to proliferate even as educators have sought more vigorously to suppress it, like an antibiotic-resistant infection.

An opposing view of invention, one in which discovery is actually recovery, in which recycling is essential to writing, is suggested by the epigraph from Sir Francis Bacon. For Murray, invention arises out of the process of writing; but for Bacon, invention arises "out of the knowledge whereof our mind is already possessed." These different perspectives imply dramatically different pedagogies. In the classical tradition, imitation is an essential part of learning, and invention involves gathering materials that an audience will recognize; in the modern tradition, students are encouraged to find their own voices and arguments. Although this opposition no doubt oversimplifies the complexities of invention (the classical tradition certainly valued originality, and modern pedagogy has often included the study of models), it does capture the fundamentally different assumptions that writing teachers must confront. This introduction therefore considers the modern "process" understanding of invention, beginning where we are now, and then surveys the classical approach. I conclude with some notes toward a synthesis and even harmony of strategies.

A harmonious synthesis was the goal of Boethius, who was unfortunately, sometime after announcing his discovery of the art of discovery, accused of sorcery and astrology, imprisoned, tortured, and eventually executed (in 523 or 524). It seems unlikely that the illiterate Ostrogoth king who silenced Boethius, Theodoric the Great, somehow mistook an invention strategy for the dark arts; but the ability to invent arguments and ideas can seem quite magical – and sufficiently powerful to make tyrants tremble.[1]

[margin handwriting: conspiracy theorists re: life]

PROCESS

The transformative events that occurred in the late 1960s and 1970s – people walking on the moon; massive protests in the United States against the Vietnam War; the emerging feminist, environmental, and Gay Rights movements; the first computer mouse; the first facelifts;

and much more – included, for some people anyway, equally momentous (and arguably not unrelated) alterations in the teaching of writing. The changes in Composition and Rhetoric seemed so exciting, so extraordinary, so revolutionary, that Maxine Hairston, writing in 1982, described them in terms of a "paradigm shift," using the concept made popular by Thomas Kuhn's 1966 book, *The Structure of Scientific Revolutions*. Hairston did not claim that composition pedagogy had achieved the same sort of grounding as the sciences, or that its new paradigm was fully in place, but by suggesting that the changes underway were comparable to the shift from a Ptolemaic to a Copernican universe, Hairston's oft-cited essay added to the confidence and enthusiasm building in the field. Kuhn and other thinkers such as Michael Polanyi in *Personal Knowledge* (1958) and Richard Rorty in *Philosophy and the Mirror of Nature* (1979) delighted many humanists in general and writing teachers in particular with the suggestions that all knowledge was personal (Polanyi), and that science and the humanities were both engaged in subjective representations of reality (Kuhn and Rorty). Writing teachers could revel in this confluence of ideas – that they were witnessing and promulgating a dramatically new and effective way of teaching writing, not unlike a scientific breakthrough; that what they were teaching, the personal making of meaning, was profoundly important; and that they might usefully investigate the mysteries of writing, given the common rhetorical ground of science and the humanities.

What was this new approach to composition? Hairston points to twelve "principal features" of "the new paradigm for teaching writing," but her first two are the most important and distinctive:

(1)   It [the new paradigm] focuses on the writing process; instructors intervene in students' writing during the process.

(2)   It teaches strategies for invention and discovery; instructors help students to generate content and discover purpose. (86)

The canons of classical rhetoric clearly had suggested a process – invent, arrange, add style, memorize, deliver. And writing, it seems obvious, is a process (what else could it be?). So how did it become possible for the idea that writing is a process to be a profound discovery, stirring teachers to believe they could intervene, especially in the crucial activity of invention, which seems to pervade the process itself? Where had the process gone that it needed to be reinvented? How did teachers conceive of writing prior to the 1960s?

[margin annotation: How is it is this shift of question???]

This is a story that we are still in the process of understanding, but some excellent work – by Sharon Crowley, Nan Johnson, Susan Miller, Thomas Miller, Robert Connors, Albert Kitzhaber, James Berlin, and many others – has shown us how key eighteenth- and nineteenth-century rhetoricians, George Campbell and Hugh Blair especially, following John Locke's philosophical lead, believed that knowledge ought to be based on empirical evidence, on what our senses and our instruments tell us, rather than on what authorities, traditions, and conventions say. Assuming that the mind naturally perceives and orders both sensory data and reflections upon them, Campbell and Blair and their legions of followers in the nineteenth century saw no need for an explicit system of invention. As Blair puts it, "Knowledge and science must furnish the materials that form the body and substance of any valuable composition. Rhetoric serves to add the polish" (*Lectures* 32). If the content for composing should come from other disciplines (history, literary criticism, psychology, ethics, etc.), or from inspiration, or from observation, then it would therefore be futile to try to teach invention. Students, according to this logic, should find things to say simply by thinking or by looking, and the teacher's role in invention should consist of advising students on how to manage and present their materials (which is not really invention per se). If Boethius found the rhetorical stone, it seems that by the late eighteenth century some rhetoricians had decided they didn't need it.

Without a need to invent, what then became important in the teaching of writing was clarity, focus, emphasis – making sure that the sentences and paragraphs were in the right "natural" order, and that the style was lucid and free from distracting errors or idiosyncrasies. Students were told in textbook after textbook (Barrett Wendell's 1891 *English Composition* is a good example) that they should select their subject, narrow it down to a workable topic, and then outline the points they would make, as if the materials that would make up the writing were pre-existing. This pedagogical approach later became known as "current-traditional rhetoric," referencing both the dominant status of the pedagogy (the current way of doing things) and its antiquated (traditional) nature.[2] When the time came to say something, students were supposed to have something to say. How? That was their problem. Out of this often-frustrating situation, current-traditional rhetoric – supposedly based on eighteenth- and nineteenth-century rhetorical theories, focusing on the completed product and the stylistic surface, reducing invention to organization – came to be the unifying enemy that informed writing teachers could agree enthusiastically to oppose.

The shift from current-traditional rhetoric to process pedagogy, then, was substantially driven by the discovery, or rediscovery, of invention, and it was the result of the efforts of many people. As early as 1912, there were articles in the *English Journal* about the process of writing, and in the 1940s Henry Sams sparked some interest in invention.[3] But it was not until 1963, when Richard Braddock, Richard Lloyd-Jones, and Lowell Schoer produced the landmark study entitled *Research in Written Composition*, that the promise of bringing serious scholarly study to various aspects of writing and its pedagogy really began to emerge. In 1965, Richard Young and Alton Becker presented a sophisticated heuristic, taken from linguistics and translation theory, called "tagmemics," a theory that would be developed in 1970 in a well-known but rarely adopted textbook entitled *Rhetoric: Discovery and Change* (many teachers did present the theory in a simplified form without using the textbook). In 1966, the important Anglo-American Conference on the Teaching of English (usually called "the Dartmouth Seminar," after the site) brought together a number of people who would play key roles in the paradigm shift: among others, James Britton, from the University

of London's Institute of Education, a former Language Arts teacher;
James Moffett, Language Arts teacher at Phillips Exeter Academy and
research associate with the Harvard Graduate School of Education;
Wayne Booth, a literary scholar whose spectacularly influential
Rhetoric of Fiction, published in 1961, helped to rehabilitate "rhetoric," and shifted critical attention from the written work as a formal entity, to the process of narrative's effects upon a reader; and
John Dixon, a British scholar interested in personal growth, whose
1967 report on the seminar, *Growth through English*, argued that
the conference had moved beyond its organizing question, "What is
English?", and was concerned instead with the problem of what students and teachers ought to be doing. The serious attention given by
such a diverse and illustrious group to the subject of what was hap-
pening when students were writing, to the processes of writing and
reading, and to teachers' activities in the writing classroom, "proved
that one can do serious work in English not only by studying literature or criticism but also by looking closely at the talk and writing
of students," as Joseph Harris puts it (17).

This "serious work" in the 1970s and 1980s, substantially
concerned with invention and the writing process, included James
Britton's *Language and Learning* (1970) and *The Development of
Writing Abilities, 11–18* (1975). Britton, acknowledging the influence of James Moffett's work, aimed to provide a "means of classifying writing according to the nature of the task and the demands
made upon the writer, and, as far as possible a way of classifying
that is both systematic and illuminating in the light it sheds upon
the writing process itself" (*Development* 3). Britton's claim (based
on the examination of several thousand samples of student writing) that writing can be classified as transactional, expressive, or
poetic, attracted scholarly attention, but his most influential idea,
I would argue, was the startling assumption that "the writing process itself" was a meaningful entity, subject to illumination.[4] Janet
Emig shared Britton's goal of "illuminating ... the writing process
itself," as indicated by the title of her 1971 study of *The Composing*

Processes of Twelfth Graders. In contrast to Britton's thousands of samples, Emig's stunningly influential work studied only eight students in a relatively narrow framework. During her first two meetings with the students, Emig asked them to write a brief essay and to talk about what they were thinking as they were composing. She also asked them, for the third meeting, to bring in any childhood writing they had saved and talk about their writing autobiographies, and for the fourth meeting, to write an imaginative piece and bring in all their draft materials. This observational and "compose-aloud" protocol would be embraced and refined by Donald Graves, Sharon Pianko, Nancy Sommers, Sondra Perl, Ann Matsuhashi, and others, who would also generally study small numbers of students (from one to twenty), observing various aspects of inventing or composing (from planning strategies to pauses).

Perhaps the most ambitious efforts to illuminate "the process itself" came from Linda Flower and John Hayes, adapting methods from cognitive scientists (in particular from the Nobel Prize winner Herbert Simon). By audio-recording experimental subjects describing what they were doing and thinking as they wrote various kinds of assignments (one prompt for instance asked participants to describe themselves for the readers of *Seventeen* magazine), Flower and Hayes elicited rich materials for analysis and produced a theoretical model of the writing process, identifying discrete tasks and processes involved in composing. However, their model looks more like a diagram for a computer operating system or a flow chart for an organization than it seems to represent a particular human being in the process of writing. Indeed, with Flower and Hayes's work, empirical research on the composing process apparently reached both its apex and its dead end. As David Bartholomae, Patricia Bizzell, Martin Nystrand, Joseph Harris, and others argued, the cognitive model in its abstraction and generality failed to capture the social and individual forces at work in particular acts of writing.[5] Lester Faigley, for instance, noted in 1985 that "within a language community, people acquire specialized kinds of discourse competence that enable them to participate in specialized groups" ("Nonacademic Writing" 238), and Martin Nystrand similarly observed that "the special relations that define written language functioning and promote its meaningful use ... are wholly circumscribed by the systematic relations that obtain in the speech community of the writer" ("Rhetoric's Audience" 17).

Thus, by the end of the 1980s, as Russell Durst notes, "writing process studies largely had dried up" (80–1), but their influence on classroom instruction persisted. Among others, the work of Donald Murray (see, for instance, his 1972 essay entitled "Teach Writing as a Process Not a Product") helped to ignite a movement that would have as its rallying cry "Teach process, not product" – a kind of a password that could be used to distinguish teachers who were "with it" from those who were hopelessly mired in the past.[6] You can infer much about what was under attack from the opening and the title of Peter Elbow's ground-breaking *Writing Without Teachers*, from 1973: "Most books on writing," Elbow says, "try to describe the characteristics of good writing so as to help you produce it, and the characteristics of bad writing to help you avoid it" (vii). The problem with that textbook approach to writing instruction, Elbow and others would maintain, is that it is product-oriented and teacher-centered. Instead of the teacher's determination whether the student's product has avoided errors and infelicities, Elbow shifted the focus to the student's process and most specifically to the act of invention. While there are, according to current-traditional rhetoric, some positive features that students' papers should have – unity and coherence, an introductory paragraph, a thesis statement, three or more supporting paragraphs, a conclusion – the old pedagogy was essentially negative, as evidenced by the "correcting" or "marking" of students' papers by teachers. Hard-working and well-intentioned teachers responded to student papers (typically in red ink) as if they were proofreading and editing them for publication, even though, ironically, the papers usually were not read by anyone other than the teacher. Typically they were returned to the students, branded with a letter grade, and an entirely new assignment would be launched. Teachers who claimed that this Sisyphean approach was exciting or even interesting for the student would generally have been considered weird by their colleagues. Process pedagogy, however, was passed on by a growing band of celebrity teachers with an almost-evangelical fervor in workshops and conferences. "I've come to bring you the good news and unleash the spirit of the writing process among you," so Tom Waldrep began in 1982 to a roomful of high school English teachers in South Carolina, who responded with delighted applause, and this kind of grassroots movement in the wake of academic publications grew from colleges and universities and National Writing Project Centers throughout the United States.[7]

The establishment that Elbow, Murray, Ken Macrorie, and others were displacing might be concretely represented by Cleanth Brooks and Robert Penn Warren's *Modern Rhetoric with Readings*, first published in 1949. In their "Letter to the Instructor," Brooks and Warren, a literary critic and a writer, explain how their book despite its "quite conventional and even old-fashioned" elements is appropriately entitled a *"modern* rhetoric," because their book "attempts to garner for composition some of the fruits" of recent "discoveries and recoveries made in criticism, in semantics, and in related fields," discoveries that have led to a "revived interest in rhetorical techniques" (xiii). But soon it is clear in the way that Brooks and Warren apply these advances and this revived interest that this hint of the future is a mirage. "The basic practice of this book," Brooks and Warren say, "and the authors' best claim to possessing a method – though it is at once more and less than any 'method' – is the constant analysis of specific passages. Indeed, this book may be described as a tissue of such analyzed passages" (xiv). Such an approach harkens back to the belletristic method of Hugh Blair, and it is easy enough to imagine how frustrating this kind of focus on written products would be for students and teachers (not to mention the evasiveness of something that is both "more and less" than a method – what does that mean?). For the student struggling mightily to find something intelligent or meaningful to say, "the constant analysis of specific passages" doesn't really appear to provide any directly useful guidance. It was as if someone were taking a course in sculpting or playing the piano, and the teacher repeatedly and constantly just analyzed great sculpture or great piano performances. In dramatic contrast, process pedagogy announced itself as all about *how to do writing*. Imagine the shock and the thrill of reading Elbow's description of a technique for how to invent material, how to get the writing process going (and then the shock and thrill of students who were actually given this assignment):

> The idea is simply to write for ten minutes (later on, perhaps fifteen or twenty). Don't stop for anything. Go quickly without rushing. Never stop to look back, to cross something out, to wonder how to spell something, to wonder what word or thought to use, or to think about what you are doing. If you can't think of a word or a spelling, just use a squiggle or else write "I can't think of it." Just put down something. The easiest thing is just to put down whatever is in your mind. If you get stuck it's fine to write "I can't think of anything to say, I can't think of anything to say" as many times as you want: or repeat the last word you wrote over and over again: or anything else. The only requirement is that you *never* stop. (*Writing Without Teachers* 3)

This invention strategy is "without" a teacher as the initiator of writing, other than perhaps to say when to start. It is also "without" the teacher's usual role as evaluator of the product. As Erika Lindemann puts it, "Needless to say, if teachers grade freewritings, they are no longer 'free.' Threatened by grades, students will shift their attention from generating and developing ideas to editing a finished product" (115). For those students, teachers, parents, and taxpayers who thought that some attention ought eventually to be paid to "editing a finished product," process pedagogy was shockingly unconcerned. "Instead of teaching finished writing," Murray said in 1972, "we should teach unfinished writing, and glory in its unfinishedness" (*Learning by Teaching* 15). Cyril Knoblauch and Lil Brannon, writing over a decade later, would agree that the teacher's role in responding to writing "is to offer perceptions of uncertainty, incompleteness, unfulfilled promises, unrealized opportunities, as motivation for more writing and therefore more learning" (123). As part of this displacement of power and resistance to closure, Knoblauch and Brannon, like many process teachers, opposed assigning grades to students' writing, saying that what matters "is not one person's estimate of improvement or degeneration, but the process of writing, responding, and writing again" (138). Invention was in other words an ongoing process, coterminous with the process of writing itself.

Thus, as Thomas Newkirk notes, "much of the process pedagogy has an anti-institutional bias," reflecting "the political era in which it was born, the turbulent years between 1966 and 1975" (xvi). To be sure, Elbow was a conscientious objector to the Vietnam War who wrote about counseling other potential conscientious objectors, but the political basis of process pedagogy is not simply oppositional. Rather, Macrorie, Elbow, Murray, William Coles, and many others were motivated by the belief that they were teaching something more profound than the mechanics of writing. "This is not a question of correct or incorrect, or etiquette or custom," Murray declared. "This is a matter of far higher importance" (*Learning by Teaching* 15). They were after nothing less than "the truth," which they believed that students could discover for themselves through the process of writing: The writer, Murray said, "doesn't test his words by a rule book, but by life. He uses language to reveal the truth to himself so that he can tell it to others." As Lad Tobin puts it, reflecting on how it felt to shift from current-traditional to process pedagogy, "I was now reading not for error and assessment but for nuance, possibility, gaps, potential. For the first time, I realized that student essays were texts to be interpreted, discussed, marveled at, and that writing students were, amazingly enough, writers" (6).

To see students as writers was indeed a powerful move with all sorts of classroom implications, including altering even the physical space of classrooms. Why should students sit in bolted-down desks, lined up in rows, staring at the teacher? Instead, students in process classrooms tend to sit in a circle or around a table, talking with each other about their writing. The classroom becomes a workshop. The teacher becomes a facilitator of conversation, a listener: one of Donald Murray's most popular essays is entitled "The Listening Eye," and it vividly chronicles the joys of meeting individually with students, reading about their lives and their ideas, and mostly listening to them talk about their writing-in-process. Murray made it seem in this essay as if the students would just about teach themselves if the teacher would just get out of the way and cheer them on. The perceived efficacy of working with students one-to-one helped fuel the rapid growth of Writing Centers in the 1970s and 1980s, where students could find tutors who would extend their teachers' intervention into their writing process.[8] For decades, the teaching of writing had been the task of the lower-class laborers of the English department, but with the advent of process pedagogy it was quickly becoming an increasingly attractive specialization. Large classes seemed incompatible with one-to-one conferences and workshops and sharing with each other. Rather than the mind-numbing work of correcting the same epidemic of errors, teachers saw themselves reading surprising, soul-searching, authentic and original writing in the process of being expressed. It's not surprising then that process pedagogy was widely embraced in the elementary, middle, and high schools, as well as colleges; in second-language learning; even in technical and business writing.

One could point to the National Writing Project (NWP) as one indicator of the new paradigm's success. In 1974 at the University of California, Berkeley, James Gray and some colleagues started the Bay Area Writing Project to "improve student achievement by improving the teaching of writing and improving learning in the nation's schools."[9] By 2008 there were over 200 Writing Project sites which have served hundreds of thousands of teachers, encouraging them to teach and to engage in the writing process. It is possible, however, to exaggerate the extent to which classroom teachers have been aware of a revolution and have altered their teaching. It's not clear how many teachers in the United States continue to teach writing by doing worksheets, learning grammar rules, identifying errors, and analyzing texts. Among informed teachers, there is a consensus that "effective classrooms always have some form of plan-draft-revise instruction," as Michael Pressley and others say in a recent volume entitled *Best Practices in Writing Instruction* – a dependence, in other words, on a conception of writing as a process (18).

But in what sense is process pedagogy a method? What is the process that teachers have embraced? The process was typically thought of as prewriting – writing – revision, which arguably adds a recursive feature to the classical progression of invention – arrangement – style. Gordon Rohman and Albert Wlecke popularized the term "prewriting" in 1965 when they introduced an assortment of specific strategies in "Pre-Writing: The Stage of Discovery in the Writing Process." Specifically, Rohman and Wlecke reported how their students used journals, meditation, and analogy to increase their creativity, generate ideas, and enhance their sense of self. Many accomplished writers keep journals, as revealed in studies of how real writers work, and process pedagogy followed Rohman and Wlecke's lead in asking students to emulate real writers in this and other respects. Although meditation as a writing strategy apparently was a bit too mystical for most teachers, parents, and students, the implicit assumption of this strategy, that the mind contains creative and generative resources that might somehow be released, was soon to be embraced by freewriting. And the use of analogies pointed toward more elaborate heuristic strategies that would be developed fairly soon after Rohman and Wlecke.

There is no question, Lad Tobin says, that "the version of process that emphasized freewriting, voice, personal narrative, and writing as a form of discovery … had the greatest influence on classroom practice and drew the most impassioned support and criticism" (9). The main appeals of freewriting were that it not only overcame the blank page, undoing "the ingrained habit of editing at the same time that you are trying to produce" (6), but it also supposedly produced better ideas, "less random, more coherent, more highly organized" (9), as Elbow surprisingly asserted. At the same time, the increasingly obvious weakness of freewriting was that it was far from clear how to get from this written brainstorming to a finished paper. In 1981, Elbow published *Writing with Power: Techniques for Mastering the Writing Process*, which addressed this issue with chapters on getting a piece of writing into a finished state, including even addressing grammatical concerns (Elbow was careful to say that such editing was the very last thing to do), as well as chapters that refined the use of freewriting to include focusing in on material. Freewriting, as Elbow envisions it, proceeds in cycles of writing and then reading (by the writer or others) to identify the most promising bits of the text. "Looping" is Elbow's term for returning to the most promising bits in a freewriting session, making these sentences, ideas, words, images, whole paragraphs, whatever, become the starting point for the next session of freewriting.

Freewriting with looping is based on the assumption that creativity is natural, and this approach – the overlapping pedagogy of Elbow, Macrorie, Murray, Graves, and others – is sometimes called the "natural process" method, or the "expressivist" approach (as students are encouraged to express themselves). What students need to write effectively and fluently, in other words, is for their obstructions to writing – their inhibitions, their editing monitors, their fears, their expectations – to be removed, and the words will flow. Expressivist teachers, I suspect, would resist the idea that they share a faith in the natural processes of the mind with those eighteenth-century empiricists, Campbell and Blair, the philosophical grandfathers of the current-traditional approach that expressivists sought so vigorously to displace. Still, at least with regard to the surface features of writing, current-traditional rhetoric and freewriting are mirror opposites: one is focused on correctness and clarity, and the other is entirely negligent; one virtually equates writing (and teaching writing) with editing, and, as Elbow says, "The main thing about freewriting is that it is *nonediting*" (emphasis by Elbow, *Writing Without Teachers* 6). Current traditional rhetoric assumes that the materials for writing will arise externally, from observation or disciplinary knowledge; and freewriting assumes that the materials will come from within, as the writer taps into what the writing process unearths. But both approaches are nonetheless equally silent about the actual working of how ideas are generated. It's mysterious. It's natural.

Although freewriting has been embraced and remains a popular classroom strategy, the research on its efficacy is somewhat disappointing. George Hillocks, authoritatively reviewing the research prior to 1986, concluded that freewriting, as "a major instructional technique," is "more effective than teaching grammar in raising the quality of student writing," but "it is less effective than any other focus of instruction examined." Even when freewriting is combined "with other features of the 'process' model of teaching writing," it is "only about two-thirds as effective as the average experimental treatment" (*Research* 249). John Hayes more recently (2006) has reviewed the research related to the efficacy of freewriting that has appeared since Hillocks's review. The most significant studies, which compare the invention strategies of writing sentences versus outlining, find that "the outline-first strategy, rather than being a problem, is actually beneficial for the kinds of assignments that students often have to do in school" ("New Directions" 33). R. T. Kellogg (1988, 1990) found that students "wrote significantly longer essays, spent significantly more time writing (exclusive of planning time), and wrote letters that were rated significantly higher in idea development and in overall quality than did the participants in the no-outline condition" (33). Another interesting study, by Galbraith and Torrance (2004), found that "more ideas were produced" when students drafted in sentences (as in freewriting), but "higher quality final drafts were produced in the organized-notes condition" (34). It is not clear, however, in any of these studies that the students had enough experience with freewriting to be comfortable and effective with it: Elbow makes clear that freewriting is counter-intuitive and requires some practice to be most effective. Still, the results, as I say, are disappointing – and no doubt disturbing to those who have campaigned so vigorously against outlining and for process pedagogy.

Freewriting, it seems clear, can be extremely valuable for some students sometimes, helping them to write those most difficult words, the first ones, and helping them to understand how real writers experiment and play around with ideas, not worrying about the final product at the outset of the process. But research supporting the benefits of outlining may suggest that all of current-traditional rhetoric was thrown overboard prematurely, since outlining is a common feature of that pedagogy. Elbow, after all, is surely overstating the case when he says, "Only at the end will you know what you want to say or the words you want to say it with" (Writing Without Teachers 15): for some occasions, some writing assignments, the writer does know more or less what he or she wants to say. For instance, if the CEO tells an employee, "I want you to defend our budget, comparing it to last year's budget, and to maintenance's budget," then the employee knows generally at the outset what to say. Outlining, it seems reasonable to say, would often be useful in sketching out how an argument or other piece of writing might be structured, and freewriting would no doubt often be useful in discovering a topic or other situations that call for brainstorming. Outlining might not be very useful if writers are required to produce a rigid plan before actually writing. But when an outline is viewed as a kind of draft, subject to change, evolving as the actual writing takes place, then it can be a powerful tool for writing. Architects often produce multiple sketches of plans, trying out different approaches to a building, and they adapt their plans as a building goes up, sometimes substantially (it is fortunately much easier for writers to start over or make basic changes). Requiring students to stick to an outline, produced before a paper was written, would be as silly as requiring them to use only what they had generated while freewriting. Thus, used reasonably, outlining and freewriting would both seem to be useful tools for engaging with a writing task. Both can be viewed as drafting with different levels of syntactic elaboration.[10]

Further, outlining draws attention to the ideas and the structural relationship between them, and so we would expect it to be most effective when at least some of the ideas are already known to some degree. Freewriting operates at the syntactic level, on words and sentences or parts of sentences, and would seem to be most effective when the writer is searching for ideas. As researchers (who were almost always also teachers) have looked for ways to help students in the prewriting phase of writing, they have identified strategies that work somewhere between the free association of freewriting and the logical structuring of outlining. In *A Writer Teaches Writing*, Donald Murray discusses the usefulness of asking students to brainstorm lists of details or observations, and then encouraging them to refine their lists into more specific, detailed, and authentic items. A similar popular technique called "clustering" moves toward finding relationships between and among such items by making a visual representation of ideas. I assigned my daughter the topic "Why I Should Read *The Great Gatsby*," which she revised to "Why I Should Play Computer Games Rather Than Read *The Great Gatsby*." Putting her topic in the center of the page, she then drew a connecting line to this idea: "*The Great Gatsby* provides a bad role model," and then offered two ideas as offshoots: "Tom, a horrid character, goes mainly unpunished," and "there are many affairs and a murder." She drew another line from the topic to the idea that computer games are better for the environment, and she connected this idea to three supporting observations: computer games use only energy, which can be taken from the sun; books require ink, which surely produces "some horrible chemicals"; and "entire forests are destroyed to produce the thick pages of *The Great Gatsby*." This heuristic, which is nothing more than arranging ideas on a page, draws on the mind's natural inventiveness, using the circles and lines to show connections and stimulate further ideas.

A more structured pre-writing approach, assuring that the writer will consider a range of related materials, emerges from the use of the reporter's questions (Who? What? When? Where? How?). Kenneth Burke, the great twentieth-century philosopher of rhetoric, combines When and Where, and adds "Why was this thing done?" – yielding his famous "pentad" of act, scene, agent, agency, and purpose (*Rhetoric of Motives* xv). Burke proposed his pentad as a heuristic to investigate human motivation, but composition teachers have used it, like the reporter's questions, as an invention strategy, asking students to think of ideas in each category. Most composition textbooks expand in some way on Burke's pentad, using more accessible terms for each category. Axelrod and Cooper for instance in the popular *St. Martin's Guide to Writing* call the pentad strategy "dramatizing," and they link each aspect to a journalistic question: Action: What? Actor: Who? Setting: When and where? Motive: Why? Method: How? (523–4). Axelrod and Cooper then offer a list of questions designed to stimulate material for composing, suggesting that the student run through the list, responding "quickly, relying on words and phrases, even drawings," and thereby better understanding their topic:

> What is the actor doing? How did the actor come to be involved in this situation? Why does the actor do what he or she does? What else might the actor do? What is the actor trying to accomplish? How do other actors influence – help or hinder – the main actor? What do the actor's actions reveal about him or her? How does the event's setting influence the actor's actions? How does the time of the event influence what the actor does? Where does this actor come from? How is this actor different now from what he or she used to be? What might this actor become? How is this actor like or unlike the other actors?[11]

A similar invention strategy that also quickly became a popular and enduring mainstay of process textbooks was presented by Gregory and Elizabeth Cowan in 1980 in *Writing*. "Cubing" asks students to brainstorm about a topic using six different categories or aspects (six sides, like a cube):

(1) Describe it (colors, shapes, sizes, etc.).
(2) Compare it (What is it similar to? In what way? How is it different?).
(3) Associate it (What does it make you think of?).
(4) Analyze it (Tell how it's made, or what parts it has).
(5) Apply it (What can you do with it? How can it be used?).
(6) Argue for or against it (Good effects, bad effects? Cost? Morality?).

Like freewriting, cubing aims to provide the writer with raw material, leapfrogging over the anxiety and frustration of beginning with a blank page. You arrive at the worksite with all the lumber, mortar, bricks, windows, shingles, pipes, etc. already delivered (the Cowans begin *Writing* with an elaborate photo essay comparing writing to building a house). Although one would not want to argue that cubing is logically exhaustive, there is the suggestion of an underlying logic, from concrete and singular to abstract and multiple; from a static view of one thing, to a comparison, to a freer association, to an analysis of the parts or origin; then opening up to a more abstract view, applying the thing, and then evaluating it.

Cubing itself is similar to (and perhaps based upon) a more rigorous invention strategy called "tagmemics," which was itself derived from a linguistic strategy for translating the Bible into unfamiliar languages. Tagmemics was adapted for composition in the 1970 textbook by Richard Young, Alton Becker, and Kenneth Pike, *Rhetoric: Discovery and Change*. Any idea, or experience, or thing can be viewed, according to tagmemics, as a particle (static, by itself), a wave (changing through time), or a field (a part of a system). Anything can also be viewed in terms of its contrast (how it differs from other things), its variation (how much it can change and still be itself), and its distribution (how does it fit into the system as a whole). Tagmemics reportedly has allowed missionaries to analyze unknown languages, and it can produce a great deal of material. The matrix (if not the textbook) was often adapted:

Particle: the thing itself, static	Contrast: its difference
Wave: the thing changing	Variation: variations of it
Field: the thing in a system	Distribution: place in a system

If your topic, for instance, is basketball, you would ask yourself these kinds of questions:

Particle: the thing itself, static	Contrast: its difference
What is basketball? Define it.	How is basketball different from
What are its features?	other sports?
Wave: the thing changing	Variation: variations of it
How has basketball changed?	In what different ways is it played?
What is its history?	E.g., college, Olympics, pick-up, etc.
Field: the thing in a system	Distribution: place in a system
How does the system of	What is basketball's place within the
basketball work?	world of sports?

The foregoing invention strategies have contributed to the widespread embrace of process pedagogy, which has transformed the field of Rhetoric and Composition – has, in fact, helped to create the field. Let's consider now the appeal of process teaching more closely by thinking about its relationship to plagiarism, the antithesis of invention.

PLAGIARISM

According to Matthew Bruccoli, the great literary biographer, "Most great writers are insecure."[12] If Fitzgerald, Hemingway, and Thomas Wolfe (the writers Bruccoli worked on most extensively) were self-doubting, why shouldn't students be apprehensive? Or terrified? The serious study of writing anxiety was one early feature of the emergence of Rhetoric and Composition as a field. In 1975, for instance, John Daly and M. D. Miller evolved instruments for measuring and analyzing writing anxiety. Perhaps, given the cure (invention strategies), composition specialists were better able to see the illness, and interesting work soon followed on various levels of writing anxiety, including its most extreme form, "writer's block."[13]

If anxiety is deleterious, research also showed us that confidence is beneficial. In fact, students' assessments of their own abilities appear to be the best predictor of their success – better than their previous success, or even, amazingly, measurements of their knowledge or skill.[14] Perhaps students who anticipate succeeding in an academic task place more value on it, and therefore put more effort into it, or perhaps they are better able to focus on the task.[15] In any event, process pedagogy's assumption that writing is in some way a teachable process (even if we say it involves creating the conditions for students to teach themselves) would in itself be reassuringly helpful to students. This optimistic core of the process movement displaced recurrent complaints about how students couldn't write, and about being assigned to teach writing (which couldn't be taught) as people began to call themselves specialists in Rhetoric and Composition and to value the writing that students performed. Further, the common process strategies of allowing students to revise their work, and grading a portfolio of the semester's work rather than individual papers, further dissipates the do-or-die doom of one-draft classrooms.

But if process pedagogy builds confidence and encourages students to write, as I am suggesting, then how do we account for the well-documented proliferation of plagiarism? Do students believe that they can do the work, but choose not to? If students are being taught a process, including invention, why do so many embrace its antithesis or absence? In "The Future of Plagiarism," Emrys Westacott has recently imagined that in the year 2030 Professors Zack and Chelsea will be lamenting their students' "cheap" plagiarizing software, which lacks "random variations in, like, vocab, grammar, quotations – all that stuff," Professor Chelsea says. Professor Zack remembers fondly the good old days when, he says, "I did my own Web search for everything I plagiarized," which "took hours sometimes." Zack is going to punish his students for their poor plagiarism efforts by giving them all Bs – the "standard procedure," which he admits is pretty tough punishment since they'll be "like, the only ones not graduating *summa cum laude.*" The serious point underlying Westacott's satire is confirmed by reports in the BBC News, *Newsweek*, *The Times* (London), *The Chronicle of Higher Education*, the *Boston Globe*, academic journals, and other places: plagiarism is rampant. Estimates of the prevalence of academic dishonesty have ranged from 75 to 90 percent.[16]

So why do students cheat? Students say it's because they desire a better grade than they believe they can earn on their own; because they don't plan ahead; because they're lazy; and because plagiarism in the Internet age is so much easier than doing the work. Invention strategies and process pedagogy might have some impact on these motivations, but how do teachers deal with laziness, convenience, and the deterioration of morality? To turn the tide of plagiarism, teachers must convince students not only that they can be successful on their own, but also that they are likely to be caught if they do cheat, and that the consequences will be serious. Teachers can also provide plagiarism-resistant assignments: instead of an analysis of a Keats poem, for instance, we might ask students to compare a Keats poem to a poem published in this week's *New Yorker*. Instead of taking up the papers at the end of the process, we can intervene at various points with editing exercises and focused feedback. By guiding them through the writing process, teachers can reassure themselves that students are evolving their own work. In addition, although students should be confident, they should also understand that writing is often difficult. Unrealistic expectations may lead students to plagiarize. Students should realize that there is nothing wrong with them if they struggle to write well: we all struggle.

There is one excuse for substituting plagiarism for invention that needs to be addressed in some detail, however. Students also say in explaining instances of plagiarism that they do not understand "the rules" or that their plagiarism has occurred "unconsciously" (whatever that means). Some composition specialists have in fact supported the idea that students often don't understand the rules – and in fact *can't* understand the rules. "*Plagiarism* is difficult, if not impossible, to define," according to Margaret Price, who points to the "perceptive, detailed questions" by her students that expose problems with identifying plagiarism, and that also reveal the spirit of entrapment underlying our policies:

> "What if you think of something and it turns out someone else already thought of it first?"
> "What if you find the same idea in two books?"
> "What if it's something you heard somewhere, but you don't remember where?" (88–9)

Price calls our attention to "critiques of the idea of [the] author, to calls for more attention to collaborative work, to arguments that the concept of plagiarism may change or lose its meaning across cultures" – all of which further complicate and undermine the idea of plagiarism, she says (89). Price is following the lead of Rebecca Moore Howard, who has also declared her subject to be "inherently indefinable" ("Sexuality" 473). "We in the academy and specifically in English studies," Howard says, "believe that the textual work required by the discourse of plagiarism is impossible, yet we continue to require that work of our students" (474).

Do we in fact believe that? Doesn't this line of thinking seem to be heading toward Professors Zack and Chelsea, toward acknowledging that plagiarism is just another invention strategy (but let's do it well)? Howard does indeed discuss the usefulness in pedagogy of what she calls "patch-writing," which is piecing together texts out of other texts, and which is not, in Howard's view, plagiarism, but is rather "a move toward membership in a discourse community"

(*Standing* vii, 70). Price, Howard, and others who have challenged the common view of plagiarism have stirred up, as you might imagine, some heated condemnation by teachers who see just another sign of a morally corrupt and indulgent culture.

What is the reality here? Can writing teachers in fact define plagiarism, and what does the answer to that question tell us about invention in particular and the teaching of writing in general? This would seem to be a crucial issue for Rhetoric and Composition. Let's focus for a moment on Price's students' questions. Are they really unanswerable? The students are asking *good* questions, indicating that they are thinking through various scenarios. Certainly, any question can be complicated and deconstructed until it is unanswerable, but in the non-quantum ordinary world, the students' questions, I would submit, do have fairly simple, workable answers. We certainly know what to do outside the world of composition if someone has an idea that it turns out has already been thought of. Let's say I have this idea that a compound made out of vitamin A, retinoic acid, will significantly reduce skin wrinkles. I could write to a pharmaceutical company proposing this idea, and I'm sure they would say it's terrific – but unfortunately this substance has already made billions of dollars as Retin-A, a modern wonder drug. Now if I'm an eighth grader, and I've never heard of Retin-A, the company might want to give me a scholarship and sign me up to come work for them later. But if I'm a dermatologist, and I'm proposing this drug as a new invention, something is wrong. I should know better. And if I'm a research scientist, and I'm trying to disguise the real nature of the compound, saying that I subject vitamin A to a special kind of laser light I invented, or I backdate my letter to suggest that I wrote it in the 1960s, then I'm asking for trouble. Plagiarism similarly depends on the situation – on what I know, on what I should know, and what I'm trying to do. So plagiarism, as most textbooks and departmental guidelines describe it, requires an element of dishonesty, as the plagiarist presents work as his or her own that is actually someone else's. If you think of an idea and then you find out that someone else has thought of it already, you can't honorably pretend you don't know that. You can use the idea, while acknowledging that someone else previously thought of it; you can assert that you actually thought of it independently but also acknowledge that someone else previously thought of it; you can see if you might be able to extend the idea, or tweak it in some original and new way, but you just want to make sure the reader understands what the situation is and how the credit should be sorted out.

Indeed, plagiarism is often ridiculously easy to identify, as I think most experienced classroom teachers would agree. In my experience: When two students in the same class turn in identical papers (they got confused on who was using which stolen paper), when a student who has been struggling with grammar and syntax turns in an extremely sophisticated essay with words that he cannot define, when a student's paper contains a paragraph that the teacher recognizes from her dissertation advisor's most recent book – these real-life examples are not ambiguous. There are, to be sure, borderline or hazy cases, but porous categories occur in the biological world as well as the semantic one. Porous boundaries do not mean non-existence. Georgia and Tennessee might argue about where the boundary is, but that doesn't mean we can't distinguish the vast majority of Georgia and Tennessee.

"Common knowledge" admittedly can pose a problem for students. They can only determine what they need to document by knowing what educated people know. This process is an essential part of engaging in a field of study. Students should also learn that good writers highlight their original ideas, making sure the reader understands the significance of what they are saying. Students can benefit from some practice in determining what is common knowledge and what needs documentation, but to avoid plagiarism the student doesn't need to figure this matter out, determining precisely what it means for a particular idea to appear in two sources: the student only needs minimally to represent accurately what has been found (that is, for instance, that an idea can be found in at least two sources). Students can always err on the side of safety as they learn what other people already know.

The third question from Price's students (What if you don't remember where you saw something?) can also be answered: it's perfectly acceptable to write in academic publications something to the effect of "I assure my reader that I read this somewhere in a reputable source, but I regret to say that I cannot at this time identify the source." You don't often see this kind of documentation in scholarly writing; usually the writer can eventually recover the source. But if you know you didn't think of an idea, but you don't know where you read it, you just need to try to find it; and if you can't, then be clear and accurate – and say "this isn't mine; I did read it somewhere; I just don't know where."

So why would Howard, Price, Patrick Scanlon, and other teachers and thinkers question the concepts of plagiarism, braving predictable charges of lapsed morals, decayed standards, well-intentioned harm? There are no doubt teachers who derive satisfaction from sleuthing and serving justice, but Price's title, "Beyond 'Gotcha!': Situating Plagiarism in Policy and Pedagogy," indicates that her goal is to move teachers toward the role of education rather than detection. So why argue that plagiarism is a situational phenomenon, shifting with time and place, rather than a violation of fundamental rules of fair play, a detestable academic crime, threatening basic issues of ownership and civilization? Before we look for political motivations or theoretical allegiances, we might consider whether there are *any* concepts that are *not* situational? Is there a term of any sort that is stable across time and culture? Meaning is of course always resolutely contextual. After Saussure, after Derrida – even after Samuel Johnson's *Dictionary* or John Locke's epistemology – it's not possible to maintain that language is stable and transparent. So "plagiarism" like any other term has meaning only within a given time and place; its meaning is always being constructed, up for grabs, subject to shifting and complication.[17] Therefore, we should acknowledge that like any socially constructed term, "plagiarism" can be difficult to define in some cases. But these cases can be addressed.

Consider, for instance, two intriguing assertions that commonly appear in plagiarism policies: that students will be held responsible whether the plagiarism is "intentional or unintentional," and that "ignorance of this plagiarism policy will not be considered an acceptable excuse." These assertions, with their quasi-legalistic flavor, understandably aim to close off easy evasions of the policy ("I didn't know that was plagiarism"; "no one ever told me this was wrong"), but isn't it hard to be entirely comfortable with these positions? How can people reasonably be held responsible for policies they may violate unintentionally or unknowingly? What if it's suddenly against the law to wear a blue shirt, and no one tells you that? If we think of plagiarism as stealing and lying, however, then it is possible to see how it is reasonable to hold people responsible. Plagiarism does violate some pervasive prohibition – one that everyone is already aware of, or should reasonably be aware of. Many teachers circulate a plagiarism policy (most programs have an official policy) and require students to sign a statement affirming that they have read and understand the policy. But do students really need a policy to tell them that they shouldn't hire someone to write a paper for them or steal someone else's words? Such an action violates a larger, well-understood, pervasive societal rule about property rights and honesty. Students can easily understand that lifting passages or ideas from someone else's text is a kind of theft. In particular situations, it may be difficult to account for all the help that one has received, but good faith efforts to give credit where it's due are all that we can ask for.

Imagine, however, a culture in which everything is considered to be community property. In such a context, could plagiarism not be assumed to be part of what everyone already knows? Have Chinese students, for example, studying in the West come from such a culture? I was once told by a colleague that it would be extremely xenophobic for me to punish a Chinese student for cutting and pasting together a paper. My colleague claimed that this kind of invention strategy was an accepted practice in China. Indeed, Stephen Stearns, a Yale University professor, recently wrote an open letter to his Chinese students about the pervasive plagiarism that he encountered while teaching there. The letter, which quickly spread around the Chinese-language Internet and then into the Western media by way of the *Chronicle of Higher Education*, accused Chinese professors and administrators of tolerating plagiarism "without serious punishment." "Disturbingly," Stearns asserted, "plagiarism fits into a larger pattern of behavior in China," noting that his own textbook, "in complete violation of international copyright agreements," was being copied and reproduced by the university where he taught as visiting faculty, "causing me to lose income, stealing from me quite directly."[18]

Although we may feel quite comfortable identifying many instances of plagiarism, our category does depend upon certain assumptions and cultural norms. Most Chinese students are taught to include the words of famous writers and poets in their own writings, and ownership and copyright are arguably unfamiliar, foreign ideas. The students are used to embracing their culture by making it their own. Thus, cultural norms, usually invisible to us, may be illuminated in certain situations when cultures are juxtaposed, as in the case of plagiarism. Similarly, our notion of the author's ownership and control over his or her text is challenged by texts without authors in the usual sense. The recognition in composition classrooms of the pervasiveness and importance of collaborative writing in the workplace has led many teachers to include such projects on their syllabi. But when a group of students turn in a paper with all their names on it, is the student who has done little or no work on the project committing plagiarism? The student is presenting someone else's work as his or her own in order to gain some benefit, yes? Further, an important feature of process pedagogy has been the transformation of the classroom into a workshop, replacing the one-to-many hierarchy of the lecture with an interactive group of peers, as students read each other's work and give constructive feedback. Sometimes students provide exceptionally good suggestions and comments, effectively transforming another student's paper. Although the teacher is aware that students are helping each other, it's often very difficult to sort out how much help has been given, and to what extent the evolving essay now is co-authored. Most colleges and universities today feature writing centers, and the advice that tutors may give students is also often difficult to track and account for. Even the assistance that a teacher gives his or her own student may blur the boundaries of the student's "own" work. But this blurring of the boundaries is almost always readily distinguishable from academic dishonesty, especially when the student is guided to make such a distinction clear.

The erosion of the "author" would seem to add another sort of complication with regard to plagiarism. According to some theorists, Vannevar Bush's invention of hypertext is a particularly transparent instance of the breakdown of the distinction between producers and consumers of texts, allowing readers dramatically more control over what they are reading, blurring the category of "author" and opening up the question of who has written and who therefore owns a particular text. In a hypertext in which the reader chooses one of multiple textual paths, or even creates and adds material, the reader arguably does participate in the author function. Such texts may have many collaborative authors who are readers. When Price is questioning the concept of plagiarism, she refers to the Web itself as "one vast hypertext, one 'publication' with millions of authors" (96). If we are all co-authors of everything that's out there, then the category of plagiarism does seem to dissipate. Do we arrive in some exotic land in which plagiarism has no meaning?

Davida Charney is not concerned with plagiarism in her essay on "The Effects of Hypertext on Processes of Reading and Writing," but her survey of the research on reading both traditional texts and hypertexts is interesting here. Charney begins by defining a "text": "Most people," Charney writes, "conceive of *text* as a collection of ideas that a writer has carefully selected, framed, and organized into a coherent sequence or pattern in hopes of influencing a reader's knowledge, attitudes, or actions" (238). What is perhaps most interesting about Charney's description is the complete absence of invention: the writer selects, frames, and organizes – but where do the ideas come from that the writer is selecting? As Charney says, champions of hypertexts have argued that they represent a kind of associative network that is not unlike the networked storage data in the human brain. And as Edward Barrett puts it, conversely, "Developers of hypertext systems are inspired by a highly Romantic, Coleridgean concept of writing," in which the human brain is itself a kind of hypertext, with material waiting in memory, waiting to be linked in any number of possible patterns (xv). If we think that hypertexts are like the brain, and vice-versa, what happens to our understanding of invention and plagiarism? Is the author simply a repository for some inspiration, for some mysterious force that works like an in-brain Google, assembling pre-existing materials without our active participation? Is a hypertext just an extension of the problematic nature of collaboratively written, work-shopped, editorially assisted writing?

We might consider at this point how Bacon's view of invention, in the epigraph to this chapter, relates to this question and our understanding of how writers work. For Bacon, inventing materials for an argument involves "finding" those resources that have previously been stored. Material has to be put into a hypertext, or the internet, or a commonplace book, or the human brain, in order for the writer to hunt it down and use it later. Plagiarism, from this perspective, is not so much the antithesis of invention as it is an overextension of it. Writers and speakers are constructing arguments out of ideas, facts, passages, examples that have been collected and placed in some sense. The plagiarist lifts this material without any finesse or style, but the adroit writer uses and adapts and acknowledges appropriately these common resources. There are, in Bacon's view of rhetorical invention, no genuinely "new" ideas – an audience

Figure 2.1 To help students learn some essential terms related to argument, logic is depicted here as a huntress. Two premises emerge from her horn in the form of roses. Her sword is labeled *"syllogismus,"* indicating that the syllogism is a major weapon. Her breastplate is made up of conclusions (*"conclusion"*). Her two dogs are truth (*"veritas"*) and falsehood (*"falsitas"*), who are chasing a *problema* in the form of a rabbit. The huntress is standing on the solid rock of Aristotle, with the head of Parmenides, a pre-Socratic philosopher, behind her. From Gregorius Reisch's *Margarita philosophica* (Basle: Johannes Scott, 1508).

in any event wouldn't be persuaded by an unknown, unrecognized assertion. Outside of science, there are only new combinations of already existing ideas and statements. The difference in these two approaches to invention is dramatically revealed in the ways that imitation is viewed. From the stance of science or process pedagogy, the writer is seeking to overcome imitation, to invent by finding an original, new insight. In process pedagogy, this originality is derived from the writer discovering his or her own individual voice. In science, the inventor makes new observations and tests novel explanations. From Bacon's stance of classical rhetoric, however, imitation takes advantage of the community's conventions and common knowledge to communicate effectively. Good writers draw on good writing.

Thus, Price, Howard, and others might also be uneasy with the project of defining plagiarism because process pedagogy, for all its appeal and power, has an implicit difficulty addressing this increasingly pervasive problem. Process pedagogy is not focused upon students acquiring an understanding of the community's conventions and common knowledge, and without some shared understanding of what writers can be expected to know, plagiarism is indeed difficult to circumscribe. We have emphasized the process of discovering original and authentic insights; we have depicted plagiarism as the most heinous of academic crimes; we have resorted to extreme threats – you'll be punished even if you are unaware of doing anything wrong, even if you didn't mean to; and yet it is far from clear how the student is supposed to know what is original and what isn't, or out of what materials to fashion original insights. For Bacon, the rhetorical hunter supposedly knows that the materials he finds have been previously stocked, and he is making use of the resources of his cultural inheritance. But for the writer who is writing in order to see what he thinks (writing as a mode of discovery), the origin of any emerging idea may well be problematic. Where do ideas come from? For the writer within Bacon's classical tradition, ideas come from the ideas previously gathered. Process pedagogy arguably offers a method without materials. The invention of ideas does seem magical, mysterious, a bit like sorcery. Let's see if we can usefully expand on these two views of invention by thinking about imitation.

IMITATION

In the classical tradition of rhetoric that Boethius inherited and helped to pass on to subsequent generations, the earliest surviving complete rhetorical treatise, covering all five canons of invention, arrangement, style, memory, and delivery, is the *Rhetorica ad Herennium* (*c*.85 BCE). This work was long thought to be by Cicero and was possibly preserved for that reason, but it is now considered anonymous.[19] Cicero did in fact write a book devoted to the first canon, *De inventione* ("On Invention"; also *c*.85 BCE), and it presents much of the same materials on invention as the *Rhetorica ad Herennium*, sometimes word for word. Both Cicero and the anonymous author of the *Rhetorica ad Herennium*, for instance, quote the same four lines from a rather obscure source to illustrate the same point, and both misunderstand the author Plautus in precisely the same way, and both criticize him for the same non-existent error.[20] The relationship between these two texts is even more interesting when we consider that they are arguably the two most influential textbooks ever written. *De inventione*, as Martin Camargo notes, "so closely defined rhetoric for the Middle Ages that it was called simply *De rhetorica*" ("Rhetoric" 98). The additional material in the *Rhetorica ad Herennium*, especially the section on style, made it an attractive supplement to Cicero's work beginning around the ninth century, but Cicero's most accomplished and sophisticated work on rhetoric, *De oratore* (55 BCE), was neglected and generally lost until the fifteenth century. Likewise, Aristotle's *Rhetoric* seems to have survived the Middle Ages only because Islamic scholars preserved it, and Quintilian's *De institutione oratoria* endured in a very fragmented version until its almost-miraculous recovery in the fifteenth century, when Poggio Bracciolini found a copy in a trunk in a Swiss monastery, an event so thrilling that he spent the next thirty-six days copying it.

What a strange situation: For sixteen centuries or so, the most important rhetorical work on how to invent material appears to share most of *its* material with the second-most-important work. The most important was repudiated by its author (Cicero later asked people to ignore this immature work, written when he was about 19), and the second has been claimed by no one. One possible explanation for this "most embarrassing" overlap in content, as William Smith calls it (*Dictionary* 727), not to mention the lack of inventiveness about invention, is that young Cicero and some other author were both taking notes from the same rhetoric teacher, each unaware that the other intended to share with the public. Perhaps the material was considered to be so commonplace, so unoriginal, that they believed no one really "owned" it. Whatever the explanation, this redundancy suggests an approach to invention that is entirely different from our modern emphasis on originality and innovation. In classical rhetoric, imitation and the deployment of pre-existing materials are crucial to invention.

If the works themselves strike us as strange, their massive success seems even more bizarre, for they describe invention strategies that were designed to assist lawyers in the Roman courts, and yet these works flourished in schools all over Europe long after the courts were gone. Newton's laws of motion and inertia do often seem to apply to education, and teachers teach what they were taught, but the persistence of a judicially based rhetoric in the absence of an open judicial arena is puzzling. What did generations of teachers see in this approach to invention in particular and rhetoric in general? Let's begin our investigation where young Cicero and Pseudo-Cicero say the orator should begin – with stasis theory, which students still find interesting and useful today.

Stasis theory and the *Dissoi Logoi*

Hermagoras of Temnos is credited with inventing stasis theory around 150 BCE, and so Cicero and the *Rhetorica ad Herennium* author clearly are drawing on a well-established doctrine, whether their source is Hermagoras or his followers. Stasis theory (the Latin is *"status"*) was designed to help defendants or their lawyers discover the crucial issue in a legal dispute. "Stasis" in Greek means both "strife" and "immobility" (compare the English word "static"), and so stasis theory helps one discover both the nature of the argument (the strife) and the tipping point of a case (the immobility), suggesting where to push. Imagine, for example, that you had been hired to defend the Enron executive Ken Lay against the charge of corporate fraud. The first stasis question you would consider has to do with the central fact of the case: Did he do it? If this is the issue that you believe the case turns upon, you'd then want to look for supporting material, challenging the factuality of the event that the prosecution attests. Note that stasis theory also works for the prosecuting attorney, who will assess each issue from the opposing point of view. If you believe that you can't argue effectively against this fact, and you've got to admit the evidence does indicate that Lay extracted over one hundred million dollars from Enron while not revealing the corporation's true situation to stockholders, then the next stasis question has to do with definition: Does the admitted act by your client fit the definition of "corporate fraud"? Perhaps neglecting to mention something or misleading the public is not technically "fraud"? Perhaps the collapse of the company was the result of poor management, or incompetent accounting, but not fraud?

If you can't argue fact or definition, then the next stasis point is quality: you acknowledge that the fraud occurred, and that your client was involved, but you attempt to characterize the quality of the act in some way that is favorable to your client. Perhaps Lay was so involved in his charity work that he was unable to think clearly about the company? Perhaps Lay's intention was only to mislead the public temporarily in order to save the company, foreseeing that thousands of people would suffer devastating financial loss if the company failed? Perhaps Lay was himself the victim of abusive and manipulative business partners? Perhaps he committed fraud only because he has a rare psychological condition that makes it impossible for him to understand numbers? If you cannot alter how the quality of the act will be seen in court, then the last resort in the stasis system concerns the law itself. Perhaps you can focus on the jurisdiction: does this court properly have authority over this case? Perhaps the crimes occurred in other places and should be tried there? Perhaps there are too many former Enron employees in the potential juror pool? Perhaps the judge owned Enron stock? Perhaps you can focus on some ambiguity in the law. Is there a difference between what the law says about corporate fraud and what was actually intended by those who wrote the law? Are there conflicting laws, or some other law that trumps the law being applied? Perhaps the blood-soaked glove found at the scene of the crime doesn't actually fit his hand? (No, wait, that's a stasis point in a different case.)

It is easy to see how this stasis strategy would be embraced by lawyers: it offers a simple decision tree that clarifies what is the issue at stake. Each of these kinds of issues – fact, definition, quality, jurisdiction – opens up different kinds of strategies. And there are sub-strategies: under jurisdiction, for instance, if all else fails, you can beg for forgiveness.

> Fact: Did it happen?
> Definition: If it happened, what is it?
> Quality: What kind of thing is it?
> Jurisdiction: Is this the right venue for judgment?

It is also easy to see how this schema would be embraced by teachers. It's straightforward, logical, and it shows students, even if they don't plan to be defendants or lawyers, the benefits of systematically assessing the persuasive potential of different positions. Identifying the issue at stake seems like the most basic step toward inventing something to say, allowing the speaker to sort out those ideas that are relevant to the case. And by focusing on the case's tipping point, the speaker can also begin to anticipate the other side of the argument. The strategy seems geared toward the *selection* of material, however, as if the speaker is going into a big-box warehouse store to pick out what will be most useful.

Aristotle believed in fact that "one should be able to argue persuasively on either side of a question ... not that we may actually do both (for one should not persuade what is debased) but in order that it may not escape our notice what the real state of the case is and that we ourselves may be able to refute it if another person uses speech unjustly" (34). Although Aristotle seems quite confident here that there is a right side and a wrong, one we might argue and another we would not, the sophists who preceded him believed that there were at least two arguable sides to every issue. An anonymous work from the late fifth century BCE entitled *Dissoi Logoi*, literally "different words," argues for the importance and the philosophical validity of looking at issues from two or more perspectives. Almost any assertion, the *Dissoi Logoi* author says, is both true and false: even "Death is bad" is "not true for the undertakers and gravediggers"; "And undoubtedly it is bad for everyone else, but good for the potters if pottery gets smashed" (Sprague 279). So if you want to argue that Ken Lay is guilty, I can argue that he is a hero who deserves our thanks for exposing a dangerous financial situation; or I will argue that you are guilty of causing more harm to the corporate economy by prosecuting Lay. Whatever one person says, the opposing person can try to turn it around or upside down. For Beth Daniell, this two-sided approach to argument has useful implications for classroom practice and for women's rhetoric, encouraging teachers and students to move beyond a competitive view of rhetoric, in which one person simply attempts to subdue another one, and toward a view in which duality and multiplicity are inherent in any issue.

Stasis theory and contrary thinking, looking for the tipping point, and looking at an argument from the other person's point of view as well as your own, look like the kinds of thinking that smart people do on their own. And rhetorical precepts at their best are, as Aristotle asserted, an attempt to analyze and organize what successful speakers and writers already do, allowing those of us who are less experienced, less gifted, to emulate them more easily (29). Although stasis theory and the *Dissoi Logoi* address legal situations, it's not a bad idea to think like a lawyer even if you're not in the courtroom, determining what is at issue in a particular situation and anticipating what might be said pro and con. Such concepts endured, it seems reasonable to assume, because teachers found them valuable. But there are many questions for which stasis theory seems not very useful (Is pleasure the greatest good? Are chilicheeseburgers worth the calories?). Stasis theory, although it might well give an inexperienced speaker a sense of confidence, only gets one started, it seems. Similarly, the "pro and con" thinking of the *Dissoi Logoi* can be stimulating, but it doesn't tell us *how* to think of alternate ideas. Thus, these heuristics are clearly not Boethius's pathway to discovery. To see what else classical rhetoric offers in the way of invention, we need to turn to a more formidable device, "the topics."

The rhetorical topics

Our sense of a "topic" as a subject, as something to write or talk about, is derived from the ancient Greeks and Romans, as well as medieval, Renaissance, and Enlightenment Europeans. According to Richard Lanham's invaluable *Handlist of Rhetorical Terms*, "The topics were for Aristotle, as they have been for rhetoricians since, both the stuff of which arguments are made and the form of those arguments" (99). If this definition seems confusing to you, then you're in good company, for scholars have been arguing about exactly what the topics are at least since Aristotle started talking about them. If topics are the bricks, mortar, and wiring of arguments (the stuff), then how are they also the plans and blueprints (the form)? Aristotle does distinguish "common" topics from "specific" or "special" topics, and the invention strategies for the question of, say, "Should the minimum voting age be sixteen?" would seem to be different from the strategies for determining, say, "At what age on average is the human brain's decision-making ability fully developed?" Anyone can have an opinion about the first question, drawing on common forms of argument and common knowledge (common topics); to address the second question most authoritatively, a special kind of scientific knowledge base and reasoning, acquired by psychologists, neurologists, biologists, philosophers, and perhaps others, would be needed. But the precise definition of a topic does not appear in Aristotle's *Rhetoric* or his *Topics* (*Topica*) or elsewhere, although he does offer hundreds of examples – which has allowed everyone to form his or her own definition, and generated a whole lot of scholarly discussion.

One particularly lucid and important presentation of the topics appears in Edward P. J. Corbett's *Classical Rhetoric for the Modern Student*, which was first published in 1965 (in later editions, Robert Connors joined Corbett) and made a huge contribution to the revival of serious scholarly interest in rhetoric and especially in invention. Corbett devotes over two hundred pages to his influential second chapter, "The Discovery of Arguments," which advises students to think of the topics as "suggesters," "prompters," or "initiators," or as a "checklist" of ideas (86, 4th edition). The topics, Corbett says, "by suggesting general strategies of development," help writers "to overcome inertia": they "prime the pump"; they "initiate a line of thought" (87). As Corbett presents them, there are five common topics, which all have sub-topics:

> 1) **Definition** (Genus, Division), 2) **Comparison** (Similarity, Difference, Degree), 3) **Relationship** (Cause and Effect, Antecedent and Consequence, Contraries, Contradictions), 4) **Circumstances** (Possible and Impossible, Past Fact and Future Fact), and 5) **Testimony** (Authority, Testimonial, Statistics, Maxims, Laws, Precedents, Examples).

Corbett explains, discusses, and provides extensive examples of each topic, showing the student for instance how Martin Luther King's "Letter from Birmingham Jail" uses "Similarity," a sub-topic of "Comparison." King argues, we see, that condemning the civil rights protesters because "they precipitate violence" is "like condemning a robbed man because his possession of money precipitated the evil act of robbery" (93). Corbett's survey of the topics thus exposes the student to many excellent passages worthy of imitation and identifies what we might think of as structural devices or argumentative techniques.

But how does the ability to recognize the topics help writers to invent material? How would understanding the topic of "similarity" enable or assist King or any other writer? How does the writer, in other words, get from the prompt of a topic to the articulated text? Corbett quotes Quintilian, the great Latin rhetorician: "it is no use considering each separate type of argument and knocking at the door of each with a view to discovering whether they may serve our point, except while we are in the position of mere learners" (*Inst. Orat.*, V, x, 122). Experienced rhetors, in other words, with study, practice, and talent, will become adept at selecting intuitively the most useful topics in a particular situation, finding (as Quintilian puts it) that arguments "spontaneously follow the thought." So the topics in classical rhetoric are a bit like a search engine, pointing the speaker or writer ("spontaneously," once the software is fully installed) to where material might be found.

For instance, with regard to the voting age issue, perhaps I have a sense, as an experienced rhetor familiar with all the various topics, that there may be some potential material "in" the topic of "definition." How might "definition" illuminate "voting rights for sixteen-year-olds"? Although I don't understand how my brain "finds" anything (any more than I understand how Google works), some ideas do in fact spontaneously pop into my head as I think in terms of defining: perhaps I can define "voting" (is it a right that should apply to everyone or a special privilege?), or I could define "age" (are we talking about chronological age, or emotional age, or biological age, or intellectual age?), or perhaps there is even some potential in defining "sixteen" (doesn't this age signify different things in different cultures?). If these ideas don't work, I can just move to another topic, or explore this one some more. Formal study of the topics, in other words, is assumed to refine our natural ability to use the topics, bringing to conscious awareness the lines of argument and materials available to us.

The intriguing notion that there is material "in" a topic, somewhere in some location, is of course metaphorical, although the Greek word *topos* means "place" or "location" (*topoi* is the plural; *locus* and *loci* are the Latin singular and plural). This geographical or spatial metaphor persists in the rhetorical tradition: Cicero would later define a topic as "the region of an argument," comparing it to "the haunts of game" (Quintilian also refers to going where ideas lurk like wild beasts, where game is hunted), or to a "storehouse" where one would go to get arguments.[21] The obscure rhetorician Theon says that a topic refers to the "headquarters," "the place from which you sally out to attack an enemy" (Cope 125). The notion that one goes to some physical "place" in order to get materials for an argument probably derives from the art of memory, which advised speakers to imagine placing the parts of a speech in a sequence of imaginary locations; then, to recall and deliver the speech, one would imagine returning to these imagined places and "finding" the pieces of the argument. Odd as this procedure may sound, it does work, as the association of one thing with another apparently helps to activate long-term memory storage.

In any event, if invention's heritage is in the art of memory, then we can see more clearly that the topics are designed to help the rhetor retrieve *pre-existing* material – as Bacon puts it, to hunt within a closed preserve – and not to generate new ideas and insights. It is no doubt reassuring for the writer or speaker *to think* of the topics as literal places that are containing material, tricking us in a sense into having the confidence to launch into inventing the ideas we need. For James Murphy, E. M. Cope, Michael Leff, Donovan Ochs, Thomas Conley, and other leading scholars of the history of rhetoric, the topics are about finding rather than creating, communicating what is already known rather than discovering anything new, although some important dissenting voices, including Janice Lauer, Carolyn Miller, and Richard Leo Enos, see the topics as part of Aristotle's system for creating probable knowledge (Murphy, *Synoptic* 57). I agree with both sides here, for the topical system certainly can help speakers to access what they know, but it can also generate new ideas by putting this information together in novel ways. Different topics may bring different ideas to your attention, just as any search engine will bring you different materials, but it can only bring you what is already out there. As Corbett puts it:

> What are the chief writers' resources when they have to find their material? Their chief resources will always be the fruits of their education, their reading, their observation, and their reflection. Both Cicero and Quintilian maintained that the most valuable background for an orator was a liberal education, because they recognized that such a broad education was best calculated to aid a person faced with the necessity of inventing arguments on a wide variety of subjects. (85)

This insight is perhaps a sobering counter to the optimism of process pedagogy, reminding us that writing as a mode of learning depends to some degree upon what the student already knows. Students are not equally able to take advantage of heuristics, and in the context of equal opportunity, it is worrying to recognize that some students who are asked to write about their personal experiences will have richer materials to draw upon than others. Asked to write about their summer experiences, the student who has picked peaches all summer and the student who has travelled all over Europe have different resources to access; both students, to be sure, may write excellent narratives, and the peach-picking student may in fact have just as much opportunity to say something important, but it seems reasonable to assume that the demands for creativity and skill are more likely to be greater as one's experience is more repetitive and narrow.

The experiential and intellectual resources that the student brings to a writing assignment include not only the student's experience but also of course the student's repertoire of previous reading. Interestingly enough, the act of reading something stimulating is not usually listed as an invention strategy in composition textbooks. In the modern writing classroom, in fact, the status of reading has been ambiguous. Nancy Nelson describes three different strands of research, beginning in the 1970s and 1980s, that sought to understand the relationship between reading and writing: (1) Intervention studies, in which students might engage in a writing exercise to increase their ability to read a syntactic feature, or a reading exercise to increase their ability to use a feature in their writing; (2) Correlational studies, in which reading and writing skills are compared; and (3) Acquisition studies, which assess whether students incorporate features into their own writing from texts that they have read. What we have learned, as Timothy Shanahan concludes in his recent summary of the research on the reading/writing relationship, is that "it is possible to teach reading so that it improves writing and to teach writing so that it improves reading, but we do not know how to do this consistently" (179). Further, Shanahan says, the research suggests that direct instruction within each ability appears to be more powerful than instruction across them. Composition specialists thus appear to have some support for shifting emphasis away from reading, making the writing classroom into a writing workshop, and thereby focusing on the students' own writing. "The primary textbook in this course will be your own and your classmates' writing": This statement or some variation of it has appeared in many syllabi over the past thirty years as the process movement has expanded, and teachers have endeavored to view their students *as writers*, as the producers of texts, revisions, editorial comments, and even self-generated assignments.

This research tends to see reading as the processing of rhetorical models, accessing sources for acquiring surface features of writing. Writing on the other hand tends to be seen as the display of such syntactic features. Reading is not generally viewed as the pursuit of general knowledge, as a lifelong engagement with the culture that one inhabits. "Rhetorical models," as Nelson says, "were a conventional component of pedagogy for centuries but have had an on-again/off-again pattern in contemporary times" (438). The movement away from rhetorical models and reading arguably stems from the modern emphasis on process, on *what the writer does* rather than *what the writer knows*. Perhaps this limited view of reading – as providing models of discourse features – has something to do with our not knowing how to use reading to improve writing "consistently," as Shanahan puts it. And perhaps the classical tradition and its use of the topics in invention suggest an alternative view. Certainly, Aristotle, Quintilian, Cicero, Erasmus, and many others would have assumed that the educated student would have read a body of material and would have shared a stock of common ideas. Some students would have amassed more ideas than others, to be sure, and thus have a distinct advantage, just as some students would have more talent, or more practice, or better teachers than others. But the "common topics" assumed the value of a foundation of shared knowledge.

In the modern era, the most controversial case for the importance of shared background knowledge arguably has been made by E. D. Hirsch, who set out in *The Philosophy of Composition* (1977), ironically, to identify a manageable number of formal features, based on empirical research, that students should master in order to improve their writing most effectively. Based on his research into the readability of texts and the comparative reading ability of university and community college students, Hirsch came to the conclusion that it is not the formal skills of reading and writing, the process strategies of encoding and comprehension, that most significantly differentiate poor from effective readers and writers. What has limited the advancement of literacy skills, and what distinguishes poor readers (and by extrapolation poor writers), Hirsch says, is a lack of the contextual knowledge needed to make sense of texts. When confronted with passages about the Civil War, university students had greater comprehension than community college students, Hirsch found, primarily because they had more knowledge about the Civil

War, not because they had intrinsically better reading skills. Thus, Hirsch argued in *Cultural Literacy* (1988) for the teaching of *What Every American Needs to Know*, as the book's subtitle put it, and he had the courage or the audacity, depending on your point of view, to identify 5,000 essential facts that educated people ought to know.

Cultural Literacy was a bestseller, so popular it was spoofed on the popular television show *Saturday Night Live*, and textbooks for each grade level (the "Core Knowledge" series) and a follow-up book, entitled *Knowledge Deficit*, have also appeared. Hirsch's ideas have not been welcomed by academics in general or composition specialists in particular, perhaps predictably, but the vehemence of the attacks has perhaps been surprising. For Margaret Spanos, for instance, Hirsch's *Philosophy of Composition*, "Stripped of its pedagogical coding devices," "may be translated into a message which leaves no doubt as to the dynamics of power involved: making damn sure the little bastards don't screw around with our language" (354). Why such acerbity? Hirsch's approach implicitly challenges the process-oriented consensus in pedagogy, devaluing the teacher's intervention in the student's behavior, adopting instead a knowledge-oriented pedagogy. More importantly, although Hirsch has identified his own politics as liberal and presented his project as an attempt to help the excluded and marginalized to achieve cultural literacy and gain access to power and prosperity, his detractors have portrayed him as a regressive conservative, striving to harden the bunkers of the dominant culture.

Thus, Hirsch's curricular proposal reinvents in a sense the general education undergirding the topical invention system, not only focusing on knowledge rather than process, but also embracing the wrong knowledge, at least according to a substantial number of composition specialists. We will return to these issues in Chapters 4 and 6 below on Style and Delivery respectively, but for the moment we should note that some specialists who have vigorously rejected Hirsch's politics (as they perceived them) have nonetheless implicitly agreed that students should be provided with materials to think about and to think with. But rather than the established canon, supposedly reflecting those in power, the content of the writing classroom should, as Charles Paine puts it, "inculcate into our students the conviction that the dominant order is repressive" (564); or, as Patricia Bizzell puts it, "interest them in a social justice project for which they may not presently see any compelling reason" (*Academic* 30). By giving reading and writing assignments that deal with progressive politics (see, e.g., Anderson or Roberts-Miller), or womanist theology (McCrary), or race and ethnicity (e.g., Lyons or Powell), or sexual orientation (see, e.g., Haggerty and Zimmerman or Malinowitz), or any other particular interest, these teachers are implicitly recognizing the heuristic value of bringing students into a "discourse community," providing them with information and materials they can employ in writing.

The liberal education that Quintilian's and Cicero's students would have drawn from, that aspired to be a foundation for any sort of more specialized endeavor, included the intensive study of literature as part of the student's knowledge base. In the classical tradition, students studied literary works as part of their grammatical study (with Grammar, Rhetoric, and Dialectic forming "the Trivium"). For many composition specialists, the place of literary study in writing instruction is problematic: literary texts in general are arguably not the best models for the kinds of things that students will need to write (imagine a letter of application influenced by Wallace Stevens, a lab report inspired by Faulkner), and literary scholars, as we have noted, have often devalued the teaching of writing by assigning this work to graduate students and adjunct faculty. The use of literature as the object of study or as the source of ideas to write about has been controversial "too long to be called a controversy" (that is, since the 1960s and 1970s), as Russell Durst puts it (98), and the trend has certainly been away from the study of literature in composition courses, as "writing about literature" courses have been positioned as the antithesis of process-oriented pedagogy. With an understanding of critical theories as invention strategies, however, writing about literature can certainly be approached as a process (see Lynn, *Texts and Contexts*). Theories such as New Criticism, Reader Response, Deconstruction, and New Historicism function as the "special topics" for writing about literature, providing different lines of argument and bringing materials to the critic's attention – and enlarging the student's fund of knowledge. But literary theories, modern heuristics, and the rhetorical topics are only a portion of the universe of invention, and we need to get a better sense of Aristotle's topics and the larger system of *inventio* that united dialectic and rhetoric, in order to better understand what we have lost.

INVENTIO

Instead of Corbett's lucid and elegant system of five common topics and their sub-topics, Aristotle's work offers a bewildering forest of topics. It's not clear how many topics Aristotle thinks there are, nor how they are organized or related to each other. In chapter 23 of Book Two of his *Rhetoric*, for instance, Aristotle discusses twenty-eight "common" topics (*koina topoi*). As Aristotle puts it, "One topic [*topos*] ... is that from opposites; for one should look to see if the opposite is true of the opposite" – a suggestion that perhaps makes more sense when illustrated: If "to be temperate is a good thing," Aristotle observes, then "to lack self-control is harmful"; "If the war is the cause of present evils, things should be set right by making peace"; if false statements can be persuasive, then truths can be incredible (191). To find material related to the issue of sixteen-year-olds voting, I could for instance ask myself what is the opposite situation. If it is a good thing to lower the voting age, would it be a bad thing to raise it? Is the opposite true of the opposite, as Aristotle says? If most of my audience would agree that we shouldn't raise the voting age, then this idea might be persuasive to them in suggesting that we might lower it. Similarly, looking at another sort of "opposite," if it is good not to have a maximum voting age, how is it good to have a minimum voting age? Obviously, the speaker needs to know what the audience believes in order to assess whether an idea is likely to be effective. Thus, in the classical tradition of invention, as we have noted, a broad liberal education is crucial: using the topics effectively depends upon knowing what the audience knows.

Another example of a common topic in the *Rhetoric* is "from the more and less," which says "If something is not the fact in a case where it would be more [expected], it is clear that it is not a fact where it would be less." Again, Aristotle's illustration makes this hazy abstraction clearer: "If not even the gods know everything, human beings can hardly do so." This topic also can be used to generate ideas about the voting issue. For instance, I believe most people would agree that it is more important for one person to decide whether to have sex, which could result in the birth of another person, than it is for one person to decide whether to vote for this or that candidate. (One person usually cannot elect a candidate, but one person can act in such a way as to create a baby and a lifetime of responsibilities.) Thus, the resulting argument (which may or may not be persuasive): If society has not decided to make sex illegal at sixteen (what is more expected), then it should not be illegal to vote (what would be less expected).

Another illustration offered by Aristotle, "a person who has beaten his father has also beaten his neighbors," seems to derive from the more and less topic in a slightly different way: in this case, as Aristotle says, "if the lesser thing is true, the greater is also" (192). If we agree that it is unlikely for someone to beat his father, but Thersites has done that, then the audience should be more willing to accept the accusation that Thersites has beaten up his neighbor. If we know someone has cheated on his taxes, we are more easily persuaded that he has cheated on a final exam. Note that this line of argument is only probable: no one who stops and thinks about it would agree that one event proves that the other has occurred. But it's persuasive, and that's what rhetoric is about. With regard to the lower voting age, if we are trying to support the case, then we are looking for activities that sixteen-year-olds might be less likely to be allowed to perform, but are; if we're opposing the case, then we want the reverse. Of course, no matter which side we support, this topic can help us anticipate what the other side might say. For instance: It seems less likely that a sixteen-year-old would be given a license to operate deadly machinery than he or she would be allowed to vote. Yet sixteen-year-olds are allowed to operate deadly machinery in the form of automobiles, which kill about 47,000 people every year in the United States. If we allow that, then how can we not allow them to vote? Or, going the other way: it seems less likely that we would limit what people can eat and drink by age, than we would limit their voting rights by age. But we do say people of certain ages cannot drink alcoholic beverages in any amount, or chew tobacco; so we should certainly restrict their ability to engage in something more important than what they consume, namely choosing our leaders.

In addition to the two examples discussed above, "from opposites" and "from more and less," Aristotle briefly discusses "from definition," "from multiple meanings of a word," "from using an opponent's own admissions against him," "from division," "from consequences," "from contrasting public statements with concealed opinions," "from the inconsistency in what an advocate chooses now with what he chose formerly," and eighteen other topics. Some, like punning on a name, or explaining the cause of prejudice, may seem odd (see Murphy *et al.*, *A Synoptic History*, 11ff). And there doesn't seem to be any organizational principle at work in the sequence. William M.A. Grimaldi has suggested that these twenty-eight topics can be sorted into three groups – Cause and Effect, More and Less, and "Some Form of Relation" – but it's not clear how revealing these categories are, especially given the bagginess of "Some Form of Relation." Aristotle does not suggest that his list of topics is exhaustive, and in the next chapter in the *Rhetoric* he covers ten invalid topics, fallacies to avoid or to spot in another person's argument, thus inventing a strategy for response. These include, for instance, using only one unrepresentative example, making assertions about the whole that are true only for a part, and ignoring important circumstances. Again, there is no reason to think that Aristotle believes he is covering all of the kinds of false arguments here. Earlier, in Book 2, Chapter 19, Aristotle has presented a different group of four *topoi* common to all subjects. The first is proving that something is possible or impossible, and Aristotle explains fifteen different ways to make such an argument, saying for instance that if the opposite of something is possible, then that thing is also possible. For instance, if a person can be healthy, it is likely to seem possible that the same person can also be sick. Aristotle also presents *topoi* for showing that some event probably occurred, that an event will occur, and for proving what is more or less.

In addition to these common topics in the *Rhetoric*, Aristotle also discusses "special topics" that are most suitable for particular kinds of arguments and audiences. Aristotle sees three kinds of speeches, each with its own distinctive *topoi*, each one associated with a different setting – the courtroom, the assembly, the ceremony: *Judicial* (or forensic) speeches focus on what is just and unjust, dealing with events in the past; *deliberative* speeches are concerned with what is advantageous or not, regarding events in the future; and *epideictic* speeches discuss what is noble and shameful in the present. For each kind of discourse, Aristotle discusses what special knowledge the speaker needs. In a legislative assembly, one might argue about "finances, war and peace, national defense, imports and exports, and the framing of laws" (53), and for each of these subjects, Aristotle points out, the speaker must have a fund of knowledge. For instance: "one who is going to give advice on finances should know what and how extensive are the revenues of the city, so that if any have been left out they may be added and if any are rather small they may be increased; and all the expenses of the city as well, so that if any is not worthwhile it may be eliminated and if any is too great it may be reduced...." (53). Further, the speaker in a deliberative setting, knowing that the ultimate goal of all such decision-making is happiness, should have studied human nature sufficiently to know what enjoyments lead to happiness, with each one suggesting the possible lines of argument. The speaker, in other words, should consider how this course of action or that will lead to wealth, good reputation, honor, beauty, a good old age, virtue, and so forth: each of these topics may suggest some material.

Any kind of speech, deliberative or judicial or ceremonial, will involve a speaker, an audience, and a subject, and Aristotle also sees that material can be generated by focusing on each element of this communication triangle. He suggests topics that will shape the way the speaker appears to the audience (his *ethos*), topics that will move the emotions (or *pathos*) of the audience, and topics that will provide compelling reasons out of the subject matter itself (*logos*). To establish a persuasive *ethos*, for instance, the speaker should say things that convey his good sense, his good will, and his good morals. To move an audience, the speaker should consider the various emotions, what sort of people are susceptible to which emotions, and what can be said to affect the variety of people. (In fact, in his extensive treatment of the kinds of emotions and kinds of people, Aristotle created what turned out to be an early classic work in psychology.)

However many rhetorical topics there are in Aristotle's system, and however they might be organized (or not), we need to recognize that Aristotle's topics are part of a larger logical system, an entire theory of reasoning. Aristotle clearly assumes that anyone engaging his *Rhetoric* is familiar with demonstrative logic, which is concerned with reasoning securely from established premises; and with dialectic, which is concerned with reasoning from probable premises in a debate format. Indeed, Aristotle influenced and shaped learning in virtually every discipline through his logic, not through his *Rhetoric*, which was neglected or lost to the West for many centuries. "When it comes to this subject" [logic, or the systematic constructing of valid arguments and making correct inferences], Aristotle says, "it is not the case that part had been worked out in advance and part had not; instead, nothing existed at all."[22] To have invented logic is a remarkable claim (at least as astonishing as saying you've invented the Internet), but we have, as Jonathan Barnes says, "no reason to dispute this" (27). There is no single work that contains Aristotle's logic, nor indeed did Aristotle have a word for logic as a whole, but a handful of works did over time come to be known as the *Organon*, the "Tool" or "Instrument," because they present, taken together, his approach to reasoning (Barnes 28): The *Prior Analytics* and the *Posterior Analytics* explain the syllogism, the method for linking statements together logically to produce scientific proofs. *On Interpretation* discusses the statements that are used in reasoning, and the *Categories* considers the terms involved in these statements. The *Topics* provides literally hundreds of "places" to look for assertions to use in debating, and even more topics are presented in *On Sophistical Refutations*, a companion to the *Topics*, which focuses on spotting fallacious arguments in debates. Aristotle's *Rhetoric* typically was not seen traditionally as part of this "tool," but some modern scholars (and I agree) believe it makes sense to think of his *Rhetoric* as part of this larger comprehensive system, which covers demonstration, dialectic, rhetoric, and sophistic.[23]

Aristotle's approach to argument distinguishes two types of reasoning, deduction and induction. An inductive argument moves from particular instances to a general conclusion. For instance, let's say that my beloved football team, the Gamecocks, lost whenever they wore black jerseys last year, and they won whenever they wore something else. So my general conclusion is "The Gamecocks lose whenever they wear black jerseys." Inductive reasoning (which we all do without studying philosophy) is powerful, but it does have some vulnerability, as you may be suspecting: How many particulars are needed before a conclusion can be drawn? What Aristotle calls a "demonstrative" proof, one that provides us with solid knowledge (what we might think of as scientific knowledge), requires that every instance be considered. With only one counter-example, then, the conclusion is collapsed. A "dialectical" proof, however, only needs to be compelling enough to use in a debate or argument. No reasonable person would accept as scientific truth my assertion that the Gamecocks will lose every time they wear black, but my assertion might be good enough to be persuasive, especially if I could provide some deductive support.

"A deduction," Aristotle says, "is an argument in which, certain things being supposed, something else ... follows of necessity ..." (*Prior Analytics*, I.i, 24a18–20). The most famous example of deductive reasoning is probably this sequence, or syllogism:

All men are mortal.   *Deductive = if x is true,*
Socrates is a man.   *then y is too*
Therefore Socrates is mortal.   *x + y are true, z is too*

Aristotle worked out rules that would allow anyone to determine whether the third statement, the conclusion, was logically drawn from the first two statements, the premises. In this case, if we assume that the first two statements are true, then the third one, something new, is also true. There are, Aristotle says, nineteen different ways to arrange three statements that are logically valid. For example: If we assume "Every horse is a mammal," and "Some dogs are not tame," then what conclusion can we draw? Aristotle's rules explain why there doesn't seem to be any inference to be drawn: the two premises do not have a term in common. If we assume however that "Every horse is a mammal," and "Sam is a horse," then we can conclude that "Sam is a mammal."

Now, we really don't need the aircraft carrier of Aristotle's *Organon* to tell us that one sequence adds up, and the other doesn't. But Aristotle provides analytical tools and rules that suggest how to build or take apart much more complicated or difficult arguments. Common sense also often tells us which sequences seem logical, but Aristotle is able to identify four possible kinds of assertions – (a) All men are handsome, (b) Some men are handsome, (c) Some men are not handsome, and (d) No men are handsome – and then identify all the logically valid relationships that are possible. Few teachers and students today are going to be willing to invest the time and energy to learn the nineteen possible logical patterns that are valid, but even this glance at Aristotle's deductive logic points us toward a strategy that we can use in inventing arguments. Namely, if you are constructing a deductive argument or attacking one, you can try to simplify the argument into a series of statements. Putting an argument into this syllogistic form, with two premises and a conclusion, makes it easier to see whether the starting points can be questioned, and whether the conclusion actually is justified. For instance: Things that are black are hard to see. The Gamecock jerseys are black. Therefore, the Gamecock jerseys are hard to see. So it stands to reason that quarterbacks throwing to receivers wearing black might have a harder time spotting them, thus supporting the idea that the team tends to lose wearing black.

In addition to deduction and induction, Aristotle thinks in terms of four levels of probability. "Demonstrative" reasoning has the highest level of certainty, beginning with established truths and yielding some equally solid insight, if the rules for constructing syllogisms are followed. Such reasoning requires starting points that are invariably true, not established by any particular circumstances or observations. Although demonstrative reasoning is sometimes referred to as the realm of science in Aristotle's epistemology, Aristotle's science is fundamentally deductive: it is not our science. There is some disagreement, however, among modern scholars whether Aristotle believes our foundational knowledge is innate or empirical in origin, and Aristotle's understanding of demonstrative reasoning is quite difficult: when James of Venice (who was in Paris) provided the first translation from the Greek of the *Posterior Analytics* in 1128, no one would lecture on it, finding it virtually incomprehensible.

Whereas demonstration endeavors to establish truth, working from previously established truth, dialectic deals with problems that may not have solid answers, only opinions. Some questions don't yield certain truth: What is the best beer? Should priests marry? Does illegal immigration ultimately help or harm an economy? More accessible and practical, "dialectical" reasoning follows the rules of argumentation, allowing one person to dispute with another and establish a winner and a loser. Dialectical disputation may help us to understand these issues better – but that depends on the skill of the two people arguing. Aristotle clearly assumes in his *Topics* that his audience knows a lot about dialectical disputation, and so what he is providing is tactical guidance. The topics in dialectical reasoning are strategies – lines of argument for winning in debate. For the modern student of writing, Aristotle's advice regarding dialectic can be unexpectedly valuable in several ways. Consider these excerpts (which, admittedly, are not easy to follow):

> Again, in the case of the contradictory opposite, look and see if it bears more than one meaning. For if this bears more than one meaning, then the opposite of it also will be used in more than one meaning; e.g. "to fail to see" a phrase with more than one meaning, viz. (1) to fail to possess the power of sight, (2) to fail to put that power to active use. But if this has more than one meaning, it follows necessarily that "to see" also has more than one meaning: for there will be an opposite to each sense of "to fail to see"; e.g. the opposite of "not to possess the power of sight" is to possess it, while of "not to put the power of sight to active use", the opposite is to put it to active use.
>
> If you are not well equipped with an argument against the assertion, look among the definitions, real or apparent, of the thing before you, and if one is not enough, draw upon several. For it will be easier to attack people when committed to a definition: for an attack is always more easily made on definitions.
>
> Moreover, look and see in regard to the thing in question, what it is whose reality conditions the reality of the thing in question, or what it is whose reality necessarily follows if the thing in question be real: if you wish to establish a view inquire what there is on whose reality the reality of the thing in question will follow (for if the former be shown to be real, then the thing in question will also have been shown to be real); while if you want

to overthrow a view, ask what it is that is real if the thing in question be real, for if we show that what follows from the thing in question is unreal, we shall have demolished the thing in question. (*Topica* ch. 15)

You can see here, I hope, that Aristotle is advising the speaker to probe his opponent's case for a weak spot. The idea is for Disputant A to get Disputant B to agree to a point that leads to the conclusion that Disputant A desires, which has become basic debating strategy.

Rhetoric, like dialectic, operates in the realm of the probable and persuasive, but instead of two opponents bound by rules, one speaker is bound by an audience's response. The speaker can appeal to the emotions, and what *seems* to be logical is more important than what is strictly valid. But rhetorical invention and reasoning can certainly draw on dialectical strategies. Aristotle's fourth kind of reasoning, false or sophistical logic, is a twisting or perverting of valid thinking. In the classical rhetorical tradition, students would have been assumed to understand dialectic (or logic), but even modern specialists in rhetoric have tended to ignore (understandably) rhetoric's counterpart. In the early nineteenth century, Richard Whately, for instance, offered one of the last incarnations of classical rhetoric, a landmark work for modern scholars. But Whately's *Logic*, obviously published as a companion to his *Rhetoric*, is largely ignored. Even in the Renaissance, someone as immensely learned as Juan Luis Vives is backing away from the edifice of Aristotle's "tool," claiming that the massive work is actually reducible to "a few brief precepts":

The logic of Aristotle consists in its entirety of a few brief precepts, namely the nature of terms as taught in the books of the *Categories*; the force of propositions in the *On Interpretation*; formulas for syllogisms in the *Prior Analytics*; the uses of persuasion and invention in the *Topics*; and subtle [misleading] argumentation in the *On Sophistical Refutations*. ... Aristotle

> does not embroil and detain his pupil in frigid and senseless
> suppositions, extensions, restrictions, and other petty terms.
> This great genius, the inventor of all those forms and syllogisms
> and indeed of all logic itself, did not consider such things
> necessary for a training in logic. (Fantazzi, 68)

Vives is directly attacking the medieval logicians who added "petty
terms" to Aristotle's logic, but he is indirectly suggesting that one
does not need all of Aristotle in order to make use of Aristotle's
approach to invention and logic. To assess this crucial notion, let's
return to Boethius and his discovery.

Before his untimely death, Boethius among many other
accomplishments had translated and written a commentary upon
Aristotle's *Topics*. Indeed, as one of the few scholars of his day fluent
in Greek, Boethius intended to translate into Latin and thereby preserve all of Aristotle's 150 or so works (about 6,000 modern pages).
Boethius had also written ("with a great deal of effort," he says) a
commentary upon Cicero's *Topics*, and his discovery of the "paths of
discovery" was in fact the result of his efforts to harmonize the work
of these two great thinkers on the topics. Boethius assumed that
any apparent conflicts or gaps between Aristotle and Cicero on the
discovery of arguments must be illusory (great minds must think
alike), and if he could just figure out how to put the two together,
he'd have the ultimate rhetorical tool.

It may seem strange for Boethius to say that his commentary
on Cicero's *Topics* took a great deal of effort, because Cicero presents
his *Topics* as an attempt to simplify and explain Aristotle's challenging work. Cicero tells us that his friend Trebatius, noticing a copy
of Aristotle's *Topica* in Cicero's library, had asked about its contents,
and when Cicero explained to him "that these books contained a
system developed by Aristotle for inventing arguments, so that
we might come upon them by a rational system without wander-
ing about," Trebatius had "begged" Cicero to teach him the subject
(383). As a lawyer, Trebatius obviously loved the idea of a routine

for inventing arguments. Cicero tells us that he urged Trebatius, "aflame with eagerness," "to read the books" for himself, "or acquire the whole system from a very learned teacher of oratory" (383). But Trebatius found himself "repelled from reading the books by their obscurity," and the "very learned" rhetoric teacher recommended by Cicero "was not acquainted with these works" (385). We may wonder why a rhetoric teacher wouldn't know about this system of discovery, but Cicero says that he was not surprised, on reflection, because these are works of philosophy, and even professed logicians, not to mention rhetoricians, are too little acquainted with them. So, we're to understand that there is a system for inventing arguments in rhetoric, but the system isn't in the field of rhetoric – it's in logic or philosophy. And it is too difficult for many rhetoricians. Very interesting.

Neither *Cliff's Notes* nor *The Complete Idiot's Guide to the Topics* had been published at this time, so, at Trebatius' urging, on July 28, 44 BCE, having arrived by ship at Rhegium, Cicero sent to his friend Trebatius a book that he had written during the voyage. We can imagine Trebatius's relief when he received Cicero's *Topica*, which would turn out to be Cicero's last work on a rhetorical subject. Now he would have access to this essential aspect of inventing arguments. And for generations of readers, reading over Trebatius's shoulder, it has proved to be an extremely influential work. What Cicero's *Topica* isn't exactly, however, is an explanation of Aristotle's *Topica*. Modern scholars agree that there is in fact "little resemblance" between Cicero's "explanation" and Aristotle's work, raising, as H. M. Hubbell, the editor of the Loeb edition of Cicero's *Topica*, puts it, "the problem of what Cicero was doing, and what he thought he was doing" (377). Cicero does point out that he took no books on this voyage, relying only on his memory, and perhaps that alone would account for the dramatic differences between Aristotle's *Topica* and Cicero's *Topica*. But Cicero had referred Trebatius to "a system for inventing arguments" (disciplinam inveniendorum argumentorum" (382, 383)), not to an individual work. Further, regarding this system,

Cicero curiously refers to those "works, which are, as I think, by Aristotle" (385). We know that Cicero knows that Aristotle's *Topica* is by Aristotle; he begins his own *Topica* by referring to that work. What Cicero really thought he was doing is lost to us, but we can say that in actuality he was explaining a list of topics similar to a list that appears in Book II of Aristotle's *Rhetoric*. In addition to "cause-effect," "definition," and "similarity," in his *Topics* Cicero also discusses "difference," "contradictories," "circumstances," "greater or less or equal," "sequence of events," "genus and species," and "division into parts" (the last two are actually a subset of definition, and I have eliminated what seemed to be redundant categories).

Boethius's discovery, which I promised to reveal at the outset of this chapter, was that he could indeed harmonize the topical systems of the two giants of argument and persuasion, Aristotle (by way of Themistius) and Cicero. Boethius created what he believed to be a simpler, user-friendlier system by grouping related topics under more general headings, which he called "maximal propositions." For example, if we want to argue about whether rulers should be chosen by lot, one topic to consider is "from proportion," Boethius says. One "maximal proposition" under "proportion" is this idea: "What occurs in one thing must occur in what is proportional to that thing." Applying this idea to our issue, we might arrive at this line of reasoning: A pilot is related to a ship as a ruler is to a city. Pilots should not be chosen by lot. Therefore, rulers should not be chosen by lot. Here's another example: Suppose we want to argue over whether English professors are secretly running the world. If we look in a topic called "from the whole," we would find this idea in Boethius's system: "Whatever is present to the genus is present to the species (and the opposite)." Applying this maximal proposition, we might get something like this: The world is ruled by God; human affairs are part of the world; therefore, human affairs are ruled by God, not English professors. The topic, in other words, offers a general structural relationship, which we can fill in with more specific examples. Where the specific examples come from is still not exactly clear, but the topic stimulates our thinking.

And how does Boethius organize the topics and their various maximal propositions? According to Boethius's modern translator and commentator, Eleonore Stump, his treatment of the topics is organized in terms of what is known as "the Porphyrian tree," a point apparently so obvious to Boethius that he neglects even to mention it. Stump has worked out in her own tree diagram how all the topics related to each other, but here we come up against a wave of reasons why Boethius's discovery of the method of discovery has not filtered down to our modern classrooms. For starters (and by way of review here) Boethius would have assumed that anyone who wanted to use his method of discovery would have stocked his (or rarely her) brain with the knowledge that educated people enjoyed. Many scholars and writers through the ages (including, for instance, Erasmus, Samuel Johnson, Thomas Jefferson, Benjamin Franklin, F. Scott Fitzgerald) have kept "commonplace" books – collections of facts, ideas, quotations, observations, and phrases. It may be, E. D. Hirsch notwithstanding, considerably more difficult to say today than in Aristotle's or Cicero's or Boethius's time what an educated person should know, although the existence of core or basic requirements in education, elementary to post-secondary, attests to our persistent desire to gather together a common foundation of knowledge.

Also, the classical approach to invention that Boethius refines is part of a larger system of reasoning. When writing teachers today ask students to compose an argument, they generally do not assume that students have any understanding of logic and argumentation. We do assume, I suppose, if we think about it, that students have somehow picked up this rationality by osmosis, by reading and analyzing arguments, or even by arguing with other people. What an awareness of Aristotelian logic suggests for modern teachers, however, is that we may be asking students to perform complicated logical tasks without explicitly addressing the underlying skills and materials needed to perform those tasks. In modern composition textbooks, the discussion of reasoning is typically reduced to a consideration of a limited number of logical fallacies. It may be helpful for students to know that they should avoid the red herring fallacy and the *post hoc ergo propter hoc* fallacy, but it might be helpful also to have some positive instruction in reasoning. Given this missing foundation, teachers may well decide to ask students to tell autobiographical stories, describe fruits and vegetables, respond to a movie – rather than construct persuasive arguments.

Most people today don't know anything about Porphyry's Tree, so we don't appreciate the beauty of Boethius's harmony of the topics. Students usually don't come into writing classes aware of the Square of Opposition, or of any of the basic rules of logic, ancient or modern, and it seems unlikely that any call to revive Aristotelian logic in all its complexity will meet with much success. But the modern writing teacher may take away from this discussion an awareness of what has been lost, as well as some useful insights from this slight acquaintance with invention in the classical tradition, juxtaposed with the modern process-oriented pedagogy. How can we put this historical knowledge to use?

APPLICATIONS

Let's try now to sum up here.

1. There are two fundamentally different ways of thinking about invention: classical and romantic, ancient and modern, formal and intuitive, procedural and process. In the classical approach, invention arises from the manipulation of shared and acquired materials. It is a kind of banking system, in which ideas are gathered from reading and study, and these ideas are then accessed when needed. This accessing can be assisted by a topical system that suggests to speakers and writers the kinds of materials they might gather, and the lines of argument that they might choose. Because students are drawing on the resources of their culture, preparing for invention means, fundamentally, learning what other people know. To be persuasive in a particular situation you need to know what your audience believes; you can't support an argument with facts or values that people don't accept. So you need to read and study what other

educated people have read and studied, not just to appropriate or imitate an effective style, but also to gain knowledge. Imitation, to be sure, is not only an essential part of learning, from this perspective, but imitation is also an effective strategy, confirming one's proficiency and preparation.

In the romantic orientation, the focus shifts from preparation and procedure to process: the act of writing will in itself produce new ideas if the student will simply draw upon the remarkable resources of the human brain. Writing is a way of learning. Although it may be difficult to escape imitation and think for oneself, it is imperative that the writer should invest the effort to seek originality and personal insight. By engaging in the process with effort and openness, the student evades that most heinous academic offense, plagiarism, the complete absence of innovation and uniqueness.

2. Should we embrace the classical or the romantic approach to invention? These are, of course, great simplifications of different ways of thinking about invention, but to the extent that they do have historical and epistemological validity, they can help us think about our pedagogical priorities. Taken together, they seem more like pendulum swings, like mirror images, like emphases on different aspects of invention to the exclusion of others. Do we want originality and personal insight, or do we want persuasive evidence? We want both, it seems clear, depending upon the writing task at hand. Innovative ideas may be helpful in persuading, and logical connection can be useful in expressive discourse. We need to draw on both process pedagogy and the classical tradition to give students the greatest flexibility and proficiency. Although writing can be a way of learning, it also seems clear that the informed writer can make better use of this process.

In practice, in the classroom, the optimism and spontaneity of process-oriented pedagogy has much to offer students and teachers, especially with those genres and assignments that call for personal knowledge and immediate observation. But students can also benefit, whatever the kind of writing, from imitation and the appropriation of pre-existing structures and materials, so long as they understand the relative ease and importance of avoiding plagiarism. Do we want our students to absorb a body of knowledge and assumptions, fitting tasks into these paradigms, thinking through problems in prescribed and socially sanctioned ways? Or do we want students to think for themselves, to arrive independently at their own individual ways of doing things and thinking through? As I say, I think we want both. Hence the value for students of reading all sorts of texts. Some careful analysis of model texts and passages can reveal for students, without layers of terminology, how various arguments have been put together. This analysis is as simple as reading the argument and then noting how it works, or fails to work: what are the assertions, what does one have to assume in order to make these assertions (what sort of audience is being addressed, in other words), and do they persuasively hang together? We can teach the topics in practice, in other words, rather than only in theory.

3. As we have seen, focusing on some aspect of invention has been a recurrent feature of the various approaches to the considerable challenge of invention. To teach invention, we might stop trying to teach it as a whole, or even defer thinking about it at all until students have control of other aspects of composing. We might start instead with style and structure, providing students with content to use, and letting them play with different ways to express the given material. We might stop worrying about whether they are expressing their unique insights and selves, and let them knowingly and openly imitate instead what other writers have done. The idea here is that it's counterproductive – it's asking too much – to have students try to invent material as they also try to arrange it and articulate it in an effective style. Benjamin Franklin, as he reported in his *Autobiography*, taught himself a great deal about writing by imitating Addison's and Steele's essays. Chapter 4 below on style offers some ideas for developing fluency that are related to Franklin's practice. The most effective approach to writing instruction, at least according to George Hillocks's extensive review of the empirical

research on writing, provides students with the information that they need in order to solve a particular problem or adopt a position. Students are given, in other words, a common stock of knowledge, a scenario for instance, allowing them all to hunt, as much as possible, within the same conceptual preserve. Similarly, freewriting and other approaches that endorse revision allow students to focus on being creative, setting aside momentarily questions of style and structure.

If invention is like going to a mental filing cabinet and finding what is already there, then the challenge of education, it would seem, is to get as much knowledge as possible crammed into those brain files, and to focus on strategies for organizing and recalling and connecting that knowledge. If invention, on the other hand, is a magical filing cabinet where stuff just creatively appears, then the writer needs only to know how to work the cabinet. Depending on the task and the writer, invention may be like one or both of these cabinets, or neither. For those of us who work in Composition and Rhetoric, the adventure is showing students the richest possible repertoire to draw upon.

Teaching Invention: some activities

Activity 1

Ask students to find instances of the topics that Corbett covers and explain to an alien who is learning about human culture and language how each topic works. I suggest the following sequence: (a) Divide the topics up and assign one or two to each student. (b) Each student presents his or her example to the class, providing copies. (Students may ask the teacher for guidance in finding examples. I'd suggest that students look first in current issues of *The New York Times*, or *The New Yorker*, or *The Economist*, or other similar magazines.) (c) The students discuss how the example works: what are the assumptions, the underlying principles, the line of argument being employed? (d) Each student writes a brief analysis of his own passage and someone else's.

Activity 2

Have students try cubing, tagmemics, and freewriting, then write a brief report about their experiences.

Activity 3

One of my teachers (and later colleague), James Dickey, had the most bizarre invention strategy for writing poetry: he asked students to pick a fruit or vegetable, carry that fruit or vegetable around with them for twenty-four hours, never losing sight of it, and then write a poem about their edible companion. This exercise invariably resulted in some amazingly inventive poems. Perhaps almost any bizarre practice will serve as an invention strategy, if the writer is willing to try it, by breaking down our inhibitions and predictable reactions. Dickey's technique can be applied to other kinds of objects that do not decay and smell, like a golf ball or a photograph.

Activity 4

Select a passage (or have the students select one) and study it closely with your students. Then ask them to set the passage aside and try to reproduce its argument or meaning or plot in their own words. This activity focuses on the intellectual activities of invention that occur after the basic idea is discovered. Students compare their version to the author's, both for ideas, logic, and style.

Activity 5

Ask students to analyze well-written passages from various genres (you may want to have the students select the passages, or some of them) in order to determine not what the passages mean, or how well they are written, but rather what the writer had to know in order to invent the material. Have students make as thorough a list as possible of what the writer knew, then select some things on the list and rewrite the passage imagining that the writer lacked the selected information. Final step: articulate how the revision is different.

Activity 6

Engage the students in a dialectical debate tournament. One person decides whether to affirm or deny the issue, another person asks questions, attempting to get the first person to contradict himself or give in to the questioner, and a third person determines the winner. Round-robin double-elimination tournament with brief written comments on the experience assigned afterward. A variation: students invent a medieval debate, creating both sides of the contest.

Activity 7

Give students a passage and ask them to summarize it with proper documentation, quote from it appropriately, and plagiarize it, clearly labeling each effort.

Activity 8

Ask students to consider how Google differs from invention in the classical tradition.

RECOMMENDATIONS FOR FURTHER READING: INVENTION

Elbow, Peter. *Everyone Can Write: Essays Toward a Hopeful Theory of Writing and Teaching Writing*. New York: Oxford University Press, 2000.

Emig, Janet. "Writing as a Mode of Learning." *College Composition and Communication* 28 (May 1977): 122–8.

Murray, Donald. *A Writer Teaches Writing*. (2nd edn.) Boston: Houghton, 1985.

Sloane, Thomas. "Reinventing *inventio*." *College English* (1989): 461–73.

Young, Richard, and Yameng Liu, eds. *Landmark Essays on Rhetorical Invention in Writing*. New York: Routledge, 1995.

The problem: Inexperienced writers often don't have a sense of how to structure their work. What should they say first – and then what? Does it matter in what order ideas are presented? How should a piece of writing end? Is there a particular formula for a particular kind of thing, or do we have basic principles for structure that govern all sorts of things?

3 Arrangement

> It is the pervading law of all things organic and inorganic, of all things physical and metaphysical, of all things human and all things superhuman, of all true manifestations of the head, of the heart, of the soul, that life is recognizable in its expression, that form ever follows function. This is the law.
>
> Louis Sullivan

> Form follows function – that has been misunderstood. Form and function should be one, joined in a spiritual union.
>
> Frank Lloyd Wright

GENRE

Arrangement, in its most narrow sense, is concerned with identifying the parts of a text and organizing those parts into a whole. Classical rhetoric focused on oral speeches, but arrangement has evolved to deal with written texts and, more recently, the visual design of texts, as well as the interplay of visual and aural design in electronic media. Although "arrangement" as a term is currently out of fashion, and the Greek and Latin terms, *taxis* and *dispositio*, are not familiar except to specialists, a cluster of overlapping terms cover essentially the same subject in a wide variety of disciplines: "form," "organization," "design," "shape," and "structure."

This subject comes second in classical rhetoric's canon, but does the form, as Louis Sullivan says in the epigraph above, really follow the function? Does the invention of ideas determine how the ideas will be arranged? Do you see what materials are available and then decide what you can build? Or, as Frank Lloyd Wright says, are the two inseparable, so that the structure determines what can be said, but the content also limits the form? For Ross

Winterowd, "Invention and arrangement are so nearly the same that they are almost indistinguishable; they are basically the same process" (*Rhetoric* 121), and J. C. McCroskey agrees that invention and arrangement are "inextricably interwoven" (215). Not only is it an open question which comes first – form or content, arrangement or invention – we should also note that one both constrains and enables the other: if language shapes reality, as Ernst Cassirer says, the reality can be articulated only in the shapes that language allows. Still, no matter how intimately they are involved, invention and arrangement are in fact not the same thing: the blueprint can be drawn, the recipe can be laid out, before or after or even at the same time the materials are gathered; each activity can influence the other. But they are fundamentally different endeavors.

This distinction is important because an understanding of arrangement in a larger sense is crucial for students' success in creating effective texts. Imagine what it would feel like to inhabit some culture in which scientific experiments must be written up in some special language that looks like English, but seems to have different grammatical rules; and an application for a job must follow an elaborate and mysterious formula. Such a culture is in fact inhabited by students who do not understand the conventions of, say, a lab report or a letter of application. Explicitly teaching students such conventions involves conveying an understanding of the parts of a text that are required, their sequence, how they are related, how they are experienced by an audience. Thus, arrangement is intimately related to genre. A genre, as Charles Bazerman puts it, is "a social construct that regularizes communication, interactions, and relations" (*Shaping Written Knowledge* 62). When a text is perceived to have structural properties that identify it as a certain type, then it is said to belong to a certain genre – laboratory report, job application letter, detective fiction, legal brief, newspaper story, etc. A newspaper story, for instance, typically begins with a tightly condensed statement of the events covered in the story, then expands into smaller details, unpacking different aspects of what has happened. Obviously, an understanding of a genre's structural properties can help to orient both the writer and the reader, shaping expression as well as comprehension. To assemble the correct parts and place them in the proper order, a writer needs to understand the kind of text being fashioned – how its arrangement relates to its purpose. As Carolyn Miller puts it, "a rhetorically sound definition of genre must be centered not on the substance or the form of the discourse but on the action it is used to accomplish" (151). Function drives form, in other words.

At the same time, as I've suggested, the perception of genre also guides the audience's awareness of function: we need to understand the conventions of a detective story to know how to react to the crime that occurs at the beginning of a story, for instance. How do writers and readers arrive at an understanding of this interplay of arrangement and genre? The first rhetorical teacher, Corax, reportedly taught a simple but powerful structure that allowed his paying clients to organize their speeches effectively.[1] Corax might have invented this structure, but it seems more likely that he observed what successful speakers did. Everyone, in fact, is to some degree already a student of rhetoric, because we are constantly exposed to verbal strategies, and we experience which structures seem more or less effective in our particular discourse community, for a particular action. To emulate what is successful and avoid what isn't, we only need to notice what is going on. Writers and speakers, in other words, can learn how to control form and genre explicitly and implicitly, from the top down and the bottom up. One can read a dozen sonnets and infer what they have in common; or read a description of a sonnet's features; or, ideally, both.

This chapter looks at arrangement from both sides, offering a brief historical overview of how form in argument has been taught, and addressing the key question of the role that form has been seen to play in communication and creativity: specifically, have people thought that form followed function? Then I'll consider how writing teachers more recently have approached the pedagogy of arrangement in a more intuitive and empirical way. And then I'll offer some suggestions for teaching arrangement, along with some sample activities.

The durability of the structure that reportedly goes all the way back to the teachings of "Corax," and that is identified with classical rhetoric, is remarkable. Although we do not have his teachings, it seems clear from later authorities that Corax advocated organizing a speech into (1) an introduction, (2) a narration, (3) a proof, and (4) a conclusion (Katula 25). A speech begins, with the application of a fixed template to various situations: the form is settled, and it is applied to various functions – specifically, to arguments in court (forensic speeches), in assemblies (deliberative speeches), and in ceremonies (epideictic speeches). By the time of Plato (427–347 BCE), this structural advice seems to have become a pervasive assumption. Both Plato and later Aristotle (384–322 BCE) complained about and thus helped to preserve (in a sense) the teachings of the earliest handbooks, which included the assertion (as Socrates reports in Plato's *Phaedrus*, paras. 266–7) that a courtroom speech has a fixed sequence of elements: (1) an introduction (as Corax indicated); (2) a statement of facts supported by witnesses, as well as by indirect evidence (corresponding to Corax's narration); (3) arguments from probability, from supplementary proof, and a refutation of countering arguments (corresponding to Corax's proof); and (4) a final refutation and recapitulation (the conclusion in Corax's scheme).

Socrates (as Plato constructs him) does not think this naming of parts will provide any help to the speaker, but the pedagogical record overwhelmingly contradicts him. Indeed, although Plato's *Phaedrus* is generally considered to be a monumentally important work in the history of rhetoric, the history of rhetorical instruction moves away from Plato's vision of a philosophical, truth-based rhetoric. Aristotle, who also obviously yearns for a philosophical rhetoric and a purely rational audience, concedes that in reality the speaker cannot rely on logic alone, but must also think about how he presents himself, and how the audience will react emotionally. Hence, although Aristotle first says that a speech need only have two parts – making a claim and then proving it (*Rhetoric* 1414b) – he concedes the necessity, given the limitations of real audiences, of four parts: an introduction, a statement of fact, an argument, and a conclusion.

By the first century BCE, in the anonymous *Rhetorica ad Herennium*, all five offices are given thorough treatment, including arrangement, "the ordering and distribution of the matter, making clear the place to which each thing is to be assigned," as the *Herennium* author puts it (7). The parts of a discourse, the *Herennium* author confidently tells us, are "the Introduction, Statement of Facts, Division, Proof, Refutation, and Conclusion" (9) – which is just a slight expansion of Aristotle's plan, unpacking the argument section into three parts: division, proof, and refutation; and also a slight variation on Corax's structure, as his "narration" becomes the "statement of facts" and "division" in the *Herennium*, and Corax's "proof" section becomes "proof" and "refutation" (a kind of counter-proof) in the *Herennium*. Cicero's *De inventione* ("On Invention"), written about the same time as the *Herennium* (around 85 BCE), assumes that to invent materials one must understand the parts of the speech for which one is generating ideas. Cicero identifies precisely the same sections of an argument as the *Herennium* author, and he discusses in detail precisely what to put into each section.[2]

Why is there such continuity in the prescribed form for a speech, stretching from the posited origin with Corax through these two most influential Latin rhetorics? One might argue that this form has endured because it works; because it is in a sense the "right" approach; because perhaps it accords with the way we process language. It does seem reasonable first to orient an audience, establishing an identity, articulating the situation, and creating a relationship with the audience, a role for them to take on; then to lay out the events leading up to the occasion of this argument; then to state one's point and indicate how the ensuing support for it will be organized; then to provide that support; then to anticipate any objections to one's argument, countering them; and then to wrap up one's case, reviewing what has been shown, and refocusing the audience's desired reaction, perhaps arousing their emotional involvement. By dividing a speech into these parts, one can think about different purposes and even different styles for the various parts. But a wider survey of form, especially beyond this Greco-Roman tradition, might suggest that there is nothing inevitable about this structure. In the *Thread of Discourse*, Joseph Grimes notes how in the Abi Consta tribe a properly made speech should begin with an assertion of the speaker's own ignorance and unfitness to offer guidance; in the Wasabiki culture, all stories should end (amazingly enough) with a pack of multi-colored dogs running away – a kind of narrative punctuation mark, we suppose (222, 261).

However our sense of "proper" structure emerges, it does seem clear that the continuation of a form is supported by the discourse community's recognition of the interplay of form and genre. A genre is recognized by the members of a cultural community as a distinct sort of discourse, and it also helps to create a community. When readers see a text that is arranged on the page like a poem, and that has fourteen lines with a particular rhyme scheme (abab cdcd efef gg, for example), then they will see this text as a sonnet, if they are familiar with that genre. Readers will then read this text against the background of the previous sonnets they've read, approaching it with certain expectations of subject matter and development, deepening their sense of the discourse community. The idea of a genre is not however limited to a set form: a detective story has a certain shape, in the sense that a crime is committed and someone (the "detective") exposes the perpetrator, but it is not only the story's structure that distinguishes it, but rather matters of plot and character. Genre is a function, in other words, of the placement of the reader and the author as well as the structural parts. Science fiction, likewise, a notoriously difficult genre to define, seems to be marked by features that relate to a variety of elements, including character, plot, style, and especially setting: we're in space, we're living under the ocean, we're in the future or some alternate past, we have friends with pointed ears and no emotions.

Kenneth Burke's oft-cited definition of "form" helps to illuminate this relationship between form and genre: "Form," Burke says in
Counter-Statement, "is an arousing and fulfillment of desire. A work
has form in so far as one part of it leads a reader to anticipate another
part, to be gratified by the sequence" (124). The genre of a public speech,
by the time of the *Rhetorica ad Herennium* and *De inventione,* clearly
seems to have involved arousing certain expectations in the audience, recognizing that certain parts of a speech would be presented
in a particular order. Some parts might be omitted, as the handbook
authors indicated, and there was considerable leeway in what could
go into a given part. But the understood template was there, as both
the handbooks and surviving speeches indicate. Thus, the stability of
this structure – Introduction, Statement of Facts, Division, Proof and
Refutation, and Conclusion – no doubt owes something to the audience's expectancy that an informed person, one who knows how to
present a speech, would employ such a form.

But when form is used to certify the speaker's competency,
is it necessarily following function? The medieval letter writer for
instance could rely upon explicit directions about the shape that his
(or rarely her) letter should take: *The Principles of Letter Writing*
(*Rationes dictandi*), published by an anonymous author around
1135, confidently dictates, "There are ... five parts of a letter: the
Salutation, the Securing of Goodwill, the Narration, the Petition,
and the Conclusion," and each part is explained in extensive detail
(Bizzell and Herzberg, *Rhetorical* 432). The salutation from a delin-
quent student asking for money from his parents, for instance,
should be quite different from the salutation of a teacher to his
pupil, but the parts of both letters should be the same, and the parts
should be five. Perhaps the medieval student could get money from
his parents without following the proper form, but a medieval letter
from one abbot to another wouldn't be accepted as authentic unless
it followed the intricate patterning of what was called the *cursus,*
an evolved version of the art of letter writing, or *ars dictaminis.*[3]
Similarly, a letter of application today, an article sent to a medical

journal, or an application for a bank loan all supposedly have to meet certain formal requirements to be accepted – formal considerations that are arguably related to but not strictly driven by their desired function. The form is arbitrary in the final analysis. The structural blueprint for a medieval sermon writer, for instance, reveals the evolution of the classical oration's form for another use. In one of the many arts of preaching manuals (*artes praedicandi*), such as Thomas of Salisbury's *Summa de arte praedicandi* ("The Ultimate Guide to the Art of Preaching," about CE 1210), the sermon writer would learn that he should have five parts in a sermon, plus an opening prayer:[4]

> Introduction of the theme, or main idea.
> Statement of the theme, a scriptural text.
> Division of the text into main points supporting the main idea.
> Development and support of the main points.
> Conclusion.

Such guidance would have been invaluable, especially for an inexperienced preacher, providing a way to organize materials, even suggesting what resources to gather. Medieval preaching and letter-writing manuals in fact came to offer such meticulously detailed descriptions of form that composing a sermon or letter might well have seemed like a fill-in-the-blank exercise.

Rather than trace this structure any further, let's jump ahead and consider: How does this kind of guidance, from these various sources over such a stretch of time, compare to more recent advice? In 1909, five Yale professors in *English Composition in Theory and Practice* compared the form of an essay to (you probably won't guess this) a railroad trestle. In between an essay's introduction and the conclusion, Henry Canby and his colleagues wrote, an essay should have a main idea, the railroad track, which is supported by three main points, the supporting trestle reaching "down at the bottom to the bedrock of facts or strong evidence" (169). Canby and his colleagues used an essay on the value of intercollegiate football to illustrate this view of an argument's form. Here is their intriguing diagram:

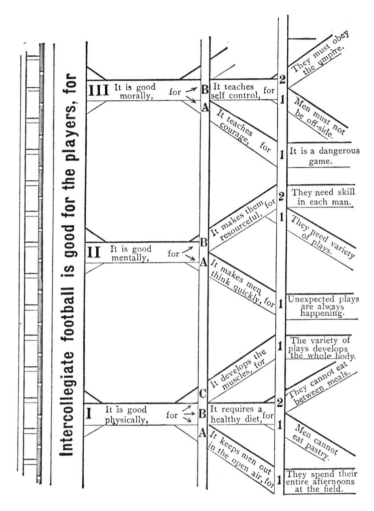

Figure 3.1 Canby's Trestle.

Aside from the mind-numbing naivete of the argument (Football is good because "It requires a healthy diet" so therefore "Men cannot eat pastry" and "cannot eat between meals"), what is perhaps most striking about this "framework," is how familiar it would have seemed to Corax, Cicero, Thomas of Salisbury, and thousands of other teachers in the two-thousand-year tradition of classical rhetoric – once they understood the meaning of "railroad."

In 1968, my high school English teacher, in Greer, South Carolina, drew the following diagram on his chalkboard:

In thousands of other classrooms, other English teachers were drawing – and continue to this day to draw – this same schematized template for an essay.[5] Why is the opening paragraph represented as a triangle? It supposedly suggests that the student should begin with a broad generalization and then narrow it down, just as the triangle narrows, to a specific thesis statement. This thesis, like the "theme" of a medieval sermon, is the central and unifying idea of the student's essay (still sometimes called a "theme" by twentieth-century writing teachers). The second, third, and fourth paragraphs, which should contain supporting points, are depicted as rectangles, suggesting perhaps the solidity desired in an argument: these are the building blocks, the foundation supporting the thesis. The fifth paragraph, an inverted triangle, adds an architectural symmetry, as the conclusion mirrors the introduction, moving from a restatement of the specific thesis outward to a broad generalization.

The structure here is a simplified but recognizable distant progeny of an oration of classical rhetoric, a distinctive genre marked by its form: the opening paragraph, with its broad and inviting start, is the introduction, leading to the statement of facts, orienting the reader, and finishing with the essay's point – the narrowed point of the triangle, representing the specific thesis statement, or the partition of the argument in classical terms. The rectangles are the confirmation and refutation, the working out of the argument's points. And the inverted triangle is the conclusion, the peroration that reverses the opening movement, from restating the claim to an opening up of its implications. The enduring appeal of this prescriptive pedagogy, for Cicero or Canby, certainly owes something to its reassuring simplicity: "Just follow this neat blueprint; just get some materials and put them in place." The continued influence of this instruction can be suggested by the website advice of a twenty-first century high school teacher, accessed in July 2008. I'm quoting only the opening paragraph of a five-paragraph essay that explains to students how to structure "the five-paragraph essay":

> The five paragraph essay follows a defined format. The first paragraph introduces us to the thesis of the essay and directs us to the three main supporting subtopics. The second through fourth paragraphs are all similar in format. They individually restate the subtopics, and are developed by giving supporting information. The fifth and last paragraph restates the main thesis idea and reminds the reader of the three main supporting ideas that were developed. All of these paragraphs are important.[6]

This teacher speaks so confidently of *"the* five paragraph essay" presumably because such an approach to teaching form seems so pervasive, as settled as the parts of an oration for Cicero. This teacher of writing has a content to teach, information to pass on to students, and this knowledge includes the prescription of form. In a popular (at least 33 printings) 1965 guide like *The Lively Art of Writing*, Lucille Vaughan Payne can refer to "The Introduction," "The Big Middle Section," and "The Conclusion" because these are, from her perspective, aspects of a standard template, expected by audiences; it works. Even in a state-of-the-art, twenty-first-century composition textbook, widely adopted and respected, the organizational advice for an argument is strikingly familiar: In *The St. Martin's Guide to Writing*, Rise Axelrod and Charles Cooper offer this pattern for "Arguing a Position": "The Beginning, Presentation of the Issue, Your Argument and Counterargument, The Ending" (274). Corax, were he alive, if he existed, would want to sue.

FORM

The five-paragraph essay, with its roots in the five (or so) parts of the classical oration, is a simple concept, yet for many students and teachers it has been seen as a powerful tool. This form is by no means the only one that students of rhetoric would have encountered in its long history. From the time of the Roman republic into the Renaissance and even the Enlightenment, for instance, students learning how to compose arguments were given a series of rhetorical exercises called *progymnasmata* – so named because they were designed to lead to the more advanced speeches and debates, the *gymnasmata*.[7] In a curriculum designed to create "good men speaking well," as Quintilian famously puts it, these exercises gave students structures and materials to piece together their own texts. Two of the earliest surviving *progymnasmata* and portions of two others are available in English translation (see Kennedy [*Progymnasmata*], Baldwin ["Elementary Exercises"], and Nadeau), and it is surprisingly easy to see how these exercises would make an engaging and effective course in composition, even today.

In fact, Frank D'Angelo's *Composition in the Classical Tradition* (2000) offers a series of twelve exercises for modern students that are drawn straight from the *progymnasmata*. D'Angelo describes part of his motivation in the preface: "We have to assume that these handbooks were more effective than other kinds of rhetorical manuals because they persisted for so many centuries."[8] One might counter of course that blood-letting to treat illness also persisted for a long time, and few people today would argue that it is effective. But as I think you'll see, these assignments still seem promising – and in any event, we ought to have some awareness of a practice with such a large historical footprint. Hermogenes' version of the writing-exercise curriculum, from the second century, asks the student to work in the following genres: a fable, a narrative, a *chria* (which is "a concise exposition of some memorable saying or deed, generally for good counsel" [Baldwin, "Elementary Exercises" 26]), an exposition of a proverb, a refutation and a confirmation, an amplification of a commonplace, an encomium (a celebration of someone, or something), a comparison, a character, a description, and a thesis (an argument). D'Angelo rearranges these assignments a bit (he begins with a narrative, a description, then a fable, for instance), and he adds some advanced rhetorical exercises – the "Speech-in-Character," in which the student invents an imaginary speech, and the argument for and against laws, in which the student is honing some political skills.

You can get a good sense of how these exercises work – how they approach the teaching of form – from this excerpt from Hermogenes, who is offering advice on how to sequence the *chria* (the translation, like the original, sounds more like lecture notes than a polished presentation):

> Let this working out be as follows: first a brief encomium of the
> sayer or doer; then paraphrase of the chria itself; then proof or

explanation. For example, Isocrates said that the root of education is bitter, but its fruit sweet: (1) encomium, "Isocrates
was wise," and you will slightly develop this topic; (2) chria,
"said, etc." and you will not leave this bare, but develop the
significance; (3) proof, (a) direct, "the greatest affairs are usually
established through toil, and, once established, bring happiness";
(b) by contrast, "those affairs which succeed by chance require
no toil and their conclusion brings no happiness; quite the contrary with things that demand our zeal"; by illustration, "as the
farmers who toil ought to reap the fruit, so with speeches"; (c)
by example, "Demosthenes, who shut himself up in his room
and labored much, finally reaped his fruit, crowns and public
proclamations." (d) You may also cite authority, as "Hesiod says,
'Before virtue, the gods have put sweat'; and another poet says,
'the gods sell all good things for labor.'" (4) Last you will put an
exhortation to follow what was said or done.

(Baldwin, "Elementary Exercises" 26–7)

It seems clear that Hermogenes is dealing with familiar, well-
established material: he refers to "the ancients," who have distinguished three different types of *chria*; and he concludes his coverage
of the *chria* by saying "So much for now; fuller instructions you will
learn later" (27). Hermogenes was probably not thinking that fuller
instructions would still be coming some 1,800- plus years later, but
D'Angelo's treatment of the *progymnasmata* offers students this
basic and most ancient pattern: Introduction, Narrative, Proposition,
Confirmation (proof), Refutation (counterproof), and Conclusion
(89). D'Angelo then gives students this more specialized structure
for amplifying a proverb:

(1)   Cite the saying.
(2)   Praise the author.
(3)   Paraphrase or explain the saying.
(4)   Give one or more reasons to support it.
(5)   Introduce an analogy.

(6) Then present a contrasting analogy.

(7) Give one or more examples.

(8) Support with the opinions of others.

(9) Draw a conclusion.

D'Angelo presents a sample essay from Hermogenes that illustrates how this structure might be applied to a particular proverb, and he also shows, with marginal headings, how this nine-part structure also fits into the more general five-part structure of the classical argument.

So, what kind of essays were the students writing eighteen centuries ago?

A Counselor Should Not Sleep All Night	
Introduction:	"A counselor should not sleep all night." One might praise the author of this saying for many things, but especially for the wise statements he made about watchfulness.
Narrative:	It is not appropriate for a person who gives advice or guidance, especially a responsible leader of a great power, to be overcome by sleep.
Proposition Proof:	A counselor should not sleep all night because sleep takes away vigilance and causes forgetfulness. Just as the helmsman at the wheel of a ship should be watchful while others are sleeping, so also should a leader of a great power be watchful for the good of his people. There is no harm done if a citizen sleeps all night, but it would be harmful if a leader is not watchful because the safety of others depends on him. In the Iliad, Hector, the son of the Trojan king Priam, was ever watchful, seldom sleeping. He sent Dolon to spy on the

Greeks who had built a fortification to protect their ships. Hector was the Trojan war leader, open, frank, and brave in adversity, who was the epitome of a wise counselor. The Roman historian Sallust, concerned about how good and bad leaders and citizens behave, agrees with this saying. "Many men," he is quoted as saying, "are wholly given to laziness, indolence, and sleep. They pass through life as public nuisances – slothful, ignorant, and uncultivated."

Conclusion: If it is fitting for a great leader to be ever watchful in the service of his country, then it should be fitting for every citizen to emulate that leader and to be ever watchful in the service of their country.

(From D'Angelo 89; text by Hermogenes; marginal headings by D'Angelo)

The vague evasiveness of the opening paragraph in this ancient student essay, and the uninspired rehearsal of the main idea in the second paragraph as well, may seem familiar to modern teachers. Here is a young writer, going through the motions, trying to please but without much to say. But the proof paragraphs at the heart of the essay seem different, each one offering a substantive example, and suggesting that the ancients might have something to teach us about inventing materials. As a whole, the essay demonstrates competence, a control over the materials, which have been arranged properly. The essay isn't really imaginative, clever, original, deeply insightful, marked by a personal voice: it isn't any of the things that we tend to associate with excellent writing today. But there is a clear sense of structure – of using a template to organize materials. And what teacher wouldn't be delighted to have a student who could cite

The Iliad and quote Sallust, not to mention create analogies and contrasts?

There is no apparent limit to the number of patterns that students might be given, and different *progymnasmata* handbooks have different numbers of exercises. Instead of the standard five-part structure, such occasional writing exercises don't appear to be presented with any claim about their singular correctness. Hermogenes and D'Angelo might well add additional steps to the description or the fable, and the exercise would still work fine. The student might be asked to re-tell the fable starting at the end, or starting in the middle, or adding additional scenes. Thus, the student isn't learning *the* structure, but is learning about form in general, as well as learning some particular sequences that can be put together.

In addition to this tradition of ad hoc and sequential exercises, writing teachers have also relied on approaches that have made claims about the comprehensiveness of the forms being presented. Frank D'Angelo's revival of the ancient *progymnasmata* grew out of his earlier work in the 1970s to describe all the types of exposition that students needed to know – which were, according to his *Conceptual Theory of Rhetoric* (1975), narration, process, cause-effect, description, definition, analysis, classification, exemplification, comparison, and analogy. By having students study examples and outlines of these patterns, D'Angelo argued that students would incorporate such structures into their own writing. A similar strategy is followed in Cheryl Glenn's *Making Sense* (2002), which identifies for students the "nine methods we all use to make sense of the world" (v). Her patterns of arrangement are also quite similar to D'Angelo's (she omits analysis and analogy, and adds "argument"), and they are unfolded in some detail as students are encouraged to employ these patterns in their essays and paragraphs. In constructing a description, for instance, Glenn tells students they may arrange their material chronologically or spatially. They may use their own point of view or the audience's as they provide a mental or physical picture of what is being described. Narratives, Glenn says, to take another example, usually reflect the chronological order of the events, yet they can also use flashbacks and "flashforwards" (136–7). Students, she says, should usually conclude a narrative with some unifying point, giving the events some significance.

We could wonder about D'Angelo's and Glenn's claim to be presenting the universe of textual patterns – why not speculation, or remembrance, or celebration, or prayer as discourse "methods" or forms to make sense of our worlds? But their claim gains some credence from the history of this kind of approach. For instance, in 1925, Joseph Thomas, Frederick Manchester, and Franklin Scott published *Composition for College Students*, a work indebted, they say in their first sentence, to a French textbook by Maurice Grigaut, *Cours de Composition* (vii). Good writing depends on subject matter and "form or technique," they say, and their book is "especially concerned" with form (1). The distinctive forms that they identify are, interestingly enough, not only almost exactly the same ones that D'Angelo and Glenn see, but Thomas, Manchester, and Scott also use virtually the same terminology: like Glenn, these 1920s authors omit analogy and add argument to D'Angelo's list; and they use "comment or criticism" for the category that D'Angelo calls "analysis" (missing in Glenn). There are intriguing correspondences among these three texts that suggest all three are perhaps talking about the same reality, rather than textual conventions. For instance, Thomas, Manchester, and Scott see two strategies for organizing a description, which they call the scientific and the artistic; these two categories are essentially the same as what Glenn calls the spatial and chronological categories.

Textbooks in the vein of Glenn, D'Angelo, and Thomas/ Manchester/Scott typically employ model essays to illustrate their kinds of patterns, asking students to read these essays carefully and incorporate the movements they see into their own work.[9]

One of the most successful examples of this models approach, based on the assumption of recurrent patterns in prose, has been Robert Schwegler's *Patterns of Exposition*, whose 17th edition appeared in 2003. This textbook represents the evolution of Randall Decker's *Patterns of Exposition* (and was called *Decker's Patterns of Exposition* into the fifteenth edition), but there are many other books that similarly group essays according to the "mode" embodied: narration, description, classification, definition, exposition, argument, and so forth. These anthologies, which also stretch back to classical times, have sometimes included student essays as models along with professional examples. Advocates of this approach believe that students will be able to identify effective patterns of form in the professional examples, and the student examples will help students incorporate these techniques into their own writing. While not always as explicitly prescriptive as Hermogenes (or Aphthonius, or Theon), these new *progymnasmata* assume that students will learn how to structure writing by observing pre-set forms.

The most ambitious and most philosophically coherent and comprehensive analysis of the kinds of texts has been James Kinneavy's *Theory of Discourse* (1971, 1982). Kinneavy's work not only raised the scholarly stakes in composition and rhetoric (arguably only Kenneth Burke's impact is comparable), but it also stimulated wide-ranging debate about the teaching of writing, from the kinds of writing assignments needed, to the content of classroom exercises, to the epistemological status of rhetorical theories. Kinneavy argued that the different kinds of writing that students needed to experience were best classified according to the elements involved in a rhetorical situation: the writer, the reader, the reality, and the text itself. Every text, Kinneavy maintained, could be classified in two ways: according to a dominant "aim," depending on which element in the rhetorical situation was most important; and according to a dominant "mode," depending on the spatial and temporal relationships created by the text. For Kinneavy, the possible modes are four:

(1) Description: One thing, stopped in time.
(2) Classification: Multiple things in relationship, stopped in time.
(3) Narrative: One thing, moving through time.
(4) Evaluation: Multiple things in relationship, moving through time.

The descriptive mode deals with space, not time, focusing on a singular entity that is unchanging. The narrative mode moves through time, relating events that are part of a singular whole. The classificatory mode deals with more than one entity, comparing and contrasting, distinguishing and defining particular items in the context of other like and unlike items. The evaluative mode compares multiple events, in the sense that an actual event is compared to an ideal event: to say how something succeeds or fails, we must imagine how it could have been better or worse. Thus, discourse is sorted out by the modes on the basis of two factors: time (stopped versus moving) and relationship (identity versus contrast). For most of Kinneavy's students and readers, the evaluative mode has seemed the most difficult to grasp, perhaps because we're not used to thinking of evaluation as a comparison between an actual and an ideal sequence of events. Each mode entails its own set of possible patterns: a description, for instance, might be structured in terms of individual features that add up to an overall picture; a classification involves organizing units into groups and defining the unifying elements of the distinctive groups, in an alternating or binary pattern; a narrative presents a series of events as part of an action; an evaluation compares two events.

Kinneavy's theory of the aims in discourse, which complements his theory of modes, allows us to identify expressive, persuasive, referential, and literary structures. In "expressive" texts, the writer is most important, whereas in "persuasive" discourse, the audience predominates. "Referential" discourse is most concerned with the world, with what is being referenced; and "literary" texts are those in which the text itself draws our attention. So, for instance, although we may see evidence of John Milton's desire to express himself in *Paradise Lost*, and although we may be persuaded to accept some concept or idea he puts forward (the attractiveness of evil, say), and although we may see various ways that Milton is referencing his own world, nevertheless the dominant aim of this text, Kinneavy might say, is literary. Kinneavy's work has sometimes been misunderstood as a claim that a work necessarily has only one aim, and he did sometimes talk about aims as if they were embedded in texts in a stable form – a position that collided with post-structuralist assumptions. Kinneavy's theory, nonetheless, provided an impressive schema that can be (and has been) used to design writing courses, to analyze texts, to develop exercises for students, and more.

For instance, Kinneavy's theory made clear that "argument" was not a category like "description" and "narration." An argument is marked by a persuasive aim; it might employ description and/or narration. Description and narration, on the other hand, are modes, not aims. Description and narration can be used for persuasion, but they can also be used for expressive, referential, and literary discourse. Another example of a practical implication of Kinneavy's theory would be to identify more clearly the kinds of textual patterns that students need to practice. What's the difference, one might ask, between the form of a narrative, a process, and a cause and effect essay? These are treated in various textbooks as distinctly different kinds of writing assignments. The standard textbook position is that narratives are usually in chronological order, but they allow for some moving back and forth in time, and some events can be skipped; a process essay, however, always moves strictly forward, step by step, with every step described; and a cause and effect essay can go in chronological or reverse chronological order, or it can organize the causes in terms of emphasis, from least to most important.

Kinneavy's theory would depart from this consensus: all three kinds of essays are in the narrative mode, and they therefore draw on the same resources of structure. Thus, there's no reason to say that a literary narrative, unlike a cause-effect essay, can't go in reverse chronological order – the film *Memento* (2000, directed by Christopher Nolan) and the play *Betrayal* (by Harold Pinter, also a 1983 movie), both narratives, tell their stories backwards. A writer might think that some scientific processes or political progressions would be easiest to understand if the narration started at the end and worked back to the beginning. Likewise, an essay that is categorizing types of causes isn't really, from Kinneavy's perspective, in the narrative mode; we would in fact expect such an essay to follow a different structural pattern – a classificatory pattern, identifying distinguishing and common features.

Structure

Despite its elegance and erudition, however, Kinneavy's *Theory* has generally not transformed the teaching of form. This major articulation of his theory, which is subtitled "The Aims of Discourse," doesn't cover the modes, and the promised companion volume that would do so never appeared. Kinneavy did publish a small textbook called *Writing: The Modes of Discourse* in 1976, but it was not widely adopted and is not well known. A thorough analysis of the kinds of patterns used in each mode would have been dauntingly complex. Discourse analysis has revealed the extraordinary difficulty of describing the form of actual discourses, and the tools for such analysis of form are specialized and difficult. Even if students could be taught the intricacies of discourse analysis, it's not clear that such analytical skill would pay off in more well-formed writing.

But there is another reason that writing teachers and rhetorical theorists have not identified and taught all the forms available to writers, and this reason has to do with the way that Composition and Rhetoric as a field has developed away from the path of Kinneavy, despite his formative influence and his status as "one of the discipline's most learned and beloved scholars," as Lynn Worsham, Sidney Dobrin, and Gary Olson put it (xx). What happened to rhetoric in the twentieth century, what led composition instruction away from patterns and templates, has its origins in the late seventeenth century. For Jonathan Swift, for example, who was born in 1667, rhetorical training was essentially what it had been for Milton, for Shakespeare, for Chaucer, for Boethius, for Augustine, for Cicero. When Swift sat down to write his famous "Modest Proposal," surely one of the world's greatest essays, he organized his argument strictly according to what he had learned about arrangement, employing an Exordium (paragraphs 1–7), a Narration (8–16), a Digression (17–19), a Proof (20–28), a Refutation (29–30), and a Peroration (31–33).[10] In fact, in many works Swift often draws on rhetorical terminology and concepts – but he often uses this expertise ironically. And the speaker who's making the modest proposal to eat the children of Ireland, inhabiting this classical form, is a madman. The apparent logic and order of his argument helps to make it so stunningly chilling. There must be something wrong, surely, with a structure that enables one to sound so rational articulating such horror. Indeed, as the eighteenth century unfolded, the teachings of classical rhetoric were increasingly challenged, and the force that was used ultimately to shipwreck classical rhetoric stemmed primarily from John Locke's monumental *Essay Concerning Human Understanding* (1690).

As W. S. Howell explains in his landmark study, *Eighteenth-Century British Logic and Rhetoric*, a shift was beginning to occur in Swift's time from a traditional, Aristotelian/Ciceronian rhetoric to a new, Lockean/scientific rhetoric. The old rhetoric concentrated on argument and persuasion, but the new rhetoric, responding to the needs of science and Locke's empirical turn, encompassed broader aims that included conveying information and investigating truth. The classical oration, resiliently effective for public argument, was awkward if not unworkable for these new purposes. In the place of the old rhetoric's formulaic arrangement, the new rhetoric advised an arrangement that reflected the flow of thought itself. By the nineteenth century, the classical rhetorical tradition was pretty much adrift – although Richard Whately made an heroic effort to salvage it. As writing pedagogy abandoned prescribed techniques for invention, arrangement, and style (memory and delivery were already sinking as writing displaced oral literacy), teachers increasingly focused on grammar and surface features. How the student was supposed to create an essay was a mystery – as all writing came to be seen as the result of inspiration. Teaching the structure of the classical oration certainly made little sense because the form of a piece of writing should be determined by the reality the writer aimed to convey, not some static pre-ordained formula.

But the teacher could mark up with rigor what was grammatically or syntactically wrong – given the time, energy, and willingness to do so. "It is absurd that a college should be obliged to teach spelling, pronunciation, grammar, construction of sentences and of paragraphs," B. S. Hurlbut argued in 1896 (I am not making up his name), and many of his colleagues agreed. But most institutions of higher learning had by the end of the nineteenth century accepted this onerous responsibility, following the lead of Harvard College, whose 1870 written entrance exam had revealed a woeful lack of basic writing abilities, and spawned one of many literacy crises to come (more on this in the next chapter). Such a focus on the basics led to a very prescriptive approach in every respect, including arrangement, even in a relatively enlightened text like Barrett Wendell's 1891 *English Composition*, which told students for instance that essays, paragraphs, and even sentences ought to move from general to specific elements. Every paragraph should have a topic sentence containing its unifying idea, and every sentence in a paragraph should support this idea.

Such constraint is not likely to have helped inspire students to write anything that teachers would willingly read. And as larger numbers of students entered colleges and universities, in need of writing instruction, that very difficult task increasingly became the work of junior, adjunct, probationary, in-training teachers. Before 1860 in the United States, classes were likely to be small, and the instruction in writing classrooms would have been based most likely on either Hugh Blair's 1783 *Lectures on Rhetoric and Belles Lettres*, an energetic effort to marry Lockean epistemology and Ciceronian techniques, or on the methods of John Walker's *The Teacher's Assistant in English Composition* (1801), which called for reading and analyzing great essays, writing themes, memorizing figures and tropes and grammatical principles and errors and types of discourse and stylistic values – a smorgasbord in other words of everything Walker could think of. After 1865, in the wake of The Morrill Act of 1862, colleges and universities in America were increasingly overwhelmed with students. The English teacher who earlier in the century had been teaching small classes, commenting on papers in tutorials with students, might find 80 to 100 students in a composition class at the turn into the twentieth century. In *one* of his composition classes.

This dismal situation led to the approach to composition pedagogy that is usually called, as we have seen above, "current-traditional rhetoric." During this period, in Robert Connors's words, "it becomes a truism that student dislike for Freshman Composition is exceeded only by the dislike of its teachers" (*Composition-Rhetoric* 13). Students were given information about words, sentences, paragraphs; about the modes of discourse (description, narration, exposition, argument); about outlining; about the importance of Unity, Coherence, and Emphasis in their writing. Their papers were written (it was unclear how) and their errors were marked (also mysterious, but abbreviations and reference systems were developed to save teachers time and ligaments). This period of pedagogical stasis, in which writing classes ranked with tonsillectomies for popularity, stretched into the 1960s. And then something momentous happened in the teaching of writing.

This transformation has already been discussed in the preceding chapter, but I want to focus here on how the shift affected the teaching of form. The popular rallying cry of composition specialists in the 1970s and 1980s to "teach process, not product" was substantially based on the rejection of static forms like the five-paragraph theme and the engagement instead with the student's own composing. Obviously, naturally occurring five-paragraph themes were rare. Real writers didn't arrange essays in that fashion. Similarly, Richard Braddock demonstrated in 1974 that in twenty-five sample essays, only 37 percent of the paragraphs contained something like a topic sentence. The resulting turn away from generalized prescriptions and toward the student's individual writing process had the fortunate effect of making large class sizes impossible: there were no longer any standard forms that could be taught to every student. Rather, the student needed to evolve his or her own form for each individual piece of writing. Compared to discussing the same structures and then marking the same errors over and over on an endless stream of student papers, the prospect of analyzing the writing behaviors of students, and intervening in those processes, seemed to many teachers quite stimulating and useful.

How the process pedagogy affected the way that form was taught can be captured in the title of Peter Elbow's *Writing Without Teachers*, published in 1973. The outside cover blurb for the twenty-fifth anniversary edition of this revolutionary book describes its approach and suggests why writing teachers would embrace a book that excludes them:

> Instead of editing and outlining material in the initial steps of the writing process, Elbow celebrates non-stop or free uncensored writing, without editorial checkpoints first, followed much later by the editorial process. This approach turns the focus towards encouraging ways of developing confidence and inspiration through free writing, multiple drafts, diaries, and notes.

There is no companion volume, *Teaching Without Students*, but the liberating effects on the teaching of structure – on teachers as well as students – is articulated succinctly in William Irmscher's *Teaching Expository Writing*, an influential 1979 book: "The job of teaching structure is not to prescribe it, but to help students realize how they can perceive and create the patterns of their own thoughts" (105). Erika Lindemann's *Rhetoric for Writing Teachers* (1982; 4th edn 2001), a popular text for training writing teachers, similarly says that teachers need to encourage students "to listen to their material and help them discover options for organizing it"; "students will discover the shape of the whole discourse as they write" (133, 131). In fact, Lindemann says, "A subject probed thoroughly enough begins to organize itself" (132) – good news for the tired teacher. This remarkable phenomenon of self-organizing subjects is motivated by the desire of process teachers to undo what their students have learned: "Writing teachers," Lindemann says, "often spend considerable time relaxing their students' grip on the five-paragraph model" (133). Interestingly, Lindemann follows this criticism of the five-paragraph model with an endorsement of Quintilian's version of the classical oration.[11] But she quickly qualifies her support for Quintilian's form, to be sure, saying that it encourages students to think of arguments as having "sides," and to think that "argumentation is a matter of 'winning' by demonstrating that one position is superior to another" (135–6) – a position that Quintilian, we can imagine, would find puzzling.

FUNCTION

Although this has been a very selective story of genre, form, and structure, the big picture that emerges can be summarized in three points.

1. From the origin of rhetorical instruction to the present day, a fairly simple structure has been presented to students as a norm, as a template to follow. Whether we call this form (or formula) the "classical oration" or "the five-paragraph theme," it has a recognizable

continuity as a template, advocating that students introduce an assertion, prove the assertion, then offer some closing remarks. This shape is oriented, obviously, toward making arguments (in the courtroom, in the assembly, in public ceremonies), and it can be expansively and intricately elaborated upon, providing for students something approaching a fill-in-the-blank strategy for writing. The detailed structural guidance of the ancient textbooks has been so durable, in fact, that all the parts of the pattern have well-known names in a variety of languages (Latin, Greek, English, French, Italian, German, and more). Although this pedagogical approach may seem to embrace a one-shape-fits-all mentality, we must admit that it has proved quite resilient. It assumes that an audience expects a certain form within a certain genre; and that writers start with form, looking for content that can be adapted to the particular occasion. From this perspective, the idea that form follows function isn't wrong; there is in fact a basic form that is derived from the function of persuading an audience.

2. We have also seen how a particular writing exercise, part of a series of extraordinarily popular exercises, also provides students with a group of simple structural patterns to follow. This kind of explicit guidance on various ways to arrange one's material is also essential to the long tradition of classical rhetoric, as is advice on how to invent material, what stylistic resources to employ, and how to recall and present one's argument. This classical tradition – teaching invention, arrangement, style, memory, delivery – has survived to the present day. While D'Angelo updates the *progymnasmata*, others have tried to preserve the ancient rhetorical instruction in as full a form as possible. Edward P. J. Corbett's and Robert Connors's *Classical Rhetoric for the Modern Student*, Winifred Horner's *Rhetoric in the Classical Tradition*, and Sharon Crowley's *Ancient Rhetorics for Contemporary Students* all enliven extremely well-tested techniques in different ways. Form still follows function, one could argue, but there are more kinds of forms and more flexibility.

3. Finally, we have noted a modern turn away from prescribed form, as the Enlightenment (in the wake of John Locke) looked to science and things, rather than rhetoric and words, for structure. Swift's famous "Modest Proposal," following the form of a classical oration, might be seen as one reflection of the tipping point away from an artificially prescribed structure, dangerously enabling the illusion of order and sanity. As this reality that language is supposed to reflect became more internalized – as truth became more subjective and constructed, in other words – the shape of writing became increasingly a reflection of the writer's thinking. Form follows function in this case in the sense that every writing occasion has a unique function for a unique writer – and hence a unique form. No one can give the student that form: it must be discovered in the process of writing.

As writing teachers, where does that leave us? How do we teach form – or can we? Should we? Although the dictum that form follows function is more famous, Frank Lloyd Wright's rethinking is more valuable: form and function, when a building or an essay or anything works well, really are united. Is such a mystical union more likely to happen if we start with a blueprint and then gather materials to build with? Or should we start by exploring what materials are available, and only then consider how to put them together? Wright's answer, it seems clear, is to deny this either/or thinking and insist on both. Wright's great pride was using local materials, suiting the building to the genius of the place and his clients, while at the same time employing those designs and forms that were already evolved and spoke most eloquently to him. So the activities below aim to come at the teaching of form in conflicting ways – both providing students with a sense of forms that already exist with content to be supplied, and also (paradoxically) conveying to students that form emerges when they give their writing content. This approach will become clearer, I hope, with the offer of some examples.

Activity 1

One thing that seems especially clear from the foregoing is that form has been taught in very different ways. To latch onto one strategy, given the multiversity of our students, seems unnecessarily limited. Some developing writers, it seems clear, are at a point that working with some prescribed forms would be very helpful. Two thousand years of classroom testing certainly make the *progymnasmata* worth considering, for some students anyway. More than anything, developing writers need confidence and commitment, which is likely to come only from a genuine sense of control and success. Asking some developing writers to invent original ideas and compelling material, usually about complex and challenging topics (isn't that what we try to assign?), while expressing these assertions in engaging and arresting language, which is of course well organized in the structure that is most effective for this particular piece of writing – asking for this kind of writing is oftentimes asking too much of our students. Therefore, writing exercises that spell out in detail the structure that students should follow can be quite valuable. Hermogenes will in fact work, but you may want to invent your own protocols for structures.

One exercise that works nicely involves deriving a set of structural instructions from an effective piece of writing. That is, you start with a good piece of writing. (You can find it, or ask your students to find examples – always an instructive option.) Then give explicit directions to your students that will allow them to fill their own ideas into the already-created form of the model. Here, for instance, is the opening paragraph of an essay by David Remnick, taken from the *New Yorker* magazine's "Talk of the Town" column February 3, 2003, a particularly momentous point in the United States's debate over going to war in Iraq:

> In recent days, as the White House speechwriters were weighing
> the language and the imagery of Tuesday's State of the Union
> address, President Bush was extemporizing his way toward

war. He declared himself (vaguely) "sick and tired of games," exasperated by the arms-inspection process in Iraq and Saddam Hussein's attempts to evade it. And (even more vaguely) he warned any Iraqi commander who launched a weapon of mass destruction, "When Iraq is liberated, you will be treated, tried, and prosecuted as a war criminal."

Here are the directions you might give to students to encourage them to imitate successfully this essay's opening structure:

(1) Your essay will be an analysis of an argument. The argument you are analyzing may be an oral argument, one that you were in or that you overheard, or it can be a written argument, from say the editorial pages of the student or local newspaper. (If you can't find an argument, ask me for help.)

(2) First, explain what the argument is (who's making it, to whom, where, etc.), orienting your reader to the occasion and the situation. One to three sentences.

(3) Second, report some statements or events that led up to the argument. What was said or done beforehand? Two to four sentences.

(4) Third, make sure you arrange the statements or events so that the reader has the feeling of the argument building up. Revise if you need to.

You can walk the students through all or part of a great piece of writing. If you show students the original, and discuss with them what you like about it, and then ask students to compare the structure of what they've written to the original, you'll have created opportunities for growth in several ways. This exercise can usefully fill an entire class period; it requires little preparation; and it can be repeated as often as desired. The students can even assess their own work (especially if that allows you or encourages you to try this: it's a sin to avoid asking students to write because we don't have time to read it): Success is determined if they have indeed followed the prescribed template. If they're unsure whether they've followed it, they can try again, or you can intervene and help.

Activity 2

Although Cicero's *Rhetorica ad Herennium* is a work of his youth, written apparently when he was a teenager, the guidance there can be, I think, quite useful for young writers. *De inventione* likewise seems effectively tailored to keep things simple but effective. Few essays do fall into the pattern of a five-paragraph theme (unless they were assigned as five-paragraph themes), but the structure of the classical oration, or more simply the structure of "Beginning – Middle – End," provides a way to think about how an essay is put together. By explaining to students what goes into each part of an argument, we can expand their repertoire of things to do and consider in their writing. An introduction, for instance, most people would agree with Cicero, should get an audience's attention and create a willingness in them to listen to what's going to be said. Should an introduction, we may ask, therefore explain what one is going to talk about? Should an introduction explain one's position? Most students will agree that introductions are supposed to do those things, but as the classical handbooks pointed out, the audience's starting orientation to one's argument should determine what's said. If one can reasonably expect the audience to be hostile or bored with one's position, then an indirect approach is likely to work better. You want to explain what you are going to argue, in other words, only if that disclosure serves your purposes.

This little piece of advice then becomes the occasion for an exercise, assigning students various positions, describing for them various audiences, and asking them to draft opening paragraphs based on the audience. In this fashion you can craft exercises for different parts of the argument, drawing ideas from the classical handbooks, or from your own common sense. The key thing you're teaching is how the audience influences the shape and the content.

Activity 3

Slice some essays into pieces, virtually or actually, using a photo-copier or a computer. Ask students to experiment with moving the pieces around into different sequences, and ask them to comment on what happens. Specifically, could the new order work? What's gained or lost? What would have to change for the new sequence to work better? The discussion should do two things: illuminate the struc-ture of the original essay, and also suggest the fluidity of structure. In some cases, a new order will work – sometimes it might even be better. Other times, it won't make sense, or will require extensive rewording or signposting. It's an interesting exploration of structure to consider with students why that is.

Activity 4

Give students a piece of writing and ask them to depict its shape, its structure, without using words. Alternately, ask students to draw somehow the shape of an imaginary argument, then ask them to write an argument that fits that shape. (This is fun – but only if you make sure students approach it in that vein. There's obviously no right answer here.)

Activity 5

My experience is that most students today will have encountered freewriting in high school, but what they may not have experienced is the way that Elbow's technique gets material from its spontan-eous, unfettered, write-without-stopping state into some organized form. In *Writing with Power* Elbow evolves his approach, explain-ing in particular how looping leads to material that will begin to fit together. Elbow's contention is that "You cannot write *really* incoher-ently if you write quickly" (16), and it's an interesting exercise to test this out. To the extent that Elbow is right (and different people will have different opinions about that), structuring writing is something that comes to us naturally. We impose coherence – especially if we don't think about it too much. This exercise is therefore reassuring to many students, who may have agonized over their form previously: write as quickly as possible for five minutes, then describe the structure of what you've written.

Activity 6

It's interesting and often illuminating to compare the structure of an essay to some other entity. You may want to give students an actual essay to compare, or just an essay outline. How is the structure of an essay, in other words, like the structure of a date? A sports event? A meal? A concert? A cathedral? A tent? Such disorienting questions can be quite useful in getting students to think about form in fresh ways.

Activity 7

Ask students to write about their experiences with structuring their writing. Do they make outlines? Do they have a template in mind? Do they struggle with form, or does it come naturally? Ask them to imagine themselves having an entirely different perspective on form – and what that would entail.

Activity 8

Ask students to bring in examples of good writing, and then focus together on their openings, endings, and middles. Ask students to imitate the opening – they should do the same thing, as much as possible, as the original. Start a list of strategies and see how many different things the essays do in the various parts. You might begin with an analysis of Swift's "Modest Proposal."

RECOMMENDATIONS FOR
FURTHER READING: ARRANGEMENT

Braddock, Richard. "The Frequency and Placement of Topic Sentences in Expository Prose." *Research in the Teaching of English* (Winter 1974): 287–302.

Eden, Rich, and Ruth Mitchell. "Paragraphing for the Reader." *CCC* 37 (December 1986): 416–30.

Miller, Carolyn. "Genre as Social Action." *Quarterly Journal of Speech* 70 (1984): 151–67.

Simons, Herbert W., and Aram Aghazarian. *Form, Genre, and the Study of Political Discourse.* Columbia: University of South Carolina Press, 1986.

The problem: You've read somewhere that Costa Rica has the most biodiversity of anyplace on the planet, but you're thinking now that the stack of student papers on your desk suggests otherwise. How could any one classroom produce so many previously unknown grammatical structures and bizarre word usages, so many different voices – such camouflage, such well-hidden ideas, such eloquence, energy, confusion, originality, insight, obtuseness, cliché? What can you do without possibly upsetting and harming the living sources of this work? If you venture into that wildness, will you ever emerge?

Perhaps it would be better to leave those papers undisturbed, in their natural state?

4 Style

> It is not surprising that we call each other names: those of us who question the value of grammar are in fact shaking the whole elaborate edifice of traditional composition instruction.
>
> Patrick Hartwell, "Grammar, Grammars, and the Teaching of Grammar" (109)

> A student sentence is an economy in miniature. It has an actor, an action, an object of that action. It is a transaction, a completed act. It is self-interested in that it seeks a good grade, seeks to demonstrate mastery of the assignment. But it also seeks to express something; it is a learner's exercise in how to trade in the market of ideas. When it is good, the writing rejoices in that exchange. There is, in any utterance, however self-interested, a residual urge to share a view of life. To see the world a certain way and to want other people to enjoy seeing it that way too. This two-way communication, self-seeking and other-seeking, is after all what makes markets fun to go to and full of life.
>
> Richard Lanham, *Economics of Attention* (266)

AUDIENCE

What is style? Consider these four requests:

(a) "Close the door."

(b) "For God's sake, will you close the dadgum door?!"

(c) "Would you please be so kind as to close the door?"

(d) "The lid on the casket holding our relationship is that door, which you now must shut."

In a famous essay in 1965, "Theories of Style and Their Implications for the Teaching of Composition," the linguist Louis Milic distinguishes three different ways to think about style. The "dualist" view of style assumes, as Milic puts it, "that ideas exist wordlessly and can be dressed in a variety of outfits" (67).[1] Style is thus simply "the way something is said." From such a perspective, it makes sense to think of the writing process in linear terms, as ideas are invented, then arranged, then dressed up in style, committed to memory, and delivered. Students thus learn how to adorn pre-existing ideas appropriately for a particular audience in a given time and place. "The persuasive is persuasive to someone," as Aristotle says (*Topics* I.ii.11). So to get the door shut most effectively, I need to know my audiences and what they will find most compelling. But what do I need to know about my audience to know the proper linguistic dress code? "To influence men's souls" (271d), Plato says in the *Phaedrus*, one must first understand the various kinds of souls, but Plato and most people who have thought carefully about it have considered such knowledge a difficult if not impossible task. Aristotle's more modest strategy involves analyzing the audience in terms of such characteristics as age, wealth, and social status, shaping the message to address the distinctive fears and desires that characterize different groups. For Kenneth Burke, the major twentieth-century rhetorical theorist, this syncing of audience and writer is so essential that the concept of "persuasion" can be usefully replaced by "identification" (*Rhetoric of Motives* 58).

From this dualist perspective on style, then, it seems clear that to persuade biologists, or privileged teenagers, or hardened criminals to shut the door (or anything else), one should speak the language of biologists, teenagers, or criminals. Interesting work has been done by Greg Myers, who has documented how two biologists, adapting to their discourse communities, made stylistic revisions in order to engage and persuade other researchers, and by A. M. Blakeslee, who has similarly shown how physicists learned to adapt their arguments for an audience of chemists by interacting directly with them. Writers, however, often cannot see, engage with, assess, and react to their audiences. As Walter Ong points out in a landmark essay, often cited by composition and rhetoric specialists, "The Writer's Audience is Always a Fiction," as his title indicates. Even when a writer can meet with his audience, or when a speaker is addressing an audience that is physically present, he or she must still nonetheless create an imaginary audience, distinct and perhaps even radically different from the actual listeners and viewers. And writers learn how to imagine their audiences, Ong asserts, from their reading of prior texts, not from their direct experience of readers. Even when there is interaction with the audience, the speaker or even the writer must draw upon a rhetorical repertoire to engage the audience as it has been imagined.

Ong's insight, which is supported by other influential explorations of the constructed nature of audiences (Edwin Black's notion of the audience as the writer's "second persona," for instance; Wayne Booth's famous concept of the "implied reader"), reinforces the idea that writing (and speaking) instruction should include rich and diverse reading (and speaking) experiences. What is at stake is not merely the capacity to envision one's audience. Rather, the writer and speaker have the capacity to create the audience, in a sense, to some degree. Andrea Lunsford and Lisa Ede distinguish between a view of the audience as a "concrete reality," the "audience addressed" as they put it (156), and an alternative view of the audience as the writer's construction, the "audience invoked." When I say "Would you please be so kind as to close the door?", I am presupposing an audience that is different from the audience supposed by "For God's sake, will you close the dadgum door?!" The former apparently invites the audience to assume a civilized relationship with the speaker, while the latter ostensibly assigns an antagonistic role to the audience. The audience is not of course obliged to accept the role posited for them: when a speaker says "You are all very intelligent people," the audience isn't required to be smart, and IQ points are not added to their scores; but the speaker can present this image. Whether it is acknowledged, aspired to, or rejected in reality, this construction of the audience arguably frames what is articulated and defines the relationship between the writer and the audience.

I say "apparently" civilized and "ostensibly" antagonistic: one might say "please" or "be so kind" in requesting door closure, but to say both starts to sound excessive, possibly ironic, as if the speaker is masking or conveying displeasure; likewise, "dadgum" is for most people not a seriously angry word, and it is easy enough to imagine the apparently polite statement being said furiously, and ostensibly angry statement being said while laughing boisterously. Even the simple request, "Close the door," can carry a vast range of meanings (it might be the prelude to a murder, romance, a music lesson, anything), and the last styling of the request is so bizarre that a good deal of creativity is required to imagine a situation in which someone might utter it. Imagining this context – the entire "rhetorical situation" to use the term Lloyd Bitzer has made famous – is in fact crucial to the making of meaning. Thus we can see how this view of style makes extraordinary and not-always-articulated demands upon student writers: The writer must imagine the audience in order to know what stylistic choices to make, but these stylistic choices can also shape the roles that the audience may assume, or reject, or adapt, or distort. Even when the audience is physically present and consists of only one person, it is ultimately unknowable, as the audience "addressed" is always to some extent also an audience "invoked." After Freud, after Saussure, after Derrida, it would be difficult to argue that the context of any utterance can be fully present to the writer. The audience is always more complex and unbounded than the speaker can limit; and in writing (and recorded speech), the actual audience is potentially infinite. Thus, when students are given writing assignments that stipulate unfamiliar or ambiguous audiences, they are being asked in a sense to imagine the imaginary – to make stylistic choices based on a mystery.

What are the pedagogical implications of this dualist view of style as the dress of thought? How can we help students to deal most effectively with these formidable challenges? Students need guidance in thinking about and writing for different kinds of audiences. Most simply, students need experience writing for explicitly and fully articulated audiences, as well as abstract and universal audiences. "The teacher" is certainly a real and unavoidable audience in the classroom, but for students to develop as writers, they need to write for other audiences also – to see, at a minimum, the teacher as playing additional roles, and optimally to address in reality a wider audience. They also need extensive reading experiences, allowing them to see the variety of ways that audiences are imagined and addressed/invoked stylistically. To see this relationship between style, audience, and effect, students need to analyze and verbalize their understanding of this interplay.

If this sounds challenging (if not overwhelmingly daunting), then you may have a clearer sense of why there is an enormous history of efforts to teach style. There is no clear path to stylistic fluency and adaptability – although, as you'll see in what follows, there are plenty of ideas to choose from. There is indeed no consensus, to begin with, that this or that particular view of style should drive our pedagogy. Milic identifies a second theory of style, the "individualist" approach, which stems from the assumption that "style is the expression of the student's mind and personality" (69). This is the view of style, in other words, famously summarized by the French naturalist Georges de Buffon as "*Le style, c'est l'homme même*," "Style is the man." Composition students, according to Winston Weathers, tend to think of style as "a kind of aesthetic luxury," a "dainty humanistic pastime" ("Teaching Style" 144, 145), but Weathers embraces the individualist view of style and exhorts teachers to say instead "that style is the proof of a human being's individuality," "a gesture of personal freedom against inflexible states of mind" (*An Alternate Style* 228). Weathers's appealing textbook, *An Alternate Style*, aims to give students "options in all areas of vocabulary, usage, sentence forms, dictional levels, paragraph types, ways of organizing material into whole compositions" (5). Although Weathers recognizes the utility of "adjustment to the diversity of communication occasions that confront us in our various lives," he clearly celebrates "mastery of the options" of style because it is "liberating." In this stance, Weathers joins other teachers and advocates such as Richard Lanham, whose *Style: An Anti-Textbook*, as his title suggests, opposes the usual textbook values of clarity, simplicity, and concreteness, embodied most famously in Strunk and White's enduring *Elements of Style*, first published in 1918. Opposing White's definition of "style" as "the rules of usage and principles of composition" (xii), Lanham contends instead that style should be "taught for and as what it is – a pleasure, a grace, a joy, a delight" (20).

In the same vein, Richard Ohmann supports stylistic freedom by attacking head-on Strunk and White's most famous dictum, "Use Definite, Specific, Concrete Language," and by exposing the ideological implications of pushing students toward "the language that most nearly reproduces the immediate experience and away from language that might be used to understand it, transform it, and relate it to everything else" (396). Peter Elbow also endorses the liberating benefits of an expressive stylistic stance in "Closing My Eyes as I Speak: An Argument for Ignoring Audience." It is often useful, Elbow says, early in the process of writing something, to ignore the real audience and write only for oneself or for imagined friends. And further, Elbow argues, sometimes writing is better because it ignores the audience throughout the process of composing, allowing the writer to find his or her own most powerful and unique voice (55).

"Voice" has often been used as a substitute or metaphor for "style," especially from within this individualist view of style. If, as Taylor Stoehr asserted in 1968, "a writer has only one voice," and "voice is the pervasive reflection, in written or spoken language, of an author's character" (150), then students must find their own unique voices or write as ventriloquists, compromising their integrity and identity. Voice, as Rohmann and Wlecke say, "in good writing, is the liberated yet controlled expression of a human being deeply committed to what he is saying" (11). We might think of Rohman and Wlecke's masculine pronoun as underscoring the significance of

Carol Gilligan's *In a Different Voice*, a classic work, often cited in feminist theory and composition studies. Gilligan considers how the reigning psychological theories of development are based on rule-driven rather than relationship-oriented "conceptions of self and morality" (2). Although Gilligan asserts that "the different voice ... is characterized not by gender but theme," she does note that "women's voices sounded distinct" (1), and her work consistently has been read as correcting a sexist bias in assessing moral development. Another feminist classic, *Women's Ways of Knowing: The Development of Self, Voice, and Mind*, by Belenky, Clinchy, Goldberger, and Tarule, has also drawn attention to the relationship between "voice" and an authentic self, influencing Elizabeth Flynn's feminist view of composition, for instance. For Flynn, voice is more than the manifestation of an authentic self; it is in fact essential to developing in women students a strong self and "a way of knowing that integrates intuition with authoritative knowledge" (429). Or, in bell hooks's terms, "the liberatory voice" is "that way of speaking that is no longer determined by one's status as object – as oppressed being" (55). Style is the woman, in other words, defined in contrast to or refutation of the dominant audience.

Both the dualist and the individualist views of style assume that content and form are separate: in the dualist view, content is shaped for the audience; in the individualist view, the writer's identity shapes the content's form, reducing the audience to the writer, in a sense. The teacher's role, from the perspective of the individualist view of style, seems obvious enough: nurturing the student to express his or her most authentic self, to develop a uniquely individual style. Weathers points to the importance of experimentation, noting that "improvement in student style comes not by osmosis, but through exercises" ("Teaching Style" 146). It may seem at first glance silly to think that students will come by way of drills and exercises to see style as an assertion of personal freedom, but they do need to enlarge their sense of the technical possibilities in order to be able to create their individual styles most distinctively. Thus, students should be engaged in the close analysis of style as well as the directed practice of various stylistic features.

Milic's third view of style, which I'll call the "organic," assumes no separation between the form and content. The four door-closing examples above, from this perspective, are not different ways of saying the same thing; instead, what they say is distinctively different. This view shifts our attention away from style as an expression of the individual, or style as the packaging for an audience, to the language itself. Are you the same person in blue jeans and in an evening gown? Are you the same person with your head shaved and a skull tattooed on your left arm? (If your head is shaved and you have a skull tattoo, then invert the question, please.) The organic view in particular highlights the power of stylistic choices. There is a situation in which simply saying "close the door" will get you what you want, but there are other situations in which one of the other articulations will be most effective – even the odd fourth option would work best in some scenario. So my approach to style in what follows aims for two things: first, heightening students' awareness of style, how the way something is said shapes the rhetorical situation – the perception of the speaker, the audience's role, the significance of what is uttered; and second, expanding students' facility with language, enlarging their syntactic and lexicographical choices – the control that they have over their writing.

GRAMMAR

Unfortunately, many students' stylistic choices are driven not by considerations of what they want to say to whom, and what they want to accomplish, but rather by a numbing fear of committing errors. They consider "What would it be correct to say?" rather than "What would be most powerful, or interesting, or effective?" We need therefore to consider first what to do about getting students out of the Den of Error, and then talk about the kinds of things that teachers can do to improve style.

Secret agents and people in witness-protection programs, so I'm told, usually respond to questions about their occupations by saying "I sell insurance." No one, apparently, asks any more questions or expresses more curiosity. English teachers, particularly those who specialize in Rhetoric and Composition, might be tempted to follow this lead, for the most common response to "I teach English" or "I teach writing" is, as any English teacher will tell you, "Oooh, I better watch what I say!" And then people often go on to talk about how much they hated English in school.

But it doesn't have to be this way. English teachers could say they're secret agents. Or, they could accept the overwhelming consensus of specialists in Rhetoric and Composition, embrace the research findings of hundreds of studies, and abandon the grammar-based pedagogy that generations of students have endured. Some progress has been made in the teaching of writing, but popular misconceptions of what teachers ought to be doing are still driving classroom practice to an astonishing degree. We'll know that pedagogy has caught up with expert knowledge when the general public stops thinking that English teachers are grammar fussies, spotting errors wherever we go, clucking self-righteously. I'm waiting for someone to say, "Oh, you teach English! You're in Rhetoric and Composition! What a fascinating job! You get to talk about great writing and work with students on expressing themselves and communicating effectively and persuading others. It must be inspiring to think about all the richness and diversity of language as people use it!"

Toward that blessed day, this section aims to answer four questions related to style:

Why do students write so poorly?
Why don't they use Standard English?
How can we help students to write Standard English?
How can we hope for more than correctness?

In an essay entitled "Grading on My Nerves," which appeared in the November 18, 2003 issue of *The Chronicle of Higher Education,* a History professor using the name of "Max Clio" laments the "illiterate and semiliterate scribbling" of his students. At least, Professor "Clio" is assigning writing, and he is working very hard to improve the writing of his students, which includes giving out many bad grades. Most depressing, "Clio" is convinced that each year the students are getting worse. Is he right? Since composition courses and arguably the field of Rhetoric and Composition began at Harvard in the 1890s, in response to shock and amazement over the terrible writing abilities of students, millions of students have been taught, and thousands of careers have been made. Have we really made any progress? What does the evidence say?

Scene One: On April 3, 2008, the *New York Times* reported on the latest installment of the National Assessment of Educational Progress, commonly known as "the nation's report card," with this dire headline: "In Test, Few Students Are Proficient Writers."[2] The reporter, Sam Dillon, covering the news conference that announced the results, quoted Will Fitzhugh, who commented that "Overall, American students' writing skills are deteriorating." Fitzhugh is the founder of the *Concord Review*, a journal that publishes research papers in history written by high school students. Dillon also quoted James Billington, who commented on "the slow destruction of the basic unit of human thought, the sentence," which is the victim, according to Billington, of cellphone texting and instant messaging. Billington, an expert in Russian history, director of the Woodrow Wilson Center from 1973 to 1987, and Librarian of Congress since 1987, asked "To what extent is students' writing getting clearer? Is that still being taught?" Billington is certainly not alone in his assumption that students are not acquiring now some writing skills that in some undefined past they were getting. But what is his evidence? He presumably had some contact with student writing as a history professor at Harvard and Princeton, but that was from 1957 to 1962, and 1964 to 1973. Fitzhugh, on the other hand, who has no doubt seen a good bit of student writing in his editorial capacity, supported his opinion by referring to "a 2006 survey of college professors, in which a large majority said that they thought most high school graduates came to college with limited writing skills." But since no one (so far as I know) has *unlimited* writing skills, it's not exactly news that most students arrive at college with some constraints. And a survey of what college professors believe about the writing skills of students tells us something about college professors, but not necessarily about the writing of students.

Given the negative slant of the story, one is surprised to read that the NAEP officials were quoted as saying they were "encouraged by the results," which – the *Times* reporter quickly adds, lest someone begin to feel hopeful – "seemed to counter other recent indicators suggesting a decline in Americans' writing abilities." Michael Casserly, executive director of the Council of Great Schools, is also quoted as saying, "These results pleased and encouraged me." Indeed, an examination of the actual results reveals that the percentage of students performing at or above the *Basic* level in the 8th grade increased from 85 percent in 2002 to 88 percent in 2007; in the 12th grade, most impressively, the increase was from 74 percent to 82 percent. Average writing scores increased, 3 points higher than in 2002 in the 8th grade, and 6 points higher than in 1998. For the 12th grade, "The average writing score was 5 points higher than in 2002 and 3 points higher than in 1998." Given this achievement, why does the *Times* have such a gloomy headline ("Few Students Are Proficient Writers")? And why is the headline followed by this assessment?

> About one-third of America's eighth-grade students, and about one in four high school seniors, are proficient writers, according to results of a nationwide test released on Thursday.
>
> The test, administered last year, showed that there were modest increases in the writing skills of low-performing students since the last time a similar exam was given, in 2002. But the skills of high-performing eighth and 12th graders remained flat or declined.

The report itself says in fact that at the worst there "was no significant change" (not a decline, as Dillon says) in the scores of students
performing at or above the proficient level. My reading of the report
really doesn't suggest that American students' writing skills are
deteriorating or that the sentence is dead. What's going on here?

Scene Two: Over three decades earlier, in September 1977, a
"blue-ribbon panel" established by the College Entrance Examination Board published a high-profile report that arrived at this
conclusion:

> More and more high school graduates show up in college class-
> rooms, employers' personnel offices, or at other common check-
> points with barely a speaking acquaintance with the English
> language and no writing facility at all. (1)

Even without seeing any of the data, most reasonable people would
have to question the characterizations here: "barely a speaking
acquaintance"? "No writing facility at all"? "More and more" is
vague, but it certainly suggests a substantial and growing number,
and therefore Stephen Judy's eloquently dismissive response, delivered in the *English Journal* a few months after the report, seems
right on target:

> Anyone who has ever listened to the babbling of two-year-olds,
> the language play of pre-schoolers, the uproar of a class of elem-
> entary children, the *tête à têtes* of high schoolers, the human
> hubbub of taverns, cocktail parties, ball games, seminars, and
> political rallies knows that virtually every speaker of English has
> far more than "barely a speaking acquaintance with English";
> native speakers have an extraordinary competence in spoken
> English. (6)

The blue-ribbon panel's observations about "no writing facility at
all" are equally puzzling, as the panel goes on to say that their "firmest conclusion is that the critical factors in the relationship between
curricular change and the SAT scores are (1) that less thoughtful and

critical reading is now being demanded and done, and (2) that careful writing has apparently about gone out of style" (26). This "firmest conclusion" would seem to be a cooked noodle at best however, as the report first acknowledges that SAT scores "are too small a window" to make an assessment of reading and writing achievements, but then goes on to do just that. The report further acknowledges that "most – probably two thirds to three fourths – of the SAT score decline between 1963 and 1970 was related to the 'compositional' changes in the group of students taking the examination" (45). Any confidence one might have had in this hazy observation – "probably two thirds to three fourths"? – is undermined by the CEEB's promotional literature about the report, which oddly shrinks those fractions, saying that "about half of the score decline is traced to the changing composition of the college-bound population."[3] Apparently the panel did not really know how much of the change results from an expansion of the pool of students taking that test, and yet it was willing to draw dire conclusions. As Judy says, we don't need "unsubstantiated, speculative, comfortable, elusive, patronizing talk" about students' writing skills (7). So, again, what's going on here?

Scene Three: One of the most famous headlines in *Newsweek*'s rich history appeared on December 8, 1975, slightly less than two years before the aforementioned CEEB report: "Why Johnny Can't Write." As the accompanying story reported, the recent National Assessment of Educational Progress (NAEP) had found widespread evidence of a substantial decline in literacy, including such things as "increases in awkwardness, run-on sentences and incoherent paragraphs" (60). All of *Newsweek*'s US bureaus had been involved in nine months of interviews with dozens of "students, parents, teachers, college professors, language experts (including Noam Chomsky) and writers who teach in schools." The article's general thrust is captured in a startling quotation from Mario Pei, a noted linguist, who lamented that American education has been dominated by people "preaching that one form of language is as good as another; that at the age of 5 anyone who is not deaf or idiotic has gained a full mastery of his language; that we must not try to correct or improve language, but must leave it alone; that the only language activity worthy of the name is speech on the colloquial, slangy, even illiterate plane; that writing is a secondary, unimportant activity" (62).

The public's outraged response to such an apparent lack of standards, morals, commitment, patriotism, and common sense was predictable. Although *Newsweek*'s editor, Merrill Sheils, surely exaggerated when he said that "hardly anyone seemed interested in the teaching of writing" before the feature, he was probably closer to the truth when he noted that afterward "there's not a week that goes by without some mention of the issue in scholarly journals and mass media, not a month without a meeting devoted to the subject."[4] For those who were not academics, who were not linguists or English teachers, the solution seemed clear: somebody needed to get serious, get " back to basics," and start preparing students for the "real world." Surely those involved in education ought to "try to correct or improve" the language of their students.

But for many of the professionals assigned to this job, the writing teachers and language experts who studied literacy, the problem was not so dismal, and the solution was not so clear. For example, Suzette Haden Elgin, a linguist, was clearly outraged by the way that *Newsweek* had, in her opinion, distorted, misled, and even fabricated. In her lengthy response to the *Newsweek* article, published in the *English Journal* in November of 1976, "Why *Newsweek* Can't Tell Us Why Johnny Can't Write," Elgin even went so far as to say, "I don't for a moment believe that Dr. Pei said what is attributed to him" (30), and she explained point by point why no linguist would ever say those things. For starters, defending Professor Pei and all linguists, Elgin asserted (in all caps), "ONE FORM OF LANGUAGE IS AS GOOD AS ANOTHER. DAMN RIGHT!" As Elgin explained, "good" is "a moral judgment," "not an esthetic or stylistic one," and "you cannot make *moral* judgments about the way that people talk and write" (31). It's not only "bad" but also "stupid," Elgin asserted, "To say to a ghetto or barrio or hill child that his or her dialect or language is not 'as good' as that of some other child who speaks a different dialect or language" (31). In setting aside judgmental questions of "good," "correct," and "educated," Elgin did at the same time acknowledge that some "'forms are language' are more useful for certain purposes than others" (31): "The speech a teenager from Harlem uses on the street is not considered appropriate for participating in a job interview. GOODNESS has nothing to do with it" (31).

But this kind of judgment was precisely what the advocates of "good" and "grammatical" English were (and apparently will forever more be) making in various handbooks and rhetorics. Consider, for instance, this passage from Warriner's classic *English Grammar and Composition* (1963):

> "Correction" of your English raises the question: Why is one word or one form correct while another is incorrect? What, in other words, is good English? Good English is the kind of English used by educated people. The fact that educated people use a different kind of English from that used by uneducated people can easily be discovered by listening. The educated person will say, for example, "Jim and I weren't able to see anything in the fog." The uneducated person might say "Jim and me wasn't able to see nothing in the fog." Although the idea expressed is clear in either form, you, as a high school student, would say it the first way, which, since it is the way an educated person would say it, is the "correct" way. (64)

It's hard to say whether Warriner's statement displays less awareness of teenagers or languages. There are certainly times and places when "Jim and I weren't able to see anything in the fog" would be considered odd. Speakers of Black English, Chicano English, or Ozark English, in various circumstances, probably would not call the speaker of this sentence "uneducated," but they might well note that the speaker wasn't part of their discourse community.

"Goodness" and "correctness," in terms of language anyway, are subjective and relative terms. Black English for instance is just as logical and grammatical as Standard English, conveying in fact tenses and nuances of meaning that Standard English cannot, as a number of linguists have shown.[5] Shirley Brice Heath's classic study, *Ways with Words: Language, Life and Work in Communities and Classrooms*, offers one particularly rich study of how children learn to use language differently in communities separated by only a few miles. What is "correct" in "Roadville" (white, multi-generational textile workers), and what is "correct" in "Trackton" (black textile workers, who in previous generations were farm workers) are often substantially different from each other – and from the "educated high school student" that Warriner imagines. Geneva Smitherman's masterful classic, *Talkin and Testifyin: The Language of Black America*, published in the same year as Elgin and Sheils's heated exchange in the *English Journal* (1977), brilliantly captures the situational nature of correctness, the relationship between "correct" and "effective" language, the unique resources of Black English, and the power of the idea of "communicative competence":

> Communicative competence, quite simply, refers to the ability to communicate effectively. At this point, however, all simplicity ends. For to be able to speak or write with power is a very complex business, involving a universe of linguistic choices and alternatives. Such a speaker or writer must use language that is appropriate to the situation and the audience. He or she must be able to answer such questions as: who can say what to whom, under what conditions? Who is my audience? What assumptions can I make about that audience? In a given act of speaking or writing, what examples or details will fit best and where? I am here talking about aspects of communication such as content and message, style, choice of words, logical development, analysis and arrangement, originality of thought and expression, and so forth. Such are the real components of language power, and

they cannot be measured or mastered by narrow conceptions of "correct grammar." While teachers frequently correct student language on the basis of such misguided conceptions, saying something correctly, and saying it well, are two entirely different Thangs. (228–9)

But "narrow conceptions of 'correct grammar,'" as Smitherman describes them, have persisted. Discovering that Carol Reed's courses at Brooklyn College included the study of Black English, to take one of many possible examples, the editors of the aptly-named *Crisis* magazine admonished "Black parents throughout this nation" to "rise up in unanimous condemnation of this insidious conspiracy to cripple their children permanently." As Reed made clear in her response to the caustic editorial, entitled "Black Nonsense," she was by no means teaching Black English to her students. The goal of her program was to enable the students to use Standard American English proficiently. But rather than trying "to eliminate Black English," her strategy aimed to "improve the students' linguistic versatility," using "the speech patterns of the students" in order "to help them gain facility in Standard English."[6]

But if Black English is as grammatical as Standard English in linguistic or moral or some other terms, then why should students adept in the former have to learn how to master the latter? Why should the desirability of linguistic versatility go only in one direction? How can teachers justify the considerable investment of time and energy required to try to give users of Black English "facility in Standard English"? Do such efforts work? Wouldn't the time be better spent studying finance, or calculus, or American history, or anything? The obvious problem, in the eyes of most linguists, writing specialists, English teachers, and the general public, is that anyone limited to Black English or any other nonstandard dialect will compete at a substantial disadvantage in a world that privileges Standard English. One response to this bias is embodied in a document published in 1974 in a special issue of *College Composition and*

Communication, the famous statement of "Students' Right to Their Own Language." The essence of this pronouncement is contained in a resolution that was adopted by the CCCC Executive Council in 1972, and by the CCCC membership in 1974 (by a vote of 79 to 20):

> We affirm the students' right to their own language – the dialects of their nurture or whatever dialects in which they find their own identity and style. Language scholars long ago denied that the myth of a standard American dialect has any validity. The claim that any one dialect is unacceptable amounts to an attempt of one social group to exert its dominance over another. Such a claim leads to false advice for speakers and writers, and immoral advice for humans. A nation proud of its diverse heritage and its cultural and racial variety will preserve its heritage of dialects. We affirm strongly that teachers must have the experiences and training that will enable them to respect diversity and uphold the right of students to their language.[7]

This was a courageous resolution, opening its authors and the CCCC to charges that they were abandoning standards, or the basics, or correctness in favor of a foolish diversity. But in concrete terms, how would "the students' right to their own language" work in the classroom? Would it mean that teachers would not correct or even notice departures from Standard English? Would this mean, given the "myth of a standard American dialect" as the 4Cs resolution puts it, that students would be taught in their own dialect, or taught to use their own dialect more effectively?

One crucial assumption here is that there is no "standard American dialect." But most people believe that there is, that the speech of people who dominate the media, political offices, educational institutions, corporate management, and much else all follow the same general "usage" of the language, despite some quirks of pronunciation (saying "nuclear" as three syllables for instance) and grammar (substituting "I" for "me," as in "He gave the check to my husband and I"). The 4Cs resolution also seems to assume that the goal of education is to prepare students to be students. But as Lisa Delpit argues in her award-winning book, *Other People's Children: Cultural Conflict in the Classroom* (1995), students who do not have access to the language used by those with resources and power, do not have access to those resources and power. As John Albertinti puts it, "a decision to deemphasize the superficial trappings of discourse (grammar, form, style) and to develop the students' writing within the language and style of the students' home (vernacular) discourse is a decision *not* to teach" (388). As Olga Welch and Carolyn Hodges find, the experience of beginning college for African American students already often feels like "standing outside on the inside," and so the question, to the extent that this conflict is related to language, is whether teachers on the one hand should try to give students the "communicative competence" to adapt to different audiences and purposes, as Smitherman puts it, or on the other hand try to change the world so that students may without prejudice use "their own language," "the dialects of their nurture or whatever dialects in which they find their own identity and style," as the CCCC resolution puts it. Are there other options?

We should do both, but teachers, it seems clear, have a much better chance of helping students achieve linguistic versatility than of teaching the world to consider everyone's usage as equally acceptable – at least in the short run. Teachers who worry that clashing languages will create identity conflicts for students will find the work of Hannah Ashley encouraging, as she documents how working-class women in one study developed a "doublevoicedness" that supplemented their own voices and identities. These women were not victims of conflict or tension or confusion; instead, they grew as writers, enlarging their repertoires. In fact, the very concept of a singular and stable voice as a reflection of the writer's self is unnecessarily essentialist and limiting, in much the same way that consigning students to "the right to their own language" would be limiting. Identity is dynamic and adaptable. Just as gender is a "socially constituted identity," which is "not monolithic, immutable, or always patriarchal," as Diane Anderson puts it (391), in a similar fashion race, class, and ethnicity also contribute to meaning and identity, which are constructed "through negotiation between author subjectivities and reader expectations," as Ryuko Kubota says (40).

When the champions of Good Grammar (as they see themselves), the Last-Best-Hopes-to-Preserve-Civilization-and-the-Language, talk about students' lack of skills, they are clearly assuming that there is some correct grammar out there, and that teachers ought to make their students adhere to it. Their obvious frustration (and emotions run high on both sides, as we've seen) no doubt stems from not understanding why in the world teachers don't just get *back to basics*. What could be simpler?! Just teach the students to spell, punctuate, coordinate their subjects and verbs, and so forth, and do the job you're being paid to do.

Certainly, students have been taught grammar for thousands of years. You'd think teachers would have that down by now. But teaching "grammar" means many different things. In an often-cited essay, "Grammar, Grammars, and the Teaching of Grammar," Patrick Hartwell identifies five different meanings of "grammar": (1) "the internalized system of rules that speakers of a language share"; (2) the branch of linguistics that is concerned with understanding and explaining (1); (3) "linguistic etiquette," or what's more commonly called "usage," a shifting and subjective set of preferences; (4) "school grammar," distinguished from the "scientific" or more rigorous grammar of 2; and (5) "stylistic grammar," the terms and rules intended to improve style, overlapping somewhat perhaps with (3), but focused on increasing effectiveness rather than avoiding error and distraction. In the classical and medieval ages, "Grammar" (4), the grammar taught in school, was that part of the Trivium concerned with literacy and, interestingly, literature, as learning the fundamentals of reading and writing included studying great literature.

Grammatical instruction in English as a part of education in Europe dates back only to the seventeenth century. Before that, people lucky enough to get an education were taught to read and write in Latin. Prior to that, and perhaps in addition to that, people were educated in Greek grammar. So there was a ready-made model for how to teach grammar, and when teachers started to include instruction in the vernacular, in English, to serve the needs of an expanded group of students, that instruction was patterned on the way that Latin and Greek were taught. That's fine, except that Latin and English are quite different languages. The traditional school grammar therefore simply doesn't work very well. It fails to describe the language effectively, as linguists have long understood – see for instance Charles Fries's *The Structure of English* (1952). As Kathryn Riley and Frank Parker show in *English Grammar*, the parts of speech and usage rules are hopelessly ambiguous and problematic. It is easy to speculate that the shortcomings of traditional school grammar (TSG) contribute to students' frustration: as Richard Meade's research has shown, most students do not enjoy formal grammar study, and even the most intelligent students (IQ 114 to 152) find it quite difficult. But it's also easy to understand why teachers keep returning, again and again, to the teaching of grammar, given the high-stakes testing that focuses on grammatical errors. As Harvard's entrance exam, the NAEP, the SAT, and whatever test is applied repeatedly reveal that students are poor writers, teachers strap on their grammatical helmets and run even harder at that wall, cheered on by parents and administrators.

What's the problem with this picture? Why do students apparently continue to write poorly, making all sorts of errors, leading intelligent people to say that Johnny can't write, that students have "barely a speaking acquaintance with English," that careful writing has just about disappeared, and so forth?

Here's the problem: In 1963, in *Research in Written Composition*, a landmark study that did much to put Rhetoric and Composition on the academic map, Richard Braddock, Richard Lloyd-Jones, and

Lowell Schoer surveyed the research that had been conducted to that point, and came to this conclusion:

> In view of the widespread agreement of research studies based upon many types of students and teachers, the conclusion can be stated in strong and unqualified terms that the teaching of formal [traditional] grammar has a negligible or, because it usually displaces some instruction and practice in actual composition, even a harmful effect on the improvement of writing. (37–8)

Braddock, Lloyd-Jones, and Schoer, to be sure, did have reservations about the methodology of much of the research, and their work helped to focus and improve subsequent studies. Over two decades later, in 1986, George Hillocks reported on his landmark overview of research, finding even more definitively and emphatically that nothing had changed – that there was even more evidence that teaching grammar doesn't work, and is a lousy idea:

> The study of traditional school grammar (i.e., the definition of parts of speech, the parsing of sentences, etc.) has no effect on raising the quality of student writing. Every other focus of instruction examined in this review is stronger. Taught in certain ways, grammar and mechanics instruction has a deleterious effect on student writing. In some studies a heavy emphasis on mechanics and usage (e.g., marking every error) resulted in significant losses in overall quality. School boards, administrators, and teachers who impose the systematic study of traditional school grammar on their students over lengthy periods of time in the name of teaching writing do them a gross disservice which should not be tolerated by anyone concerned with the effective teaching of good writing. We need to learn how to teach standard usage and mechanics after careful task analysis and with minimal grammar. (248–9)

In 2006, in Bazerman's *Handbook of Research on Writing*, Michael Smith and Julie Cheville join George Hillocks in yet another survey, updating the research on grammar and writing instruction. "Current tests," they say, "place a high emphasis on the standard of correctness that TSG [Traditional School Grammar] is designed to provide," but there continues to be "a wealth of evidence" that TSG does not help students eliminate errors in their writing or have any other positive effect (264). Smith, Cheville, and Hillocks confirm the earlier overviews, and the only substantive advancement in the research is concerned with documenting "students' strong negative reaction to the teaching of grammar" (266). But what about other approaches to grammar? Perhaps some new approach to grammar will provide the benefits we seek? Smith, Cheville, and Hillocks explain structural grammars, transformational-generative grammar, systemic functional linguistics, and "more progressive" versions of TSG, and they consider what research has revealed about their effectiveness in the writing classroom. Sentence combining (which we'll cover in a moment) seems to help students to write more complex sentences, but it doesn't seem to improve the quality of their writing. Indeed, they must conclude that "No empirical evidence yet suggests that alternative approaches to TSG actually contribute to students' writing development" (272). And yet, what is perhaps most surprising, even these researchers seem to be drifting a little in their final sentences toward the popular assumption that surely there must be some way to teach grammar that will work, as they note the "anecdotal evidence offered by teachers at regional and national conferences," indicating "at the very least, the considerable professional interests in synthetic approaches that situate grammar instruction in the context of process instruction" (272). Grammar is an alluring vampire.

We have seen a few instances (which could easily have been multiplied) of the mainstream media and the public repeatedly decrying the awful writing of students. We have an ongoing literacy crisis, and we've got to get back to the basics, back to grammar, back to correctness and clarity. Unfortunately, if we agree that we do want to enable students to use Standard English fluently and effectively, we have mountains of evidence showing that teaching grammar and mechanics not only doesn't work – it actually causes harm. Some teachers and researchers have justified continuing to teach grammar: James Williams says for instance that "The real issue is how grammar should be taught, not whether it should be taught," arguing that students "deserve an opportunity to learn about the language that they speak" (180). "Given the right approach," Williams says, "students are as interested in grammar as they are in social sciences, and for many of the same reasons" (180). It would be difficult to find someone, I think, who would argue that students do not deserve an opportunity to learn about the language that they speak, but one could substitute "their musical heritage," "their religious faith," or "their cell histology" as subject matter and also arguably have a case. Isn't the real "real issue," at least in terms of Rhetoric and Composition, whether grammar should be taught *as a way of improving writing*? If the aim of a course or sequence of courses is advancing students' writing abilities (or reading, or thinking, or arguing, or persuading, or communicating), what role should the direct study of grammar have?

The answer, according to dozens and dozens of research studies, would seem to be "none." But writing teachers, even well-informed ones, have had a difficult time taking that leap, arguing for instance that "effective teaching" "must differentiate between grammar and usage," noting that grammar is concerned with a language's structure, and usage with its production. But research doesn't support the efficacy of lectures and exercises and worksheets on usage and sentence diagramming any more than it supports teaching grammar. Since the teaching of grammar is usually designed to enhance usage, the distinction seems unimportant in terms of pedagogical strategies.

So if we somehow don't teach grammar, if we can turn away from its Undead Appeal, what can we do to help students improve their writing?

FLUENCY

Obviously, some students do learn how to write well. Some students do not hate English. Some students even major in English and writing. So let's start with those students. How did they acquire their fluency?

Just as the most powerful second language acquisition involves immersion, children acquire their first language by being born into it, living in it, hearing it daily, hour after hour, making their own sounds, experimenting until they hit upon a meaningful articulation. Children somehow come to understand grammatical rules, even though they're not taught them. Ask any native speaker to use "French," "athletic," and "young" to describe "the girl" in a sentence, and he or she will most likely say "the athletic young French girl." For some reason, "the French athletic young girl" sounds odd to native speakers of English. "The wise old British general" also sounds right, whereas "the old British wise general" doesn't. Native English speakers have a rule inside their heads that no one taught them explicitly, that they probably cannot articulate, and that they can apply effortlessly. People who are learning English will have to memorize this rule relating to ordering adjectives. When children are exposed to a language early enough in life, they are able not only to master the sounds of that language, speaking with no accent, but they are also able to internalize the language's rules. It's amazing. As they get older, it is increasingly harder to restructure the brain (if that is what happens) as the language is acquired, until at some point, it is very difficult for most people to learn to speak a new language effortlessly without any accent.

With about 6,500 languages spoken on the planet, the human brain obviously has an incredible capacity to learn languages, but languages do have to be learned: they're not already in our heads. My daughter's first word was "wight," which is meaningful only if you know she was pointing at a light bulb. As you can imagine, no one told her that she had said the word poorly – we danced with delight. And we said the word back to her, "light," emphasizing the "l" sound, allowing her perhaps to hear the difference. When we said one day, "The car's pooped out," explaining why we couldn't drive around some more, our three-year-old got out of the car and crawled underneath it, yelling "Dere's no poop under heah! No poop!" We didn't chide her for taking the word in the wrong sense. Instead, we just hugged her, laughed our heads off, and explained that "pooped" can also mean "tired." In most families in which children are being raised reasonably and responsibly, people know that they are learning to use the language, and usually the errors that they make are considered to be charming. Specialists in language acquisition have noted that parents are constantly repeating what children have said, allowing them to hear the sounds, rewarding their efforts with attention. When language users are corrected too much or too harshly, they may become self-conscious and insecure. They may stop using some constructions, limit their vocabularies, and in essence pull back their language experimentation. Hypercorrection is a common phenomenon in which speakers unwittingly introduce errors in order to be, they believe, more formally correct – as when someone says "between you and I," or "Give the key to Ted and I," for instance. Speakers with more education, interestingly enough, actually make some kinds of errors more often, saying for instance "I feel badly" (suggesting that their sensory system works poorly) when they mean "I feel bad." You have probably already anticipated my point: the way that we teach writing is bizarrely different from the way that we "teach" children to speak and listen. If they thought about language acquisition, teachers would assume that students are going to make mistakes – that if they're not making mistakes, they're probably not developing as quickly and fully as they could. Children learn to talk and listen by (drum-roll please) being encouraged to talk and listen. We don't drill them on sounds, and then on words, and have them practice arranging words into sentences. We encourage them to experiment, to engage in communication: we talk to them; we listen to them; we allow them to listen. We are, generally speaking, delighted with their efforts to join the discursive community.

So grammar instruction, although it seems commonsensical ("get back to the basics"), doesn't work because that isn't the way human beings learn to communicate. Some writing teachers have argued that writing is unnatural, and therefore extrapolations from first-language oral acquisition are misleading, but research into the development of writing abilities suggests otherwise. Even the acquisition of sign language works best by focusing on using the language – through immersion, in other words. Students come into the writing classroom, in the elementary through post-secondary grades, with grammar already installed in their brains. That's great – except when the grammar that's in there isn't Standard English, and the course requires (as most people think it should) acquiring facility in Standard English. Quintilian, many centuries ago, obviously understood the importance of early language acquisition, writing at the outset of the *The Institutes*:

> Before all things, let the talk of the child's nurses not be
> ungrammatical.... It is they that the child will hear first; it is
> their words that he will try to form by imitation. We are by
> nature most tenacious of what we have imbibed in our infant
> years; as the flavor, with which you scent vessels when new,
> remains in them; nor can the colors of wool, for which its plain
> whiteness has been exchanged, be effaced; and those very
> habits, which are of a more objectionable nature, adhere with
> the greater tenacity; for good ones are easily changed for the
> worse, but when will you change bad ones into good? Let the
> child not be accustomed, therefore, even while he is yet an
> infant, to phraseology which must be unlearned.

I've had colleagues who graded the writing of their students without mercy, exacting substantial penalties for any stylistic error, and as a result often flunking over half of their students in many classes. Such a practice, given what we know about language and dialects, seems a bit like flunking shorter people because they can't jump as high.

But the situation is a little more hopeful than that. If the direct teaching of grammar is ineffective, and students have established their neural networks for languages early in life, it is nonetheless the case that immersion at any point can have transformative effects. I'm just going to present here some illustrative activities that research or direct experience or compelling anecdotal evidence indicates can help students to improve their stylistic fluency and general writing ability.

1. *Write often, and write all sorts of different kinds of things for different kinds of audiences.* Write rough drafts, not worrying about anything, and write final revisions, getting everything exactly right.

In the most extensive investigation of the writing done in American secondary schools, Arthur Applebee found in the early 1980s that students "were spending only about 3% of their school time – in class or for homework – on writing of a paragraph or longer" (*Writing* 30). Still, writing in all subject matters occupied "an average of 44% of the observed lesson time," but this writing overwhelmingly involved "fill-in-the-blank exercises, worksheets requiring only short responses, translation from one language to another, and the like" (2). Even when students did write essays, "the essays were treated as tests of previous learning," requiring the students to repeat information "that had already been organized by the teacher or textbook," rather than extend or integrate "new learning for themselves" (3). When students were not being asked simply to rehearse information they had been given, they were often asked, Applebee says, "to write on topics that were in a real sense impossible," such as (a real assignment) describing "the political, economic, social and cultural changes that Europe was going through at the time of the Reformation" (4). Fewer than one-third of the teachers asked for more than one draft (80), and about 3 percent of the English teachers had students brainstorm before they started writing. If writing teachers were teaching tennis instead, and they had their students playing tennis less than 3 percent of the time, focusing instead on taking quizzes on tennis and drawing pictures of tennis balls, and using a 75-foot high net, or no net, when they did actually play – we would question their sanity and demand new and different teachers.

Is this why there has been no comparable study since Applebee's work in the 1980s – English teachers, already depressed by all those airplane and party conversations about grammar, are afraid of what might be uncovered? For whatever reason, one could plausibly argue that we know more about certain areas of Mars than we know about the average American writing class-room. Hillocks's study in 2002 of state writing tests in Illinois, Kentucky, New York, Oregon, and Texas, entitled *The Testing Trap*, does provide some possible comparisons chronologically and geo-graphically. By examining state preparation and testing materials, and interviewing over 60 teachers and 20 administrators in each state, Hillocks concluded that students in high schools are writing far more than they did 20 years ago. Although the focus clearly has moved beyond writing individual sentences or filling in blanks, the five-paragraph theme still appears to be the goal in many districts, Hillocks says, thus constraining dramatically the development of writing abilities. Emphasis on grammar may also have declined somewhat, as only 5 percent of the teachers Hillocks interviewed considered grammar to be their major focus, but more than 70 per-cent considered grammar to be a secondary focus of their teaching. What will it take for teachers to focus on engaging in the richness and diversity of writing – not five-paragraph themes, not grammar drills – as the foundation of writing instruction? Where is that wooden stake?

Perhaps two excerpts from the website of the Assembly for the Teaching of Grammar (ATEG), an organization within the National Council of Teachers of English, established around 1984, provide an especially interesting vantage point from which to judge the progress that has been made. ATEG's "Frequently Asked Questions and Answers" section includes this one:

> *Grammar workbook exercises get pretty dull, but they do cover the basics. Are they worthwhile? How should I use them?*
>
>   Traditional drill and practice will be the most meaningful to students when they are anchored in the context of writing assignments or the study of literary models. Students find grammar most interesting when they apply it to authentic texts. Try using texts of different kinds, such as newspapers and the students' own writing, as sources for grammar examples and exercises. This approach helps make grammar relevant and alive. It also avoids the artificiality of studying sentences in isolation, a problem with grammar books; in real texts, students can see how sentences connect and contrast to each other through their grammar.

On the positive side, we should note that the straw-person questioner does acknowledge that grammar exercises are "pretty dull" and questions whether they're "worthwhile." On the negative side, we see the enduring desire for "the basics" and the respondent's evasion of the question of whether, in what way, such exercises are worthwhile, sliding over instead to answer the question of how to use them. The respondent says how such drill for skill will be "most meaningful to students" (in the context of writing or literary study), how it will be "most interesting" (applied to "authentic texts"), where to find examples (in newspapers and students' own writing), but the respondent in the final analysis does not say explicitly "yes, they're worthwhile."

Even more promising is this "exchange," which seems roughly analogous to the Flat Earth Society saying that maps are useful in understanding a three-dimensional spherical planet:

> *I hear that teaching grammar doesn't help students to make fewer errors. But students make so many mistakes in their writing. What should I do?*

Teaching grammar will not make writing errors go away. Students make errors in the process of learning, and as they learn about writing, they often make new errors, not necessarily fewer ones. But knowing basic grammatical terminology does provide students with a tool for thinking about and discussing sentences. And lots of discussion of language, along with lots of reading and lots of writing, are the three ingredients for helping students write in accordance with the conventions of standard English.

If "basic grammatical terminology" does indeed make the discussion of sentences more insightful or useful, or even convenient, we can take comfort in knowing that such information can be imparted in an hour or so. Most students are supposedly taught in elementary school about nouns, verbs, adverbs, adjectives, and prepositions. There would seem to be no need to keep repeating this information at every grade level, nor to spend months refining it, or to extend it to learn about passive periphrastic conjugations. There will be lots more time freed up, then, for writing. We'll consider in a moment (and in Chapter 6 below on Delivery) the kinds of assignments teachers might employ and how they might react to them (what to do with all the writing?), but the key point here is that students need to write – as much as possible – to improve their writing.

2. *Read, read, read.* In various disciplines – psychology, education, literary criticism, neuroscience – reading has increasingly been seen, especially since the 1970s, as the active making of meaning rather than its passive reception. Our understanding of reading as an open-ended, generative, constructive process has come from sources as different as reader-response criticism, artificial intelligence, and deconstruction, with the result that reading and writing seem in many ways to share fundamentally similar cognitive operations. The writer is a reader not only of other prior texts but also of the text that he or she is making. The reader must not only write about the text to register his or her reading, but must also "write"

the text in some sense in order to read it. The notion that writing and reading are intimately related is certainly supported by research. Not only has reading research helped us to understand writing, and vice-versa, but substantial research also supports the commonsensical notion that writing and reading strongly correlate – that good writers are good readers, and vice-versa, in other words.[8] Imaginative research has also indicated that even specific textual features tend to be transferred from reading to writing.[9] In other words, the use of models in writing classes – that is, asking students to read exemplary texts in the hope that writing abilities will be absorbed by some kind of osmosis – is validated. Indeed, better writers, according to Nancy Sommers's research, re-read what they have written more often than poorer writers.

In some ways, the conventions of the classroom have not served us well in the cultivation of reading. Why do we assign the same work to every student in a classroom? Do we believe that they have the same interests and concerns, the same level of reading ability? There is, to be sure, something quite valuable about having students discuss what they've read, as Gordon Mills argued compellingly in *Hamlet's Castle* (a work that deserves to be better known), but students do not need to discuss every work they read thoroughly. And life is full of opportunities to talk about things that one person has read and others have not. These are often the most important and meaningful kinds of conversations. In far too many classrooms, students are spending long stretches of time struggling to read through a work that is ill-suited for their abilities and their imaginations – only to produce a few pages of writing that are too likely to be adapted from someone else's work. We may need legislation prohibiting students from undertaking Shakespeare until they have obtained a license proving they're ready for such a challenge. Or, as a compromise, we need teachers who combine some carefully chosen common works with individually-tailored reading assignments. The world has too many wonderful books for any student to say "I don't like reading." Even for students with reading disabilities, there is some text that will light up their sky. If we want to help students write fluently, correctly, effectively, we've got to help them become readers. With efforts to champion Writing Across the Curriculum (WAC) and Writing In the Disciplines (WID), many writing teachers have recognized that teachers in every subject need to help us teach writing and reading. But the writing teacher has a special role to play here.

3. *Understand the logic of errors and cultivate correctness.* It's wonderful to say that students should read and write copiously, and have grammatically correct nursemaids, but imagine that the following passage, which Mina Shaughnessy received while teaching at the City University of New York, was turned in to you by a student: what you would say?

> First of all the system, don't really care about the students,
> schools are always overcrowded and the students get the impres-
> sion that really there are some teachers, just like the students
> just to Be there, and the children performing below par is mainly
> the parents fault too, they really don't stress How important is,
> and that when they go to school they should try to do the Best
> they can instead they are encourage to learned Basketball, But
> in all the fault would lie on the state and government officials,
> Because really they don't care about children Education they're
> more concerned about what's your color or do your family have a
> good Income? and really with all the pressure society put on the
> children ... [the passage continues] (19–20)

Shaughnessy's approach to the writing of this and many other students who were accepted into CUNY's open university profoundly influenced the teaching of writing (a major prize in Rhetoric and Composition is named for her), as she asserted that the teacher, "confronted by what at first appears to be a hopeless tangle of errors and inadequacies, must learn to see below the surface of these failures the intelligence and linguistic aptitudes of his students" (292). Shaughnessy's great insight in *Errors and Expectations*, published in 1977, was to look for the logic and intelligence underlying errors. A "careful reading of an incorrectly punctuated passage," Shaughnessy wrote, "often reflects a design which, once perceived, can be translated into conventional punctuation" (21). Regarding the passage above, Shaughnessy says, for instance:

> The writer ... appears not to have learned the convention for ending sentences. The capital B that dominates the passage probably reflects some difficulty with forming the lower-case *b* and has no significance as punctuation. Note, too, how the comma plays into the writer's aversion to closure, allowing him to create strings of conjunctions (mainly with *but*).

This kind of analysis requires no special expertise and is based on Shaughnessy's patient and observant intelligence, along with her assumption that errors are usually not random, that there is some underlying thoughtfulness. By seeking to understand the logic of errors, Shaughnessy is able to provide targeted exercises and explanations that are designed to help students master specific problems, rather than trying to cover every possible grammar and usage issue. Shaughnessy's fascinating study, based on the analysis of thousands of student papers, considers very basic problems, such as why "basic writers" (students who are learning the fundamentals) often omit words or use the wrong word ("skips and misses," as she calls them). Shaughnessy also tackles the most complex issues, such as the thinking that underlies an argument. I can't begin to convey here the wealth of useful information, tips, strategies, encouragements, cautions, and wise counsel that Shaughnessy's masterful study conveys, but I would like to give some sense of the topics she covers, and commend her book to anyone with any interest in writing instruction. Chapters in *Errors and Expectations* deal with "Handwriting and Punctuation" (Shaughnessy argues that many of these students' problems stem from or are complicated by difficulties controlling writing instruments – often they just need more practice), "Syntax" (she asserts that "process and practice" rather than "direct grammatical instruction" will improve syntax most effectively [88]),

"Common Errors" (they are often, "no matter how peculiar they may sound to a teacher," the result "not of carelessness or irrationality but of *thinking*" [105]), "Spelling" (it can be taught, although there is no one way to teach it), "Vocabulary" (although there appear to be "stubborn" limits on the pace at which words can enter a person's active vocabulary, teachers working across disciplines can inspire students to expand their linguistic resources significantly [224]), and "Beyond the Sentence" (students "need to experience consciously the process whereby a writer arrives at a main idea or point"; they "need to practice seeing and creating structure in written language"; and they "need to recognize specific patterns of thought that lie embedded in sentences and that point to ways of developing large numbers of sentences into paragraphs and essays" [274]).

Shaughnessy, to be sure, does advocate some general exercises to deal with common grammatical problems, and the startling popularity of books about grammar and correctness may suggest that some writers find such explanations useful, or at least interesting. There may also be an element of superiority or even snobbery in the sales success of books such as Lynn Truss's *Eats, Shoots, and Leaves: The Zero Tolerance Approach to Punctuation*, June Casagrande's *Grammar Snobs Are Great Big Meanies: A Guide to Language for Fun and Spite*, Patricia O'Connor's *Woe Is I: The Grammarphobe's Guide to Better English in Plain English*, and many others, including the granddaddy of style manuals, Strunk and White's classic (and now controversial) *Elements of Style*. For students with complex deficiencies in standard English (often called Basic Writers), any approach that can give them hope and good humor about the non-standard features of their language is exceedingly valuable.

4. *Nurture students' awareness of the effects of stylistic choices.* There are tools or strategies, beyond simply reading and discussing, that can heighten students' understanding of the choices writers are making and the effects upon the reader. One of my favorites, extremely popular with students, is Walker Gibson's

"Model T Style Machine," as he terms it in *Tough, Sweet, and Stuffy: An Essay on Modern American Prose Styles*. By "style," Gibson says he means the way that a writer "presents himself to a reader," the "self-dramatizations in language" that allow the reader to construct a voice out of a set of linguistic choices. Gibson finds, writing in 1966, three distinct kinds of personalities that inhabit American prose: the Tough Talker, the Sweet Talker, and the Stuffy Talker. In a series of brilliantly entertaining and revealing analyses of sample passages, Gibson identifies the stylistic features that distinguish these three kinds of personalities. He vividly brings to life, in a sense, the personalities dramatized in particular passages, and shows us *how* they are created. For instance, just to give you some sense of what Gibson does, consider the following sentence from the United States government's 1964 report on "Smoking and Health":

> Cigarette smoking is causally related to lung cancer in men; the magnitude of the effect of cigarette smoking far outweighs all other factors.

And now consider this sample of Gibson's analysis of that sentence:

> Causally related? Probably there is some good reason why the committee could not say simply "Cigarette smoking causes lung cancer in men." What good reason might there be? Perhaps the latter phrasing suggests that smoking is the *only* cause of lung cancer? Perhaps it suggests that all smoking necessarily causes lung cancer? But our faint understanding of the committee's anxiety for caution and clarity, in the light of its complex audience, should not prevent us from deploring the alternative. For by using the passive verb (*is related to*) and its odd modifier (*causally*), the writers deprive their language not only of strength but of responsibility. Note that in this sentence the committee's voice isn't doing any relating itself; all it's saying is that something is or has been related to something – by someone else. Very scientific, very "objective." Then we read on (to

finish the first sentence): "the magnitude of the effect far out-
weighs all other factors." The magnitude is doing the outweigh-
ing, not the austere members of this committee ... Explained
in these terms, we can understand why the voice in the first
paragraph sounds so disembodied and the wording sounds so
awkward. (93–4)

After working his way through a healthy sampling of passages, Gibson
presents sixteen questions that help to clarify the basis for each of
the three kinds of voices. For instance, here is Gibson's last question: "How many occurrences are there of these marks of punctuation: italics, parentheses, dashes, question marks, and exclamation
points?" Simply counting these features gives us some information
about how a particular self is being dramatized. Dashes for instance
tend to create a sense of closeness. With dashes, "relations between
parts of a sentence ... remain logically in the air, another characteristic of our elliptical and loose syntax in conversation" (133). This
sort of closeness, of "intimate discourse," is characteristic of sweet
talkers, Gibson says – a finding that is supported by his sampling
of 25 passages: 11 dashes appear; nine in passages that Gibson characterizes as "Sweet," two in "Tough" talking passages, and none
in "Stuffy" talkers. Gibson also shows how some writers combine
voices ("mostly stuffy," "mixed," "mostly sweet," etc.). And he also
includes a chapter on "Being Serious Without Being Stuffy."

The passages alone are a valuable resource for writing teachers,
and getting students to identify the features that contribute to stylistic effects can, at the very least, get them more interested in style.
(Here is a reason to learn some grammatical terms.) A lively class
can always be produced by asking students to bring in contemporary
passages to update Gibson, seeing whether there are other types of
voices pervasive today, or if Gibson's triumvirate still works.

5. *Explore various approaches to characterizing style.*   Cicero
identified three levels of style – the plain, the middle, and the grand –
and he linked each style to one of the three "duties" of an orator.

Thus, the plain style is supposedly best for teaching; the middle style is best for delighting; and the grand style is best for moving. This simple schema can be used to get students thinking about the relationship between types of style and different purposes, but I suspect that modern students will want to poke holes in Cicero's formulation. Is it unreasonable to expect, for instance, that the teacher should move and delight in order to teach most effectively? In *The Five Clocks*, Martin Joos offers what might be seen as a modern extension and complication of Cicero's approach, identifying five different levels that also reflect degrees of formality, ranging from Intimate to Casual to Consultative to Formal to Frozen. Joos's scheme in any detail is probably too complicated for students not planning to major in Linguistics, but the categories can get students thinking about which features mark language as casual or formal. Edward Corbett's analytical method, explained in *Classical Rhetoric for the Modern Student* (296ff), is even more detailed and complex, but it was designed for classroom use and is easy enough to implement. It involves, as Corbett illustrates with an analysis of Swift's "Modest Proposal," a good bit of "tedious counting and tabulating," as students must count, for instance, the total number of words in the passage, the total number of sentences, the number of words in the longest sentence, and in the shortest sentence, the average sentence length, etc. Corbett's method repays this accountancy with a stylistic profile of the shape of sentences and paragraphs, the types of sentences, the kinds of sentence openers, and the diction. Corbett suggests using his method to have students compare their own style to that of a professional writer. A student might find for instance that his sentences range from 11 to 28 words, while the professional writer's sample contains sentences that range from 4 to 51 words. This kind of finding might be more persuasive than a teacher saying "You need to vary the length of your sentences more."

In the tradition of classical rhetoric, in addition to the levels of style, students were also given lists of figures of speech, which they were supposed to identify in exemplary works and use in their own exercises. For instance, the oldest complete Latin textbook on rhetoric, the anonymous *Rhetorica ad Herennium* (about 90 BCE), presents 64 different ways to vary one's speech in order "to confer distinction [*dignitas*]" on one's style, making it "ornate, embellishing it by variety" (IV.xiii.18). For Quintilian, a figure is "any deviation, either in thought or expression, from the ordinary and simple method of speaking" (*Inst. Oratoria* IX.i.11). The author of the *Rhetorica* offers definitions and examples of 45 figures of diction and 19 figures of thought. For instance, the figure of an "apostrophe" occurs when the speaker addresses some person or thing that is not literally the audience, as when Percy Shelley addresses the West Wind in his "Ode to the West Wind." "Hyperbole," to offer one more example, is the term for an overstatement for rhetorical effect: "He weighs a ton." "He's no bigger than a gnat." Oddly, the *Rhetorica* author lists hyperbole as a figure of speech and as a figure of thought. "Antithesis," the joining of contradictory ideas, is also listed as both, and in fact, although these categories seem to be logical and organized at first glance, rhetoricians over the centuries have struggled to determine the number and the nature of the figures, with Henry Peacham in his seventeenth-century *Garden of Eloquence* identifying some 184 figures. Obviously, I am not advocating that students be forced to memorize this or that exhaustive list of figures, but students who notice figures of speech may want to know the names of the most important figures, and are more likely in turn to notice figures when they read them in model passages – and they are perhaps more likely to use those figures effectively.

    6. *Try Sentence Combining and Erasmus's copiousness.* In 1969 John Mellon published a study showing, he thought, that teaching a new kind of grammar (transformational-generative grammar, to be precise) increased students' abilities to write complex sentences. In 1973 Frank O'Hare's research suggested that the gains came from students' practice combining very simple sentences into more complicated sentences, and not from any linguistic theory. Subsequent research, including some of the best experimental studies conducted

in composition, confirmed the efficacy of sentence combining. Classroom materials developed by William Strong, by Daiker, Kerek, and Morenberg, and by others, provided coherent and thorough programs of sentence combining. Students of almost any age, from the second grade to adulthood, could easily combine sentence kernels into various patterns. Any teacher, without mastering daunting linguistic terms or concepts, could take students through a series of exercises likely to increase their syntactic facility. In their review of the research on sentence combining, Hillocks and Mavrogenes found in 1986 that "the overwhelming majority" of the studies showed "significant advances ... on measures of syntactic maturity" (142–3).

How does sentence combining work? Students are given very simple sentences and asked to combine them, either in some prescribed way or freestyle. For instance, students might be given these bits about *Spore*, a new computer game:

> *Spore* provokes the user.
> *Spore* amuses the user.
> *Spore* is an intelligent romp.
> *Spore* deals with science, mythology, and religion.[10]

Students might be told simply to combine these bits into one long sentence, or they might be shown examples of, say, sentences that use subordinate clauses and asked to follow that pattern. Like this:

> Although *Spore* provokes and amuses the user, it is an intelligent romp that deals with science, mythology, and religion.

Or this:

> Although *Spore* deals with science, mythology, and religion, it is a provocatively and amusingly intelligent romp.

Or any number of other possible combinations. Teachers can easily invent their own exercises by dividing well-written sentences into simple sentences. By comparing the students' various reconstructions with each other and with the original version, teachers can provide rich exposure to the variety of sentence construction. Since students are given the content to use, and directed to write sentences more complex than they might choose on their own, they are able to focus on the syntax, gaining control of new structures that they would otherwise not attempt.

If sentence combining (SC) works and it is easy enough to do, then why isn't it the basis of all writing instruction? For one thing, it is not clear to everyone that more complex sentences equals better writing. Although some research has indicated that syntactic maturity correlates with writing quality, Nold and Freeman as early as 1977 found very little correlation between perceived quality and the average length of clauses. According to Hake and Williams in 1979, basic writing students' sentences actually become shorter and simpler as they become competent. Even more intriguing, Smith and Combs in a 1980 experiment told students that they were writing for an audience that would be impressed by long sentences, and the students were also given two days of SC exercises. The increases in the number of words per clause, resulting from this week of interventions, was comparable to the increases seen from a semester of SC work. If Smith and Combs suggested that a week of instruction might replace a semester of SC work, a 1980 study by Morenberg, Daiker, and Kerek, following up on their 1978 research, found that after 28 months the control group, given no SC training, also increased their syntactic fluency significantly, suggesting that SC is simply quickening a process that would otherwise occur naturally. The obvious question: Is it a good idea to speed up a natural process? Further, studies by Maimon and Nodine (1978, 1979) suggested that SC exercises produce more errors when students try to revise their work. Hake and Williams's study also found in 1979 that the number of errors increased as sentence lengths increase. Is that bad?

Sentence combining skeptics have also worried about the question of purpose. SC may help students to have more syntactic options as writers, but what do they learn about choosing one structure rather than another? This issue was addressed by SC textbooks that included the materials for students to combine whole passages and even essays. But even as SC was incorporating a more sophisticated rhetorical component, it was losing steam in the classroom. Part of the problem was of course the studies just cited and others that raised various questions about SC. Most significantly: Does SC really improve the quality of writing? Does it do something that would otherwise happen naturally or might be stimulated more efficiently? But there is another reason, I suspect, underlying the reluctance of classroom teachers to embrace SC. It's just not much fun. Although writing teachers may complain about the papers they have to read and respond to, teachers are able to assign their own topics. If the papers are boring, then the teacher can at least hope to assign a more stimulating topic next time, or work with the students' invention strategies, or at least have the satisfaction of dispensing wake-up-call grades. With SC exercises, the content is the same for every student. Every single student is combining the same bits of information, and if the students are practicing a particular pattern, then the redundancy is mind-numbing, if the students are doing it right. During the semester I tried using SC extensively, I found myself longing for students to go astray somehow, just to give me something to think about. I began to think that a set of "What I Did on My Summer Vacation" papers would be a spa-resort vacation in itself.

So I do not recommend giving your classes over to SC, but I do suggest that brief exercises, focusing on particular syntactic and rhetorical strategies, can be a useful part of the thoughtful teacher's style toolbox.

The goal of complexity is not of course more complicated sentences, but rather, greater facility by the writer. We want students to have more options and more control as they compose. Many centuries ago, in 1512, Desiderius Erasmus advocated a different approach to the same goal of fluency. Erasmus suggested that students cultivate "copiousness" (or complexity or fluency) by trying to say the same thing in many different ways. To illustrate, Erasmus offered dozens of variations on the statement, "Your letter delighted me greatly." Here's a small sample:

> Your friendly letter brought me incredible pleasure. I was delighted to an unparalleled degree by your letter. Your pages suffused me with unspeakable joy. Faustus' letter to Erasmus could not but be highly pleasant. Your writings were in no way unwelcome to me. Your lines were as sweet to me as the sweetest things of all. I read through your letter with much delight. Good heavens, how many causes for rejoicing your letter to me provided! The mail carrier delivered a lot of pleasure to me. Your writings flooded me with a copious quantity of joy. As I read what you wrote to me, an amazing happiness crept into my soul. May I die if anything more delightful than your letter has ever happened. What laughter, what applause, and what dancing your letter brought to us! Your letter to me was pure honey. Whenever a letter issues from you, I think it flows with cane-juice and honey. At the lavish banquet of your letter, I dined in princely fashion.[11]

In the right spirit of playfulness and experimentation, Erasmus's exercise can be both fun and instructive. Although Erasmus and his contemporaries clearly were delighted by language variation and exuberance (think of Shakespeare's indulgence in his comedies), the idea was not simply to pile up more words. Rather, copiousness was about providing options, building stylistic fluency that would allow writers to draw upon a large array of articulations, choosing the most desirable. If students have difficulty being creative, or if you want to nudge them beyond their comfortable structures, you can bring in models. Rather than trying to show students formulas for varying a sentence, you can let students see what Erasmus or someone else (you, previous students) has done, and suggest that the students imitate (which takes us to the next strategy).

7. *Imitation – it's not just for sincere flattery.* Imitation is a powerful way to expand students' stylistic options. One especially appealing strategy, described by Phyllis Brooks in an essay called "Mimesis: Grammar and the Echoing Voice," asks students to imitate the structure of a passage, providing their own content. Like SC, students experience directly, without terminology or linguistic concepts, syntactic structures that may not be part of their repertoires. They learn how to use these structures by, well, using them. The upside for everyone is that they also get to supply their own content. This "structural imitation" tends to be more challenging for students than SC because they are inventing content and acquiring a structure, so it is important for teachers to adjust the complexity of the imitated passage to the level of the student.[12] Start with simpler passages and move to more complex ones. I've also had good success with allowing students to select their own passages to imitate, so long as they are guided to choose passages with interesting stylistic features that they would like to try out and acquire. Here's how it works (using a sophisticated, challenging passage).

Suppose that you assign the following excerpt from Leo Rosten's *Many Worlds of Leo Rosten:*

I'm wild about walking. I don't mean health-nut hiking with set
jaw, exposed teeth, challenging chest, stern eyes fixed on an
athletic horizon. Shucks, ma'am, I never walk like a scoutmaster.
Actually, I don't walk so much as meander: I amble, I ramble,
I mosey along, often humming, sometimes whistling, with a
happy, idiot glaze on my features: and when anything strikes
my fancy – a child in a doorway, a ring in a window, a niche,
medallion, entablature on a wall – I stop and enrich my reveries.
I am no purposeful perambulator, Pedro: I dawdle, I gape, I gawk,
which is a perfect name for a firm of English tailors. What
man could resist having a suit made by Dawdle, Gape, and
Gawk? (234)

What can students learn from this passage? Rosten is daring and play-ful, apparently willing to stand on his hand and juggle dirty walking shoes to amuse his reader. A dose of his risk-taking fun should be good for students, perhaps helping them to have the courage to try syntactic structures. He uses a wide range of stylistic features – long and short sentences, high and low vocabulary, alliteration, dashes, colons, parallel structures, personification, vivid description, sim-ile and more. Taken all together, the passage is a tour de force, far beyond what any but the very most gifted writing students would be capable of. And yet, here is one of hundreds of imitations my stu-dents have written, given only a few examples of original passages and imitations, and told to follow the sentence structure and punc-tuation of the original as closely as possible:

> I'm wild about eating. I don't mean stuff-your-face gorging with
> bulging cheeks, drooling lips, sweaty brow, beady eyes fixed on
> an obese horizon. Burp! Excuse me, sir, I never eat like a pig.
> Actually, I don't eat so much as linger: I sniff, I examine, I taste,
> often sighing, sometimes exclaiming, with a silly smile on my
> mouth; and when anything tantalizes my tastebuds – a cream
> sauce on cauliflower, a chocolate mousse in a champagne glass,
> a cherry, slice of lemon, twist of lime in a drink – I stop and
> savor the flavor. I am no gastronomical gourmet, Gus: I slurp,
> I grind, I gulp, which is a perfect name for a firm of American
> lawyers. Who could resist being represented by Slurp, Grind,
> and Gulp?

Julie Barry's imitation here is a remarkable piece of writing in its own right, using effectively a dazzling array of stylistic devices. In my experience, students are themselves often amazed by the quality of what they have written, and teachers who use this strategy are often amazed by how frequently the imitated features show up in writing of their students.

There are of course other ways to carry out an imitation: Benjamin Franklin in his *Autobiography*, for instance, talks about reading and rereading a particular *Spectator* essay, and then setting it aside and attempting to re-create it. My experience, like Franklin's, is that this activity very efficiently engages the neophyte writer in stylistic and semantic choices.

8. *Practice revision strategies, creating tighter, brighter, and sharper prose.* Although grammar exercises are not effective, there is some reason to think that revision exercises will often help. Obviously, not every student will benefit equally from every kind of exercise: a student who is writing shrunken, too-simple sentences probably will not get much out of exercises designed to help students generate leaner, clearer sentences. Richard Lanham, for instance, in the very successful *Revising Prose* and its spin-off, *Revising Business Prose*, provides valuable advice on getting the flab out of your sentences. Lanham's target is what he calls "The Official Style" – the bloated, obscure, bureaucratic style that, Lanham says, pervades business, government, and academia. Consider this sentence:

> (a) The situation is one in which still more landfills will be forced to close, following the EPA requirements introduced last September.

Many students and teachers might be perfectly happy with this sentence, but Lanham's method would produce something like this revision:

> (b) EPA requirements introduced last September will force still more landfills to close.

The difference is not only 22 words versus 11, but the second version also focuses the reader's attention on "EPA requirements" versus "The situation." To say which version is better, you'd really have to see the context of this sentence: what is the paragraph about? EPA requirements or the situation? Or perhaps the focus should be on landfills, like this:

(c) More landfills will be forced to close, following the EPA requirements introduced last September.

Lanham's point is that people who adopt the Official Style often write things like "There is a kicking situation taking place between John and Bill," attempting to sound sophisticated and important, when what they really mean is something like "John is kicking Bill." The notion that the subject of the sentence should be what the sentence is really about is just one of Lanham's tips in a packed toolbox of revising strategies. Others include looking for phrases that can be replaced by a word or at least a shorter phrase, looking for prepositional phrases that can be collapsed or eliminated, and looking out for unnecessarily large words and stilted phrasings.

Recently Lanham published *The Economics of Attention: Style and Substance in the Age of Information.* After spending much of his career getting people to think more effectively about style, Lanham now believes that the digital age is going to make us even more "acutely aware of style" (258). For one thing, Lanham notes what is quickly becoming a commonplace, that we are "drowning" in information. We lack the "attention needed to make sense of it all," and therefore, in the information economy, "Attention is the commodity in short supply," not information. Tips for revising prose are, in a sense, advice on how to get and keep a reader's attention. Clear and elegant prose can certainly help, and Joseph Williams's *Style: Ten Lessons in Clarity and Grace* is, among the many guides to style, especially useful. Teachers will also find useful exercises, analysis, and tips to pass along in William Zinsser's sensible *On Writing Well* and in John Trimble's delightful *Writing with Style.*

Some of the research underlying these style guides has been concerned with the way that texts order and link together ideas – in other words, how they hold a reader's attention. Effective writers use cohesive devices like referential pronouns and demonstratives (pronouns that take the place of particular nouns, and "pointing" words like "this" or "that"), but they also create coherence by the ordering and flowing of ideas. In the late 1970s and 1980s especially, linguists and composition researchers studied how high-rated and low-rated essays differed from each other with regard to coherence. Readers, as you can imagine, tend to like writing that seems connected, that flows. In terms of style, teachers can help students to notice how effective pieces of writing repeat words and ideas, set up and follow patterns of ideas (problem – solution, given information – new information, for instance) and provide explicit cues to readers on how to relate various items.

Any reader can of course tell a writer "You lost me here" or "I had a hard time following this part" or "I don't see what this has to do with that." Any reader can say "This seems a little dull" or "I wish you'd think of another word or phrase here" or "Look at this piece of writing; can you try to sound a little more like that?" The most effective stylistic intervention is having a reader. The reader doesn't have to be brilliant. In fact, if you're writing for a general audience, there are advantages in having all sorts of readers give you feedback. An honest reader can tell a writer a great deal about the style – but at the same time, a writer also needs to realize the limitations of any one reader. Or, arguably, if you are writing for the ages, any one generation of readers! Within the field of Rhetoric and Composition, style is intimately bound up with helping students to develop their tools, preparing them for whatever writing tasks life may hold. In the next two chapters we will turn more directly to teaching, among other things: first, how it has been done over the centuries, in "Memory"; and second, what your options are today, in "Delivery."

RECOMMENDATIONS FOR
FURTHER READING: STYLE

Gibson, Walker. *Tough, Sweet and Stuffy: An Essay on Modern American Prose Styles.* Bloomington: Indiana University Press, 1966.

Lanham, Richard. *Revising Prose.* (4th edn.) New York: Longman, 1999.

Trimble, John. *Writing with Style.* (2nd edn.) Upper Saddle River, NJ: Prentice-Hall, 2000.

Weathers, Winston. *An Alternate Style: Options in Composition.* Portsmouth, NH: Boynton/Cook, 1980.

Williams, Joseph. *Style: Ten Lessons in Clarity and Grace.* (7th edn.) New York: Longman, 2002.

The problem: There is a vast history of this field, covering thousands of years and who-knows-how-many people. Shouldn't you know something about it? How can you even begin to get a sense of this past? What is worth remembering? Is there an art of remembering in all this memory?

5 Memory

Before the widespread use of neural implants in the 2040s, the term "memory" referred to ideas and concepts that were stored in living brain cells. Obviously, such organic processes of retrieving information and analyzing data were haphazard endeavors at best, subject to random interference and data decay. Learning how to write effectively consequently took many years and much effort.

Cambridge Introduction to Composition and Rhetoric, 24th edition

The study of memory encompasses not just ideas of memory at a particular historical moment, but entire regimes of memory, ways of privileging certain types of knowledge, certain values, certain ideas, beliefs, symbols – in short, an entire cultural ethnography coalesces around the apparently innocuous ability to remember the past.

William West

Have you heard the startling survey results that most people fear public speaking more than death? The comedian Jerry Seinfeld, who has made a career of pointing out how dumb we are, notes the absurdity – that most people at a funeral would rather be in the casket than deliver the eulogy. The origin of this popular knowledge appears to be the blockbuster *Book of Lists*, which in 1972 referred vaguely to "American marketers," who had uncovered this insight. I don't believe for a moment that most people, asked to choose between sudden death or making a public speech, really would opt for the Grim Reaper, but the fact that so many people have accepted and repeated this ranking (many of them, to be sure, speech coaches and executive consultants) does suggest that many people do find public speaking to be frightening.[1] And if ancient peoples were anything like us in this regard, the art of rhetoric would have been very popular just for the training it offered in memory alone. For a speaker without a teleprompter, without a manuscript to read from, any effective strategy for recalling what one wanted to say – or anything intelligent to say! – would have been precious indeed. In a courtroom setting, with all sorts of distractions, questions, and interruptions, keeping track of what to say would be even more difficult and crucial.

This chapter begins by looking briefly at "Memory" in this sense, as the ancient art that was the fourth canon of Rhetoric, designed to help speakers remember what to say, or remember materials so they could fashion something persuasive to say. This chapter also considers "memory" in the more expansive sense of history. Every academic field is in some sense the culmination of its history, so by learning something about Mendeleyev or Darwin, we might arguably better understand the periodic table and evolution. But most students in Chemistry and Biology, to be sure, don't usually spend much time on how we came to know something, or what we used to think. We know more today than Mendeleyev or Darwin, our logic goes, and so the sciences tend to focus on the current state of knowledge, using history only as a prop to assist our understanding. In the humanities, however, history is an especially powerful way of knowing. Aristotle's *Rhetoric* may contain some examples that are outdated, some terms and concepts that are foreign, but the approach that Aristotle offers has not been disproved or superseded, and the terms and concepts may usefully expand our insights. If a biologist today were to say "My approach is Aristotelian," his colleagues would probably wonder what in the world he meant, but an Aristotelian approach to rhetoric would not be incomprehensible at all. Memory in the sense of history is thus a kind of map, a way to know where you have been, where you are, and even where you are going.

ART

The art of memory that was intended to help speakers remember what they wanted to say has generally withered away as mnemonic technologies have expanded: writing, printing, and computing, have all arguably diminished the necessity of certain kinds of remembering. It appears that the greatest impact has come from writing and printing, as word processing in itself seems to have a "minimal impact on written products," according to Charles MacArthur's recent review of the research (260). Computers do encourage students to edit more, and powerful ways of accessing and organizing data, transforming the writing process, may well be on the way. At any rate, we do depend upon technology to enhance or even provide our memory. Even scholars in the field(s) of Rhetoric and Speech Communication usually share their research at conferences by reading aloud: most if not all do not give speeches without notes. Without our manuscripts or powerpoints, would we recall what to say? At such scholarly conferences, the question-and-answer period is usually where the action is. Thus, we still do especially value the ability to recall information, to make analyses and assessments on the fly, to speak without notes. Students comment favorably on teachers who don't use lecture notes, or who refer to them infrequently. Indeed, politicians, ministers, lawyers, football coaches – anyone who can speak directly to the audience, seemingly "off the cuff," usually is considered somehow to be more in control of their material, more accomplished and committed. Without an organizing intelligence, making sense of memory, there is no meaning – only data – and we value this ability to manage the material in our minds.

Memory in the largest sense of the fourth canon of rhetoric refers to the capacity not only to remember a speech verbatim, or to remember the ideas one wants to present, but also the capacity to retrieve ideas and facts and use them. In other words, "Memory" is intimately bound up with every other aspect of rhetoric. There is no invention, arrangement, style, or delivery without memory. Everything starts, really, in a sense, with memory. Quintilian recognized this, saying, "Our whole discipline relies on memory" (11.2.1), and he begins his discussion of memory by calling it "the treasure-house of ideas supplied by Invention." So the task for rhetoric is to determine whether there is an art to storing material and to searching in our own minds for what we know, and for making use of what we recall. Or is memory simply a natural ability?

The ancients' accumulated wisdom about memory is captured most fully in the anonymous *Rhetorica ad Herennium*, in Cicero's *De oratore*, and in Quintilian's *Institutio Oratoria*. Earlier Greek works dealing with memory have been lost. These and other authorities agreed that the art of memory could only assist a person's natural memory, not replace it. The oldest mnemonic strategy seems in fact to pile more stress onto one's natural memory, but many people will join me in affirming that this method does work.

First, the speaker needs to identify a setting or a sequence, which could be a mansion, or a landscape, or any series of items. Some friends of mine use what they call their "alphabet circus," which consists of an anteater, a bear, a crocodile, a deer, a fox, and so forth – a line of animals marching in alphabetical order. Second, the speaker needs to associate an image of some kind with each idea that he or she desires to remember, and then each image needs to be "placed" within the setting or sequence. So, if I wanted to remember to begin a speech by referring to Jerry Seinfeld's comment about death and the fear of public speaking, I might imagine Seinfeld lying in a casket. Then I would imaginatively "place" that casket with Seinfeld in the entry foyer of my memory mansion, or riding atop my anteater, or in any other initial position. The more outrageous the image, the better, as the author of the *Rhetorica ad Herennium* says, since "ordinary things easily slip from the memory while the striking and the novel stay longer in the mind":

> We ought, then, to set up images that are not many or vague but active; if we assign to them exceptional beauty or singular ugliness; if we ornament some of them, as with crowns or purple cloaks, so that the similitude may be more distinct to us; or if we somehow disfigure them, as by introducing one stained with blood or soiled with mud or smeared with red paint so that its form is more striking, or by assigning certain comic effects to our images, for that, too, will ensure our remembrance of them more readily. The things we easily remember when they are real we likewise remember without difficulty when they are figments. (9–10)

Figure 5.1 This example of a mnemonic alphabet is from Johannes Romberch, *Congestorium Artificiose Memorie*, published in Venice, 1533.

Even though it means remembering two or three things rather than one, this cumbersome system actually works. Perhaps just focusing on the ideas long enough to associate them helps to make them memorable, or perhaps associated ideas are somehow more easily retrieved than isolated ones, or something else. Let's turn now to the other sense of "history," the record of ideas and events.

HISTORY

The most familiar historical map of rhetoric is divided into six conventional chronological periods: Classical, Medieval, Renaissance, Enlightenment, Nineteenth-Century, and Modern/Postmodern. There is some disagreement about when these periods begin and end, but most people would agree that the following timeline is not bizarre, and that the main figures for each period at least include the ones listed below. Recklessly, I will offer here a key idea associated with each figure.

Classical: fifth-century BCE to 410 CE (from the beginnings of formal instruction to the fall of Rome).

Gorgias   (*c*.480 to *c*.380 BCE), most famous of the Sophists: Language creates what we can know – which means our knowledge is contingent, provisional, rhetorical.

Aspasia   (*fl*. fifth-century BCE), known only by surviving fragments of dialogue, various sources indicate that she taught the Socratic method to Socrates and was a brilliant rhetorical teacher.

Isocrates   (436–338 BCE), an educator who saw rhetoric as powerfully useful for pursuing probable knowledge and for moving the public to act for the common good.

Plato   (428–357 BCE), founded the Academy, where he taught that transcendent truth is knowable, and should be a prerequisite for persuading others; his *Gorgias* condemns false rhetoric, and his *Phaedrus* offers a vision of a true rhetoric.

Aristotle   (384–322 BCE), first teacher of rhetoric in Plato's Academy, theorized three major rhetorical appeals – *logos* (logic), *ethos* (self-presentation), *pathos* (audience's feelings) – and influenced virtually every intellectual endeavor.

Cicero   (106–43 BCE), a lawyer, moved from a practical, how-to view of rhetoric (*De inventione*) to a more philosophical consideration of eloquence (*De oratore*).

Quintilian   (35–96 CE), lawyer and teacher, whose *Institutes* summarizes classical rhetoric; he is noted for his insistence that the good speaker must also be a good man.

Medieval: 410 to *c*.1300 (from the fall of Rome to the renaissance of learning in Europe).

Augustine   (354–430), lawyer and teacher of rhetoric who converted to Christianity and argued for the value of

	classical learning, including rhetoric, for Christianity; *On Christian Doctrine* offers advice on interpreting scripture and persuading various audiences.
Boethius	(480–524) attempted to preserve Greco-Roman learning; his work on topical invention, well-known throughout the Middle Ages, drew especially on the *Rhetorica ad Herennium*.
Geoffrey of Vinsauf	(*fl. c.*1200), author of an "art of poetry" mentioned by Chaucer, an example of the many "arts" of the period providing basic guidance for preachers, poets, letter-writers.
Christine de Pizan	(*c.*1364–*c.*1430), widowed at an early age, turned to writing to help support her family, producing brief biographies and other works that advocated for the eloquence and education of women.

Renaissance:	fourteenth century to 1660s (from the birth of Petrach, who epitomizes the pursuit of classical wisdom and eloquence, to the founding of the Royal Society in London).
Desiderius Erasmus	(1469–1536), a great humanist scholar whose Greek New Testament set a new standard for accuracy, and whose *On Copia* displayed his vast learning and his eloquent Latin style.
Peter Ramus	(1515–72), believing that reasoning is innate and need not be taught, attacked humanist and classical thinkers alike, advocating a simple method of division that he believed to be universally applicable.
Thomas Wilson	(*c.*1523–81) wrote the first logic text in English, *The Rule of Reason* (1551), and

	the first rhetoric text in English, *The Arte of Rhetorique* (1553), drawing primarily on Cicero, Quintilian, and Erasmus.
Francis Bacon	(1561–1626) influenced virtually every branch of learning by endorsing observation and experiment, and questioning misleading and ambiguous language.
Margaret Fell	(1614–1702) contributed to the opening up of education for women, publishing her forceful *Women's Speaking Justified, Proved, and Allowed by Scriptures* in 1666.

Enlightenment: 1660 to 1800 (from the Restoration of the Stuarts in England, and the founding of the Royal Society, to the end of the eighteenth century and the turn to Romanticism).	
John Locke	(1632–1704), philosopher, whose insight that words stand for the ideas in our heads, not for the things in the world, had a profound impact on rhetoric and epistemology, leading to an emphasis on clarity and perspicuity.
Mary Astell	(1666–1731), often called the first English feminist, proposed a college for women and a broad educational program that included attention to persuasion and logic.
Giambattista Vico	(1668–1744) attempted to unite humanism and science, arguing for the importance of language and culture in the making of knowledge.
Thomas Sheridan	(1719–88), who began as a stage actor, turned to elocution, focusing on correct language, good taste, and effective nonverbal communication.

George Campbell	(1719–96), in his *Philosophy of Rhetoric* (1776), argued that persuasion addresses four mental faculties: the understanding, imagination, passion, and will. The topics, syllogistic logic, and much of classical rhetoric, Campbell believed, do not address these faculties.
Hugh Blair	(1718–1800), whose *Lectures on Rhetoric and Belles Lettres* (1783) became one of the most popular textbooks in history, focused on the cultivation of taste, especially by means of studying literature – thus devaluing classical rhetoric and its strategies of invention, arrangement, and style.

Nineteenth Century:	1800–1900.
Richard Whately	(1787–1863), in his *Elements of Rhetoric* (1828) and *Elements of Logic* (1826), endorses Aristotle's rhetoric and logic, but also makes use of Campbell's psychological orientation.
Sarah Grimké	(1792–1873), an American activist against slavery, was important for the history of rhetoric as a woman practitioner, and as an advocate for the education of women.
Frederick Douglass	(1818–95), a renowned orator in the abolitionist movement, also wrote a classic autobiography, drawing on rhetorical examples and principles in *The Columbian Orator* (1797).
Alexander Bain	(1818–1903), who helped to found modern psychology, followed Campbell in applying faculty psychology to rhetoric; his *English Composition and Rhetoric* (1866)

> established four modes of writing (description, narration, exposition, and persuasion) and popularized the importance of unified paragraphs with topic sentences.

Modern/Postmodern: 1900 to the present.

Mikhail Bakhtin	(1895–1975) insisted that language and meaning must be seen as a dialogue, within a social context, as multiple meanings are explored.
I. A. Richards	(1893–1979), an important literary critic, who also contributed to rhetoric with *The Philosophy of Rhetoric* (1936) and subsequent works; the latter part of his life was devoted to developing "Basic English," a minimal vocabulary that can speed learning of English as a second language.
Kenneth Burke	(1897–1993) applied rhetorical analysis to every kind of discourse, including literary criticism, generating conceptual frameworks for making sense of human motives and actions.
Chaim Perelman	(1912–84), working with Lucie Olbrechts-Tyteca, developed in *The New Rhetoric* (1958) a theory of value judgments in arguments, illuminating the logical, structural, and stylistic features in persuasive (especially legal) discourse.
Stephen Toulmin	(1922–2009) focused on practical reasoning (as opposed to formal logic), providing a theory in *The Uses of Argument* (1958) for understanding how arguments in all fields are put together.

Jacques Derrida	(1930–2004), one of the most influential and controversial twentieth-century philosophers, poses a challenge to the study of rhetoric as purposeful discourse, arguing that language cannot be transcended and refers only to itself (and not to some negotiated, constructed meaning).
Wayne Booth	(1921–2005), in *The Rhetoric of Fiction* (1961), shows how authors imagine audiences, and readers assume those roles; in his later work, Booth considers how people reason and persuade, supplementing the work of Perelman and Toulmin.
Henry Louis Gates	(b. 1950), in *The Signifying Monkey: A Theory of Afro-American Literary Criticism* (1988) draws attention to the rhetoric of Black English, using sociolinguistics to identify distinctive speech genres and strategies.

What resources are available to help us understand rhetorical history? The field's standard historical anthology, Patricia Bizzell and Bruce Herzberg's *The Rhetorical Tradition: Readings from Classical Times to the Present* (2nd edn. 2001), in addition to a canon-confirming and canon-forming selection of readings, offers a nice historical survey in the "General Introduction" and detailed introductions to each period. Susan Miller's monumental *Norton Book of Composition Studies* offers a rich current introduction, gathering 101 essays and excerpts that include both essential landmarks and unexpected gems. Thomas Conley's *Rhetoric in the European Tradition* (1990) provides a single-volume historical overview that is especially useful for the bibliographical notes suggesting further reading, the outlines and tables of contents for key works, and the brief summaries of key works. Two themes guide Conley's survey: First, that rhetoric has been "particularly important to people during times of strife and crisis, political and intellectual" (ix), and therefore Conley focuses on texts "in that context." Second, there is not, in Conley's view, "a single, unitary art or discipline called 'Rhetoric,'" but rather a variety of responses to political and intellectual crises, with one response dominant in one period, and another dominant later. In other words, although Conley divides Rhetoric's story into chronological periods, he traces "various perennial responses" as they shift in importance through time. In *The Bedford Bibliography for Teachers of Writing*, Bizzell and Herzberg, joined by Nedra Reynolds (6th edn 2004), present "A Brief History of Rhetoric and Composition" (1–18), and they annotate 70 key books and articles on rhetorical history, as well as 81 items on "Rhetoric and Composition Theory" (in all their categories, 704 items are included).

Although an updated edition is overdue, Winifred Bryan Horner's 1990 volume, *The Present State of Scholarship in Historical and Contemporary Rhetoric*, provides a still-useful guide to the scholarship on each period, with bibliographical essays for each of the traditional periods written by major authorities: "The Classical Period" is by Richard Leo Enos and Ann Blakeslee, "The Middle Ages" by James Murphy and Martin Camargo, "The Renaissance" by Don Paul Abbott, "The Eighteenth Century" by Horner and Kerri Morris Barton, "The Nineteenth Century" by Donald Stewart, and "Contemporary Rhetoric" by James Kinneavy. James Murphy's indispensable *Short History of Writing Instruction* (2nd edn 2001) also features chapters written by major scholars on writing instruction in each of the following periods (note the recurrence of names from Horner's collection): Ancient Greece (Richard Leo Enos), Ancient Rome (Murphy), from Late Antiquity to the twelfth century (Carol Dana Lanham), the later Middle Ages (Marjorie Curry Woods), the Renaissance (Abbott), the eighteenth and nineteenth centuries (Linda Ferreira-Buckley and Winifred Bryan Horner), up to 1900 in America (Elizabethada Wright and S. Michael Halloran), and the twentieth century (Catherine Hobbs and James Berlin). A much more condensed but nonetheless rich survey is offered in "Teaching of Writing and Writing Teachers Through the Ages," a chapter by Duane Roen, Maureen Daly Goggin, and Jennifer Clary-Lemon in the *Handbook of Research on Writing*. Edward Corbett, with Robert Connors in later editions (1965, 4th edn 1999), also includes a brief "Survey of Rhetoric" in the landmark *Classical Rhetoric for the Modern Student*, and Erika Lindemann's fine *Rhetoric for Writing Teachers* includes a brief historical survey in a chapter entitled "What Do Teachers Need to Know about Rhetoric?"

The Encyclopedia of Rhetoric and Composition: Communication from Ancient Times to the Information Age, edited by Theresa Enos and published in 1996, is a magnificent resource, with extensive historical entries on periods, people, concepts, and works. *The Encyclopedia of Rhetoric*, edited by Thomas Sloane and published in 2001, is also an excellent and significantly different work. The entries for important topics in Sloane's volume are generously expansive: "classical rhetoric" gets almost twenty-two pages, for instance, written by George Kennedy, unquestionably one of the most important scholars of classical rhetoric. Even the *ad hominem* argument gets over three substantial pages; a fascinating entry on "Chinese Rhetoric" gets almost seven columns. This depth comes at a price, as there are no entries on people – "not even Aristotle, not even Nietzsche," as Sloane says in his preface (xi). This peculiarity is driven, Sloane says, by the "effort to abstract rhetoric" as much as possible, "not only from this or that discipline but also from this or that theorist, time, place, culture, and to endeavor to search for its principles." But Sloane also acknowledges that this policy sets his work apart from Enos's *Encyclopedia* as well as Heinrich Lausberg's *Handbuch der literarischen Rhetorik*. The whole enterprise of doing rhetorical history – what we might learn from it, how we use and abuse history – is addressed in three edited collections of essays: Takis Poulakos's *Rethinking the Rhetorical Tradition: Historiographies of Rhetoric and Histories of the Classical Rhetorical Tradition* [Denver, CO: Westview, 1993], Victor Vitanza's *Writing*

Histories of Rhetoric [Carbondale: SIUP, 1994], and Theresa Enos's *Learning from the History of Rhetoric: Essays in Honor of Winifred Bryan Horner* [SIUP, 1993]. Finally, Andrea Lunsford, Kirt Wilson, and Rosa Eberly have collected an outstanding group of 33 essays in *The Sage Handbook of Rhetorical Studies*, organized under four headings: "Historical Studies in Rhetoric," "Rhetoric across the Disciplines," "Rhetoric and Pedagogy," and "Rhetoric and Public Discourse." Likewise, Walter Jost and Wendy Olmsted's *Companion to Rhetoric and Rhetorical Criticism* brings together an equally impressive group of 31 essays, organized into historical, conceptual, critical, and miscellaneous sections. Olmsted's *Rhetoric* is a good one-volume history, a solid counterpart to Conley.

With all these general introductions and resources, and many more, it may seem unnecessary to attempt here any sort of chrono-logical overview or period-by-period discussion myself. But rather than send you immediately to some other text or cluster of texts, what I want to offer, for each period and its major figures, is a thumb-nail sketch as well as a very brief guide to some of the most important scholarly resources. Such a fly-over, admittedly objectionable for its omissions and distortions, may serve three purposes, I hope: First, this survey may serve to provide a clearer context for all the history in the preceding chapters; second, I want to provide some sense of the specialized historical resources available for each period; and third, for the reader who has an immediate need-to-know, even a very brief history can suggest some implications for current practice.

Classical Rhetoric. As George Kennedy says at the outset of his essential *Classical Rhetoric and Its Christian and Secular Tradition from Ancient to Modern Times*, "Classical rhetoric is superficially very easy to describe. It is that theory of discourse developed by Greeks and Romans of the classical period, applied both in oratory and in literary genres, and taught in schools in antiquity, in the Greek and western Middle Ages, and throughout the Renaissance and early modern period" (3). However, any attempt to describe the detailed characteristics of classical rhetoric, captured in thousands and thousands of printed pages, quickly runs into trouble, as Kennedy immediately points out. For starters: Aristotle is the most famous figure in classical rhetoric from a modern point of view, but his rhetoric was pretty much ignored for two thousand years. The Ciceronian rhetoric that dominated education contained little that originated with Cicero, and was unknown in the Greek-speaking East.

There is however one cultural shift that does underlie the various permutations of rhetoric in the classical period, and that shift involves the pervasive introduction of writing into an oral culture. Apparently, most ancient Greeks did not read silently, and a written text thus had an essentially oral quality. Writing instruction was in the service of orality as the early Greek rhetoricians wrote speeches to be delivered orally. Still, the effect of introducing writing into an oral culture, as Eric Havelock in particular has argued, is more profound than simply preserving speech, assisting oratory. Writing facilitates abstract thought, according to Havelock (in a contested but generally accepted assertion). Of the thousands of language systems that are known to have existed, only a hundred or so have developed writing – and, as Walter Ong has noted, those writing systems have profoundly affected the legal, educational, political, and social development of those literate societies.

Plato famously distrusted writing, warning against its harmful effects upon the memory, human interaction, and the intellect. And he likewise assailed rhetoric, likening it in *Gorgias* to deceit and flattery, and to disguising bad food with heavy spices. But the case against writing and rhetoric is made by Plato *in writing* with masterful rhetorical skill; it is "spoken" by "Socrates" only on the page, creating the illusion only of a conversation. The Sophists, the targets of Plato's attack, taught writing as a powerful tool for oratory. Writing allowed the Sophists to teach primarily by example rather than precept, as students could practice various stylistic flourishes and dramatic tactics. The Sophists apparently did not see writing as a way of getting at the truth – their philosophical relativism or skepticism in fact questioned the possibility of truth. But writing was useful in learning how to produce the ornate eloquence, the poetic prose, that made them such famous and popular teachers, sort of like nomadic rock stars, performing verbal music on tour.

Aristotle is apparently not very interested in writing. His *Rhetoric* explicitly aims to move beyond the surface of language and reveal the rational processes involved in creating a persuasive argument in a particular situation, although he also acknowledges the emotional and aesthetic resources that the realistic rhetorician will need to employ. Aristotle says that writing is most appropriate for composing ceremonial speeches to be read aloud, and that writing is helpful in refining one's style (1414a, 1413b). The real flowering of "rhetoric and composition" in our sense occurs not in Aristotle but in Isocrates' educational program.

Isocrates is often called the father of liberal arts education because he believed that all knowledge was essential to preparing an effective public speaker. In his early work *Against the Sophists* as well as his later *Antidosis*, written when he was 82, Isocrates advocates, as Richard Enos puts it, "a broadly based education that included such subjects as history, political science, poetry, ethics, geography, literary studies, mathematics, and oral and written rhetoric" ("Ancient Greek" 32). Not only did Isocrates see writing as a way of understanding, but much else about his pedagogy would sound familiar and desirable to a modern writing teacher. Isocrates, for instance, used peer responses, asking students to evaluate each other. He stressed small classes, probably no more than eight at a time, allowing for lots of practice and feedback. His students studied exemplary texts and imitated them; they wrote speeches out and then practiced giving them.

The Romans took the Greek educational program, organized it, and used it as a tool to tie their empire together. There were some hiccups, as the Roman senate expelled all the rhetoricians and philosophers from Rome in 161 BCE, and prohibited the teaching of rhetoric in Latin (Greek was okay) in 92 BCE, but such fears of rhetorical skill were overwhelmed by an awareness of its value. In his day, Cicero was a dazzling lawyer and a powerful statesman, but for many later generations he was most importantly the author of a profoundly influential and practical work on invention, *De inventione*, written about 86 BCE, and he was thought to be the author of the *Rhetorica ad Herennium*, the first full treatment of all five activities (or canons, or faculties). Interestingly, Cicero would later disparage his youthful work, but its very simplicity and clarity was extremely appealing to teachers.

The fullest educational expression of the Roman system, the *Institutes of Oratory*, was written in 95 CE by Quintilian, who lays out a cradle-to-grave curriculum for eloquence, grounded in virtue. The important role of writing is stressed, as Quintilian asserts for instance, that "our speech will never become forcible and energetic unless it acquires strength from great practice in writing; and the labor of writing, if left destitute of models from reading, passes away without effect, as having no director" (*Institutio* X.i.i). Like Isocrates, Quintilian saw that a broad foundation of learning was essential to rhetorical training – "nothing is unnecessary to the art of oratory," he says (Preface 5). In addition to grammar, invention, arrangement, elocution, memory, and pronunciation, Quintilian also discusses what the morals of the orator ought to be, and even what he should do with himself after retirement.

Quintilian's precepts, his imitation exercises, and his writing assignments are all still very effective. There is something satisfying about giving students an assignment that has been classroom-tested for over two thousand years. The basic writing assignments were widely known as the *progymnasmata* (although Quintilian, interestingly, does not use that term): A *gymnasma* in Greek was a declamation or fictitious speech, and so these exercises are the pre-declamations (*progymnasmata*), preparing students for the most advanced rhetorical study. Apparently the exercises were already so familiar to Quintilian's audience that he explains them very briefly. Hermogenes of Tarsus and Apthonius offer more detailed descriptions that were quite popular in succeeding centuries. Here's the sequence (Quintilian adds "Cause and Effect" to this list):[2]

(1) Fable: The student starts by retelling fables from Aesop, either condensing or expanding (with dialogue or more events).

(2) Tale: Next the student tells a story in his own words, either a true history or a literary story.

(3) Chreia: The student elaborates on a maxim or pithy anecdote, such as Diogenes beating the tutor of a student who was misbehaving, saying, "Why are you teaching him such things?"

(4) Proverb: Very similar to Chreia.

(5) Refutation and Confirmation: The student undertakes to prove or disprove a narrative, analyzing what might be incredible, or impossible, or inconsistent, etc.

(6) Commonplace: The student practices adding emotional appeal and vivacity to an established fact (this is an uncommon use of "commonplace").

(7) Encomium: A speech praising or criticizing a thing or a person.

(8) Comparison: Two encomia, allowing the student to draw comparisons.

(9) Impersonation: The student pretends to be someone else in a particular situation, often famous, and says what he imagines that person might have said. What might Niobe say over the dead bodies of her children, for instance?

(10) Description: The student should endeavor to bring the object vividly before the eyes of the audience.

(11) Thesis: An answer to a general question, such as "Should a man marry?"

(12) Laws: The student argues for or against a particular law.

Since this educational system aimed to produce good citizens ("a good man speaking well," Quintilian says in his final book), and women had little legal status, we have little evidence of the involvement of women in Greek or Roman rhetorical education. Plato, we know, did admit some women to his Academy, but that apparently was remarkable. There was a school for wealthy Greek girls run by the poet Sappho, and there are educated women appearing here and there in classical history – Aspasia, for instance, the mistress of Pericles, is said to have been a superb teacher of rhetoric. H. I. Marrou notes that schools for indigent children, boys and girls, were begun by the emperor Trajan, and Robert Cape has recently suggested that women were in fact widely educated in Rome, and their abilities in private conversations were especially valued.

Several collections have enlarged our sense of women's contributions and also questioned the traditional boundaries of "rhetoric": *Listening to Their Voices: The Rhetorical Activities of Historical Women* (1997), edited by Molly Meijer Wertheimer; *Reclaiming Rhetorica: Women in the Rhetorical Tradition* (1995), edited by Andrea Lunsford; and *The Changing Tradition: Women in the History of Rhetoric* (1999), edited by Christine Mason Sutherland and Rebecca Sutcliffe. Cheryl Glenn offers a useful consideration of what we know about the education of women and their contribution to philosophy and rhetoric in *Rhetoric Retold: Regendering the Tradition from Antiquity Through the Renaissance* (1997). The story of Verginia, for instance, which is recounted by Cicero, Livy, and Dionysius of Halicarnassus, confirms that ordinary women received some education, for Verginia was the daughter of a plebeian centurion, a working-class position, and she encountered Appius Claudius, who was chief of the ruling oligarchy, the decemvirs, as she was on her way to see her schoolmaster, according to the story. But the episode also confirms how constrained and oppressed women were, because Appius was unable to control his passion for the beautiful Verginia, and so he had her declared to be the daughter of his slave, and therefore also his slave. Appius had himself approved the law prohibiting the marriage of plebeians and patricians, so rather than violate his own law, he violated Verginia's liberty. Even more pitiful and illustrative of the status of women is the ending of the story, in which Verginia's father kills her rather than have her become Appius's slave.

The best place to begin studying classical rhetoric, in addition to the materials gathered in Bizzell and Herzberg's anthology (*The Rhetorical Tradition*), arguably would be the essays collected in James Murphy's *Synoptic History of Classical Rhetoric* (3rd edn, 2003; co-edited by Richard Katula with Forbes Hill and Donovan Ochs). George Kennedy's masterful *New History of Classical Rhetoric* (1994) is also essential reading: it revises, abridges, and supplements three previous landmark books by Kennedy (all still worth reading on their own) – *The Art of Persuasion in Greece* (1963), *The Art of Rhetoric in the Roman World*, and *Greek Rhetoric under Christian Emperors*. For convenient access to translations of primary materials related to classical rhetoric, see Thomas Benson and Michael Prosser's *Readings in Classical Rhetoric* (1969) and Patricia Matsen, Philip Rollinson, and Marion Sousa's *Readings from Classical Rhetoric* (1990). Rollinson and Richard Geckle's *Guide to Classical Rhetoric* (1998) provides handy brief essays on the major and many minor figures. Donald Clark's *Rhetoric in Greco-Roman Education* (1957) is a book "about teaching," "written primarily for teachers," containing a lucid and entertaining discussion of how ancient students learned to speak and write. The chapters on "Imitation," "The Elementary Exercises," and "Declamation" are especially valuable. Rhys Roberts's *Greek Rhetoric and Literary Criticism* (1928) is also still useful, as is Charles Baldwin's *Ancient Rhetoric and Poetic* (1924). On the importance of the Sophists, see Susan Jarratt's *Rereading the Sophists: Classical Rhetoric Reconfigured* (1991), and John Poulakos's *Sophistical Rhetoric in Classical Greece* (1995).

Essential specialized studies of the early history of rhetoric include Robert Wardy's *The Birth of Rhetoric: Gorgias, Plato, and Their Successors* (1996), Richard Leo Enos's *Greek Rhetoric before Aristotle* (1993), Scott Consigny's *Gorgias: Sophist and Artist* (2001), Janet Atwill's *Rhetoric Reclaimed: Aristotle and the Liberal Arts Tradition* (1998), Jasper Neel's *Plato, Derrida, and Writing* (1998), and the collection of essays edited by Edward Schiappa, *Landmark Essays on Classical Greek Rhetoric* (1994). For Aristotle, George

Kennedy's new translation and edition, *Aristotle On Rhetoric: A Theory of Civic Discourse* (1991) is now the standard, but the Loeb editions (with facing pages of original text and English translation) of Aristotle, Cicero, Quintilian and all other Latin and Greek works are invaluable. The *Cambridge Companion to Aristotle* (1995), edited by Jonathan Barnes, is also excellent. Cecil Wooten's translation and edition of *Hermogenes' On Types of Style* (1987) provides a fascinating view of an alternative to Cicero's high, middle, and low approach to style. For the classroom teacher, four collections of essays are especially appealing: James Murphy's *The Rhetorical Tradition and Modern Writing* (1982); Theresa Enos's *Learning from the Histories of Rhetoric: Essays in Honor of Winifred Bryan Horner* (1993); Robert Connors, Lisa Ede, and Andrea Lunsford's *Essays on Classical Rhetoric and Modern Discourse* (1984); and Winifred Bryan Horner, Michael Leff and James Murphy's *Rhetoric and Pedagogy: Its History, Philosophy, and Practice* (1995).

Medieval Rhetoric. In the standard history of this period, *Rhetoric in the Middle Ages* (1974), James Murphy describes four ancient traditions of rhetoric that feed into the Middle Ages: (1) Greek Rhetoric, dominated by Aristotle, adopting a philosophical approach, as dialectic and rhetoric shared invention strategies; (2) Roman Rhetoric, dominated by Cicero, emphasizing techniques more than principles, given its richest humanities grounding in Quintilian; (3) Grammatical and Literary Rhetoric, dominated by Horace and Donatus (the grammarian), emphasizing correctness and the use of figures of speech; and (4) the Second Sophistic, dominated by various oratorical teachers and performers, emphasizing the dramatic display of ceremonial language. All pagan learning, as Murphy notes, even grammar, was under attack by some Christian thinkers, such as Arnobius (*fl.* 303), for instance, who asserted that the truth was not affected by grammatical errors, or Hilary of Poiters (d. 367), who similarly says that the truth is not affected by purported flaws of logic. Tertullian, a professional rhetorician before he became one of the Church Fathers, repudiated his classical training, famously asking, "What has Athens to do with Jerusalem? What concord is there between the Academy and the Church?" Jerome (d. 420), another Church Father, also trained in rhetoric, reports a dream in which at the final judgment he's told "thou art not a Christian, but a Ciceronian. Where thy treasure is, there is thy heart also." In fact, in 392 CE Theodosius abolished paganism by decree, and the Fourth Council of Carthage forbade bishops to read pagan literature unless it was necessary. For Lactantius, pagan works were "sweets which contain poison."

Yet the Church clearly needed verbal warriors to help stamp out proliferating heresies – Manichean, Pelagian, Donatist, and others. Augustine (354–430 CE) played an important role in authorizing the preservation of classical learning. In his autobiography, the *Confessions* (c.398), Augustine confesses that he was "a teacher of the art of rhetoric" [*artem rhetoricam*], and that "Love of money had gained the better of me and for it I sold to others the means of coming off the better in debate" (251). But Augustine recognized that it would be foolish not to take advantage of the intellectual riches of the Greeks and Romans: if evil people know how to use Ciceronian rhetorical strategies to render an audience well-disposed, attentive, and docile, then good people should learn how to do this also. Thus, in *On Christian Doctrine* (*De Doctrina Christiana*; c.397, 427), Augustine argues that classical learning ought to be a powerful resource for Christianity, and his approach to preaching and biblical interpretation is heavily indebted to his rhetorical training.

But Augustine did not attempt to preserve the entirety of rhetoric or pagan learning. Indeed, according to Thomas Sloane, he "Christianized pagan rhetoric by shattering its theoretical integrity" (*Donne* 104), dispensing for example with invention in Cicero's sense of identifying arguments and appeals, embracing instead an invention that is based on God's pre-existent truth. For Quintilian, the end of rhetoric is rhetoric (*non persuadendi sed bene dicendi*, "not persuasion but speaking well"), but for Augustine the goal of rhetoric is to compel people to accept the truth. Toward this end, Augustine believes that imitation is more powerful than the rules; one should learn the rules quickly when young, but don't try to rely too much on your own abilities. In fact, Augustine says, it's okay to plagiarize if necessary – the important thing is to convey the Christian truth (416). Augustine probably did not foresee how deep a wilderness civilization was entering into, but as he was dying in Hippo, in North Africa, barbarian Vandals were attacking his Episcopal seat. Augustine thus advocated summaries and condensations of classical learning, selecting what was most useful, making it more accessible, preserving what one reasonably could in the wilderness of what would come to be known as the Dark Ages. Martianus Capella for instance, in *De nuptiis Philologiae et Mercurii* (*The Marriage of Philology and Mercury*, between 410 and 439), imagines that the arts of grammar, dialectic, rhetoric, geometry, arithmetic, astronomy, and music are female figures who attend this allegorical marriage. This frame gives Martianus an excuse to describe each art in some detail. Lady Rhetoric, for example, is presented as a stunning and colorful woman, but the theory that Martianus attaches to her is dull and unoriginal.

Still, Martianus's popularity derived from his convenience, gathering together a compendium of knowledge. Isidore of Seville, for instance, another encyclopedist, outlines the trivium (grammar, dialectic, rhetoric) and the quadrivium (geometry, arithmetic, astronomy, and music) in the first three books of his *Etymologiae* (c.616). He offers a brief discussion of rhetoric that is based on the *Introduction to Divine and Human Readings* (c.551) by Cassiodorus, another encyclopedist. The treatment of rhetoric in these compendiums offers basic information on the kinds of speeches, the parts of a speech, the offices of rhetoric, stasis theory, the syllogism, and the figures of thought and speech. The approach, in other words, is classificatory and fundamental, echoing Boethius's *Overview of the Structure of Rhetoric*. In his *Metalogicon* (c.1156), John of Salisbury describes the method of his teacher, Bernard of Chartres, who would lecture on a classical text, explaining the grammatical problems, pointing out the figures of speech, and then assigning a theme for composition to help his students assimilate what they had learned.

From the fifth to the eighth centuries, the old Roman civilization continued to collapse, leaving only monastic and private education, usually at only a rudimentary level, but from the ninth through the twelfth centuries, the liberal arts began to revive at various times and places, especially in Italy and France. A new attitude toward the pagan past began to take root, leading to the development of an educational system to employ that classical heritage. Disputation – that is, arguing according to dialectical rules, based on Aristotle's logic – was central to all disciplines. In rhetoric, the authority of Cicero's early works continued, but rhetoric was merely, as R. R. Bolgar puts it, "the gateway through which medieval scholars came to dialectic, law, and literary achievement" (iii). In fact the subordination of rhetoric and the interest in classifying knowledge can be seen in the various explanations of rhetoric's relationship to logic and dialectic. For Isidore and Gerbert, logic has two parts: dialectic and rhetoric. For Pseudo-Rabunus Maurus, logic has three parts: grammar, rhetoric, and dialectic. Hugh of St. Victor divides the playing field into rational logic, which consists of parts of dialectic and rhetoric, and verbal logic, which consists of grammar and the rest of dialectic and rhetoric. William of Conches believes that the study of eloquence contains the study of logic, which is composed of grammar, reasoning (*ratio disserendi*), and rhetoric. And Roger Bacon sees logic as comprised of theoretical rhetoric and poetic, and moral philosophy is made up of applied rhetoric and poetic.[3]

Richard McKeon in a classic essay on medieval rhetoric describes the situation this way:

> Since its discipline was gradually limited by the transfer of the commonplaces, definition, and finally, proof – even in the rhetorical formulations they had received from Cicero, Victorinus, and Boethius – to the domain of dialectic, and since its subject matter was limited by the transfer of moral and political

questions to theology, rhetoric developed ... along three separate
lines: as a part of logic, or as the art of stating truths certified by
theology, or as a simple art of words. (276)

This transfer of rhetoric's substance, along with the impetus to
organize and classify what was left, would in fact seem to call into
question the whole notion of development in rhetoric. But there were
new developments in the arts of discourse that emerged outside of
the classical tradition but did nonetheless draw upon it. Sometime
around 1087, manuals on the art of writing letters, the *ars dictaminis*,
began to appear, applying Ciceronian arrangement and style to letters, and offering model letters for various occasions (how a scholar
should ask his father for more money if his father is aware that he
has been goofing off at school, for instance). About 1175, manuals on
writing poetry, *ars poetriae*, started to appear: Geoffrey of Vinsauf's
Poetria Nova, written between 1200 and 1216, is the most famous
because Geoffrey Chaucer refers to the preceding Geoffrey as his
"deere maister soverayne" and translates the opening lines of the
Poetria Nova in his *Troilus*. Around 1200, the art of preaching, *ars
praedicandi*, began to change as manuals advocating a more rhetorical
approach started to appear. Alain de Lille's *De Arte Praedicandatoria*
(c.1199) suggests a tripartite structural pattern, a style adapted to the
audience, and invention based on biblical interpretation.

In addition to Murphy's indispensable *Rhetoric in the Middle
Ages*, other useful historical overviews include Martin Camargo's
"Rhetoric" in *The Liberal Arts in the Middle Ages*; George
Kennedy's medieval chapters in *Classical Rhetoric*, especially
"Greek Rhetoric in the Middle Ages" (chapter 8) and "Latin Rhetoric
in the Middle Ages" (chapter 9); McKeon's "Rhetoric in the Middle
Ages"; Bolgar's "The Teaching of Rhetoric in the Middle Ages" in
Brian Vickers's *Rhetoric Revalued*; and the chapter on "Medieval
Fragmentation" in Vickers's *In Defence of Rhetoric*. In addition to
Bizzell and Herzberg's anthology, Miller, Prosser, and Benson have
compiled *Readings in Medieval Rhetoric*, and Murphy has edited

Three Medieval Rhetorical Arts, providing English access to letter writing, preaching, and poetry manuals, plus excerpts from medieval textbooks on Aristotelian dialectic. Eleonore Stump has translated and provided excellent notes and appendixes for Boethius's *De topicis differentiis* and his *In Ciceronis Topica*. Traugott Lawler has translated *The Parisiana poetria of John of Garland*, and Marjorie Curry Woods has edited and translated *An Early Commentary on the Poetria nova of Geoffrey of Vinsauf.*

The "Middle Ages" survey in Horner's *Present State of Scholarship* is ably done by Luke Reinsma. Rita Copeland's "Medieval Rhetoric: An Overview" in Sloane's *Encyclopedia of Rhetoric* sees rhetoric playing a vital role in the period's intellectual and institutional formation, and Jan Ziolkowski's entry on "Medieval Grammar" is also worth attention. In Murphy's *Short History of Writing Instruction*, Carol Dana Lanham discusses "Writing Instruction from Late Antiquity to the Twelfth Century," and Marjorie Curry Woods covers "The Teaching of Poetic Composition in the Later Middle Ages." Valuable collections of essays include Vickers's *Rhetoric Revalued*, Harry Caplan's *Of Eloquence: Studies in Ancient and Medieval Rhetoric* (a collection of Caplan's essays), and Murphy's outstanding collection, *Medieval Eloquence: Studies in the Theory and Practice of Medieval Rhetoric*. For the interplay of rhetoric and early Christianity, see James Kinneavy's *Greek Rhetorical Origins of Christian Faith* and Averil Cameron's *Christianity and the Rhetoric of Empire: The Development of Christian Discourse*. On the art of letter writing, see Martin Camargo's *Ars Dictaminis, Ars Dictandi*; on the art of poetry, see Douglas Kelly's *The Art of Poetry and Prose*; and on preaching, see Marianne Briscoe and Barbara Jaye's *Artes Praedicandi* and *Artes Orandi*. Jody Enders provides an interesting perspective in *Rhetoric and the Origins of Medieval Drama*, and John Ward's massively learned *Ciceronian Rhetoric in Treatise, Scholion, and Commentary* opens up the medieval world of manuscripts and education.

Renaissance Rhetoric. If a hurricane in Texas can result from the movements of a butterfly in South America, as chaos theory apparently attests, then perhaps we can believe that the discovery of some personal letters, over a thousand years old, led to massive cultural change and the flowering of a civilization. The origins of the Renaissance are indeed often tied to Petrarch (Francesco Petrarca, 1304–74), an Italian poet, who in 1345 discovered Cicero's letters to Atticus, and also two of Cicero's speeches. These letters with their easy elegance and eloquence exposed for many the rigidity and ugliness of medieval learning and the *ars dictaminis*. These letters also illustrated the wonderful possibility of recovering the intellectual riches of the ancient world.

Cicero was already the leading authority on rhetoric – for his juvenile and prescriptive *De inventione* and *Rhetorica ad Herennium* (the latter, as it turned out, was not his work). But this new vision of a mature Cicero, speaking so beautifully and wisely on a personal level in his letters, was so compelling that over a century later Pietro Bembo (1470–1547) would urge scholars to study only Cicero, and Christophe de Longueil (1488–1522) would aspire to write only in Cicero's language and style. The excesses of such Ciceronians prompted Erasmus to ridicule them in his *Ciceronianus* (1528), which prompted much controversy and consternation, including Nizolio's *Thesaurus Ciceronianus* (1535), which had 70 editions before 1620, Peter Ramus's *Ciceronianus* (1557), Gabriel Harvey's *Ciceronianus* (1576), and many other works. Gerardo Landriani, the bishop of Lodi, discovered Cicero's *De oratore, Brutus*, and *Orator*; Coluccio Salutati discovered more letters; Poggio Bracciolini (1380–1459) discovered the complete text of the fullest pedagogical expression of Cicero's rhetoric, Quintilian's *Institutio oratoria*; and these and many other works, partially or entirely lost or generally unknown, were soon published and distributed widely. Cicero's *De oratore*, for instance, was published in Subiaco in 1465 and had at least 22 more editions at different places up to the 1696 edition published at Oxford.

Those Renaissance thinkers who placed rhetoric at the heart of education have usually been called "humanists," champions of Cicero's *"humanitas,"* that program of learning going back to the Greeks that became our "humanities." There was indeed also a rebirth of interest in Greek eloquence as well as Latin. Greek works were rediscovered and translated into Latin: the collection of *Rhetorices graeci*, published in 1508 and 1509, made a wide range of Greek works accessible. Greek letter collections were also quite popular: in the 1470s, for instance, Francesco Zambeccari translated 109 letters of Libanius; he also forged another 430 letters – striking evidence of the market for Greek letters![4] Popular forgeries of speeches purportedly by Demosthenes also appeared. And yet, despite a flood of authentically new classical sources, fifteenth-century humanism was in an important sense also conservative. The Renaissance was a revolution that was also a rebirth. Even George Trebizond, for instance, who in 1433 had himself published a five-canon rhetorical treatise more sophisticated than the *Rhetorica ad Herennium* (*RaH*), was nonetheless still lecturing on the *RaH* in the 1460s. Even medieval commentaries upon it were the subjects of lectures, and even doubts about Cicero's authorship, which began to emerge in the fifteenth century, did not expeditiously displace the *RaH*. And Thomas Wilson's *The Arte of Rhetorique*, published in 1553, is a five-canon rhetoric in English – the first – that is based extensively on the Ciceronian tradition, plus Quintilian and Erasmus.

Why were the humanists so interested in preserving and recovering Greek and Roman learning? For one thing, the classical works provided an alternative or a supplement to the Catholic Church's world view. Although there were many notable exceptions, the hierarchy of the Catholic Church did not tend towards tolerance and open-mindedness. Reformers faced stiff resistance: John Wycliffe's works were condemned in 1382, and John Hus was burned for heresy in 1415, Galileo Galilei was placed under house arrest in 1634 for espousing a sun-centered universe, to pick only three of many examples. The humanists, however, with a world view rooted in rhetoric, tended to endorse argument and open inquiry. To a vertical world, in which man looked up to God, the humanists added a horizontal dimension, in which human beings exercised the creative power of language. Take, for instance, Castiglione's famous *Book of the Courtier* (1528), which had more than 80 editions in several languages before 1619. According to Castiglione, the most important influence on *The Courtier* was Cicero's *De oratore*. Both are multi-sided conversations exploring how a broad education enables one to achieve power and influence for the greater good. Both works see a fundamentally rhetorical world in which human relationships are crucial. The self that an orator or a courtier puts forward is a performance, as Stephen Greenblatt's influential study of *Renaissance Self-Fashioning* reveals. In Cicero's world, the ideal orator constructs a self that persuades his audience directly; but in Castiglione's world, the ideal courtier must influence his patron and his companions more indirectly, entertaining, deferring, gently nudging. Renaissance monarchies did not have the ancient forum or senate that called for public oratorical skill. Instead, engaging on a personal level, the courtier needed a different kind of persuasiveness, emphasizing intimate charm and artfulness that appeared artless and effortless (*sprezzatura* was the term for this hidden proficiency).

Charles V, Holy Roman Emperor from 1519 to 1556, supposedly kept a copy of *The Courtier* beside his bed, along with the Bible and Machiavelli's *The Prince*. Charles was at war against Pope Clement VII, Henry VIII of England, Francis I of France, and the Venetians; he confirmed the 1521 Edict of Worms that condemned Martin Luther; and so he needed the Bible, no matter his own level of piety, just to understand his enemies, one might argue. Machiavelli's work is both a kind of mirror image of Castiglione and an extension of his insights. Whereas Castiglione imagines how the courtier's performance can maximize his influence, Machiavelli explains how the ruler should fashion and present himself in order to rule his subjects most effectively. The admirable characters in Castiglione's discussion agree that the good courtier will refuse to obey evil commands, but Machiavelli's ruler has no such scruples: he cannot afford to have inflexible morals and character. He should be religious if that is useful, or kind, or ruthless, using ceremonies and public appearances like dramatic performances – whatever would be most effective and persuasive.

In this context of self-fashioning and performance, the goal in language training would logically involve cultivating the greatest fluency and flexibility. A broad general education in history, literature, theology, science – becoming a Renaissance man in other words – would provide one with the expansive resources to influence other people most effectively. Training in the technical aspects of rhetoric would also be helpful – invention strategies, conventional structures, figures of speech: We can get some sense from Shakespeare's often-astonishing wordplay how the Renaissance valued verbal dexterity and imagination. Consider the career of Erasmus (1469–1536), a monk whose work profoundly influenced humanism and education. In his *Adagia* (1508), Erasmus helpfully collected some three thousand classical proverbs, providing a treasure trove for other writers and thinkers to draw upon. His *Ecclesiastes* (1535) gave preachers rhetorical training and encouraged them to employ all the resources of language in their sermons, relying not only on God's intervention but also upon their own human exertions. *The Praise of Folly* (1511) is a powerful demonstration of the delights of a humanistic orientation. Folly comes to life in this work and delivers a dazzling oration in praise of herself, in which Erasmus satirically pokes fun at the foolishness of humankind and at the same time praises the folly that underlies love and ultimately even faith. Erasmus's *De Copia Verborum ac Rerum* (1512) was designed as a textbook to show students how to develop a "copious" or abundant style. It is a brilliant explanation of how to amplify, elaborate, and enliven one's thoughts. Erasmus shows students, for instance, how to say the same thing in a wide variety of ways, taking for example the statement "Your letter pleased me greatly" and producing 195 quite different assertions. As Erasmus says, when we are called upon to speak, "If in these circumstances we find ourselves destitute of verbal riches and hesitate, or keep singing out the same old phrase like a cuckoo, and are unable to clothe our thought in other colors or other forms, we shall look ridiculous when we show ourselves to be so tongue-tied, and we shall also bore our wretched audience to death."

As a humanist, Erasmus was especially inspired to recover classical learning. His work on copiousness owes much to Quintilian, who has a chapter in his *Oratoria* that is entitled "de copia verborum." But the Renaissance thinkers did more than simply try to replace medieval thinking with classical ideas. Peter Ramus (1515–72) for instance, a professor at the University of Paris, vehemently attacked in serial volumes Aristotle, Cicero, and Quintilian, even going so far as to downplay the importance of studying classical languages and publishing his works in French as well as Latin. Ramus was wildly popular and unpopular, as you might imagine. Most famously, in terms of the rhetorical tradition, he assigned "rhetoric" to cover only style and delivery, giving invention and arrangement to dialectic. Ramus simplified invention and arrangement by advocating an analytical strategy of dichotomous thinking, breaking any subject down into binary-branching trees. He also simplified style, viewing it as adornment and advocating for serious subjects the use of simplicity and clarity. Ramus's career ended supposedly as a Protestant martyr, killed during the St. Bartholomew's Day Massacre, when a Catholic mob attacked French Protestants, but there were rumors that his colleagues, no doubt tired of his unrelenting academic assault, pointed the mob toward his house.

In any event, Ramus contributed to the dislodgement of medieval, scholastic thinking (which, one might argue, is still ongoing). This shift toward humanistic thinking and rhetoric involved the embrace of argument and persuasion, the sensual appreciation of language and literature, and a certain tolerance and inclusiveness. Most of the humanist schools educated young boys and girls, and there was a significant number of learned women in the Renaissance, including Laura Cereta (1469–99), Cassandra Fedele (d. 1558), and Margaret Fell (1614–1702), to name only three. But the inclusiveness had its limits even for the humanists, and educated women were expected to exchange letters with learned men and do scholarly work only as youthful marvels. As they became adults, they were expected to lay aside their scholarly work and tend to their husbands and their domestic chores. As Anthony Grafton and Lisa Jardine note, Isotta Nogarola (d. 1466), who tried to maintain her scholarly studies, had to endure a published attack that asserted "the woman of fluent tongue is never chaste" (40).

Nogarola and other scholarly women are considered in Margaret King's "Thwarted Ambitions: Six Learned Women of the Italian Renaissance," and also in Grafton and Jardine's *From Humanism to the Humanities*. Women in the English Renaissance are discussed in Cheryl Glenn's "Inscribed in the Margins: Renaissance Women and Rhetorical Culture," in *Rhetoric Retold: Regendering the Tradition from Antiquity through the Renaissance*. For an overview of education, see Bruce Kimball's *Orators and Philosophers: A History of the Idea of Liberal Education*. On the education of the courtier, Charles Singleton's translation of Castiglione is the modern standard; Sir Thomas Hoby's Renaissance translation is available in *Three Renaissance Classics*, edited by Burton Milligan, which also contains Machiavelli's *The Prince* and Erasmus's *Utopia*. Wayne Rebhorn's essay, "Baldesar Castiglione, Thomas Wilson, and the Courtly Body of Renaissance Rhetoric," is essential reading on Castiglione. On Machiavelli, see Victoria Kahn's *Machiavellian Rhetoric: From the Counter-Reformation to Milton* (1994), and on Erasmus see Thomas Sloane's *On the Contrary: The Protocol of Traditional Rhetoric*. Sloane's *Donne, Milton, and the End of Humanistic Rhetoric* is also an excellent far-ranging work connecting poetry and rhetoric. In that vein, Brian Vickers's *Classical Rhetoric in English Poetry* is a classic work.

James Murphy has collected an extremely useful group of essays in *Renaissance Eloquence*, and Peter Mack's subsequent collection, *Renaissance Rhetoric*, is also quite helpful. Essential introductory essays are by Don Paul Abbott, in Horner's *Present State of Scholarship*; by Charles Stanford in Horner's *Historical Rhetoric*;

and by John Monfasani in Rabil's *Renaissance Humanism*. The standard modern edition of *On Copia* is in the University of Toronto's *Collected Works of Erasmus*, volume 2. Ramus is available in two English translations: Carole Newlands' renderings of *Arguments in Rhetoric against Quintilian* and *Peter Ramus's Attack on Cicero*. For Thomas Wilson's *Arte of Rhetorique*, see Peter Medine's edition.

Enlightenment Rhetoric. Revolutionary changes in science and philosophy drove dramatic changes in rhetoric during this period. During the Enlightenment, stretching through the seventeenth and eighteenth centuries, new ways of thinking about the world and human knowledge of it emerged. The simplest way to think about this change would be to say that the power of science and technology became manifest. As the microscope, the telescope, and many other instruments for perceiving and measuring the world made clear, humankind could organize, understand, and manipulate nature to an amazing degree. What did all this information mean? What was its status with regard to truth? Francis Bacon (1561–1626), Descartes (1596–1650), John Locke (1632–1704), and many other thinkers addressed these questions with profoundly invigorating consequences. "Words," as John Locke puts it in his *Essay concerning Human Understanding* (1690), arguably the most influential book throughout the eighteenth century, have "naturally no signification." Words "have all their signification from the arbitrary imposition of Men" (347). Furthermore, Locke argues that the human mind begins as a blank slate, a *tabula rasa*. We are not born with a set of innate ideas about good and evil, for instance. We learn from our experiences, from our reflections upon our experiences, and from the culture and language we inherit. Descartes' famous starting point, "I think, therefore I am" ("Cogito, ergo sum"), reflects an effort to determine what we can know on our own.

Thus, the meaning of all the information gathered by the scientific method is always going to be subject to interpretation, manipulation, rhetoric. As Locke puts it, drawing the juridical implications:

> And hence we see, that in the interpretation of Laws, whether Divine or humane, there is no end; Comments beget Comments, and Explications make new matter for Explications: and of limiting, distinguishing, varying the signification of these moral Words, there is no end. (3.9.9)

Even words that refer to "Substances," to natural classes and particular things, are uncertain because our ideas vary from person to person, and things are not knowable in any total or essential way. Presciently, Locke notes that even the most basic, simple term, like "life," rarely seems to have "a clear distinct settled *Idea* in men's minds" (3.9.11). If mankind understood "the imperfections of Language, as the Instrument of Knowledge," then "a great many of the Controversies that make such a noise in the World, would of themselves cease; and the way to Knowledge, and, perhaps, Peace too, lie a great deal opener than it does" (3.9.21–22).

Locke, who had lectured on rhetoric in 1663 at Oxford, concluded that "if we would speak of things as they are, we must allow that all the art of rhetoric, besides order and clearness; all the artificial and figurative application of words eloquence hath invented, are for nothing else but to insinuate wrong ideas, move the passions, and thereby mislead the judgment; and so indeed are perfect cheats" (370). The fact that rhetoric, "that powerful instrument of error and deceit, has its established professors, is publicly taught, and has always been had in great reputation," just illustrates, Locke says, "how much men love to deceive and be deceived." Locke's philosophy did not immediately collapse the study of classical rhetoric and scholastic logic, but it certainly contributed to a process of change. From the perspective of the new science, the best ornamentation would be none. As Thomas Sprat says in his *History of the Royal Society*, the members of the Society, devoted to using empirical science to advance knowledge, resolved to speak plainly and clearly. Sprat attacks "this vicious abundance of Phrase, this trick of Metaphors, this volubility of Tongue" that "makes so great a noise in the world" and obstructs learning and understanding (112). The more ambitious and loony language reformers advocated inventing or adopting languages so that words and things would link more directly together.[5]

The shift from a traditional, Aristotelian/Ciceronian rhetoric to a new, Lockean/scientific rhetoric can be quickly sketched.[6] The old rhetoric concentrated on persuasion, whereas the new rhetoric, partly in response to the needs of science, encompassed broader aims that included conveying information and investigating truth. While the old rhetoric advocated beginning with commonplaces, with established truths, which are then subjected to deductive manipulation, the new rhetoric grounded discourse upon experience and inferential reasoning. Proof derived from authorities and words contended against truth derived from reality and individual reasoning. The old rhetoric offered writers a formulaic arrangement, but in the new rhetoric *dispositio* followed the flow of thought. The grand style was valued by the old rhetoric; the plain style by the new. In the old rhetoric, disputation was seen as a way to truth; in the new rhetoric, disputation only sharpens one's ability to dispute, going nowhere. Thus, while the old rhetoric considered the *topoi* useful, the new rhetoric consulted facts, not a set of commonplaces. In sum, the old rhetoric saw truth as equal to verbal consistency, and the new rhetoric recognized a gap between words and things.

This summary is of course far too neat and orderly. There were efforts to revive classical rhetoric such as John Ward's *System of Oratory* (1759) or John Holmes's *The Art of Rhetoric Made Easy* (1755). Holmes included material from Longinus's *On the Sublime* and presented his material in rhyming couplets. Also, with invention relegated to scientific inquiry, and arrangement limited to a clear rehearsal of the process of discovery, rhetoric became essentially a stylistic matter. John Stirling's *System of Rhetoric* (1733) focused on figures of speech, for instance. The new science and philosophy also left delivery, in addition to style, within the purview of rhetoric; and elocution (the study of delivery) emerged as a distinct enterprise, as we shall see in the next chapter.

The most important "new" rhetoric appeared in Hugh Blair's *Lectures on Rhetoric and Belles Lettres* (1789), which went through an astonishing 110 editions. Blair's impact arguably stems from the influence of Henry Home, Lord Kames, who enticed Adam Smith to lecture on rhetoric and literature (belle lettres) at the University of Edinburgh from 1748 to 1751 (this was the same Adam Smith who would write the economic classic *The Wealth of Nations*, championing the free market). Blair followed Smith and Robert Watson in this position, and was named Regius Professor of Rhetoric and Belles Lettres in 1762. The location is significant, because, as Thomas Miller has shown, the academic interests that would become the field of English did not begin in Oxford or Cambridge, but in Scotland and in independent academies, called the Dissenting Academies because the students and teachers did not swear allegiance to the Church of England. Oxford and Cambridge had in fact degenerated into a "preserve for the idle and the rich," as H. C. Barnard says in *A History of English Education from 1760* (24). Scottish students and Dissenting Academy students apparently desired to cultivate good taste, correct writing, cultural refinement, and an appreciation for fine literature. Blair offers extensive analysis of literary language and syntax, taking Addison and Steele's *Spectator* papers as a model of good writing. Blair does discuss the eloquence of the courtroom, the pulpit, and the ceremony; he discusses the parts of a speech, following the classical structure; but these traditional features of rhetoric are approached in terms of critical evaluation. Blair recognizes that students want to generate writing and speeches, but he believes that cultivating good taste is essential to that capacity. Invention, Blair believes, cannot be taught – it's a natural ability. And arrangement should follow the structure of the subject, not some predetermined convention.

George Campbell's *Philosophy of Rhetoric* (1776), more philosophical and less popular than Blair, was also focused upon cultivating taste and correctness. Campbell's assertion that grammar should be "current, national, and reputable" was especially influential, addressing the questions of whether the English should try to recover some more eloquent past from the Renaissance; whether the language of some privileged geographical or social segment should be adopted; and whether grammar instruction should be descriptive or prescriptive. Campbell and Blair were part of a larger grammatical and stylistic picture, of course: In 1755, the publication of Samuel Johnson's great *Dictionary of the English Language* was in part the result of a desire to "fix" the English language – to stabilize it, and to correct it (a task Johnson came to see as impossible). Subsequent dictionary authors, including especially Noah Webster, contributed to the new rhetoric's emphasis on clarity and correctness, on language that aspired to be transparent in some sense – not a celebration of itself, of copiousness, of linguistic richness, but rather a window to ideas and things. Take John Witherspoon, for example, who graduated with Blair in 1739 at Edinburgh, and who became president of Princeton University in 1768. Witherspoon's lectures on rhetoric offered basic tips on writing and emphasized improving one's taste through critical analysis and reading. James Madison was among Witherspoon's students, and the other founding fathers were taught or influenced by followers of Blair and the Scottish new rhetoric.

A number of ideas come together in the eighteenth century: a standardized language, purposeful and accessible to all; knowledge from experience and observation, available to anyone ("common sense"); fundamental rights – "life, liberty, and estate" as Locke put it (*Two Treatises of Government*), related to our shared common sense; optimistic faith that humankind could improve itself by cultivating everything from good taste to exotic fruits and vegetables. Women made considerable progress in this period, as more began writing for publication in various genres and speaking out. Margaret Fox's *Women's Speaking Justified, Proved and Allowed by the Scriptures* (1666) and Mary Wollstonecraft's *A Vindication of the Rights of Woman* (1792) give some indication of the ongoing struggle for equality.

Wilbur S. Howell's *Eighteenth-Century British Logic and Rhetoric*, from 1971, is still the most thorough survey, providing summaries of most major and minor works. Also helpful in assessing the big picture, Michael Moran has edited a collection of short biographies, commentaries, and bibliographies, *Eighteenth-Century British and American Rhetorics and Rhetoricians*. Winifred Horner and Kerri Barton survey the eighteenth century in *The Present State of Scholarship in Historical and Contemporary Rhetoric*. Useful chapters on this period appear in Conley's *Rhetoric in the European Tradition* and Kennedy's *Classical Rhetoric and Its Christian and Secular Tradition*.

Thomas Miller's *The Formation of College English: Rhetoric and Belles Lettres in the British Cultural Provinces* (1997) masterfully shows how the field of English arose out of the Scottish universities and Dissenting Academies, and Ian Michael covers the introduction of writing, rhetoric, and literature into the British schools in *The Teaching of English: From the Sixteenth Century to 1870*. Different aspects of rhetoric, language, and epistemology are explored in three excellent studies: Carey McIntosh's *The Evolution of English Prose, 1700–1800: Style, Politeness, and Print Culture*; Barbara Warnick's *The Sixth Canon: Belletristic Rhetorical Theory and Its French Antecedents*; and H. Lewis Ulman's *Things, Thoughts, Words, and Actions: The Problem of Language in Late Eighteenth-Century British Rhetorical Theory*. A facsimile edition of Blair is available, edited by Harold Harding, and an abridged edition is forthcoming edited by Linda F. Buckley and S. Michael Halloran. Lloyd Bitzer's edition of Campbell's *Philosophy of Rhetoric*, Thomas Miller's edition of Witherspoon's *Selected Writings*, and J. C. Bryce's edition of Adam Smith's *Lectures on Rhetoric and Belles Lettres* are all quite useful.

Nineteenth-Century Rhetoric. How did English departments become an essential part of higher education, and the study of English literature pervasively required throughout the curriculum? One answer is that educators followed the implications of Hugh

Blair's work, supplemented by the contributions of George Campbell, Richard Whately, and a host of nineteenth-century rhetoricians. The study of rhetoric and belles lettres, these Enlightenment rhetoricians believed, would develop students' moral character, refine their taste, advance their insight and intelligence, enrich their cultural awareness – not to mention increase their ability to write and speak effectively. Rhetoric not only had a large improving effect, but it was also concerned with all kinds of communication, from letter writing to poetry, from oratory to literary criticism. Thus, it made sense to think that every educated person might improve themselves by studying rhetoric and fine literature. Technology and science became part of the mainstream curriculum in Europe and the United States, and composition in the vernacular languages finally began to displace the focus on Latin. Change was embraced at different paces in different places – England, for instance, was slow to change at Oxford and Cambridge, and the classics continued to be important in elite schools and universities. In Scotland and the United States, the new curriculum was readily adopted.

The appeal to a growing middle class and the culture of self-improvement is suggested for instance by the titles of Samuel Newman's *A Practical System of Rhetoric* (1834) and John Genung's *Practical Elements of Rhetoric* (1886). With this focus on the utilitarian, much of the classical curriculum, including much of classical rhetoric, seemed increasingly irrelevant or at least less crucial. Richard Whately's influential *Elements of Rhetoric* (1828), for instance, was designed in part to educate future clergy. So Whately sees classical invention primarily in terms of convincing a diverse public audience of the truth of revealed religion. Thus, Cicero's emphasis on the probable and the judicial is not shared by Whately, who focuses on providing an audience with the grounds for assenting to the truth. Whately's treatment of the Burden of Proof, for example, innovatively drew attention to which party in an argument has the presumption of being correct: who is challenging what sort of an accepted notion, and how does that affect the argumentative strategy? The affinities of rhetoric to psychology are especially evident in Whately's complete title: *Elements of Rhetoric, Comprising an Analysis of the Laws of Moral Evidence and of Persuasion, with Rules for Argumentative Composition and Elocution.* Whately includes both oral and written argument, and he provides both theoretical analysis of what constitutes proof, and also pragmatic rules for speaking or writing effectively. The pervasive motivation for rhetorical theory and pedagogy, Whately's included, is adapting the message for the audience, as the speaker or writer becomes a manager of information. The different modes of discourse, which are both kinds of writing and approaches to a subject, reflect different faculties in the mind. Thus, adapting a message for an audience involves using description, narration, exposition, and/or argumentation to "enlighten the understanding, to please the imagination, to move the passions or to influence the will," to use George Campbell's popular phrasing (1).

To get experience in adapting material for audiences, many people joined literary and debating societies during the nineteenth century, supplementing their formal training. At least two hundred such societies appear to have been active in the United States during the 1870s and 1880s. Also, the practical issue of finding the form for the audience is highlighted in works like *Martine's Sensible Letter-Writer* (1866) and *The Universal Self-Instructor: An Epitome of Forms and General Reference Manual* (1882). These guides were a continuation, to be sure, of the medieval *ars dictaminis*, but in the nineteenth century an unprecedented number of writers were advancing their own education. Women were increasingly literate, starting from perhaps a fifty percent literacy rate at the beginning of the nineteenth century. Some were able to justify speaking out by pointing to the social issues that they were addressing, including especially slavery. Margaret Fell in the late seventeenth century led the way for many Quaker women who would become socially active through the eighteenth and nineteenth centuries. Sarah and Angelina Grimké, for instance, bravely led a public assault in the nineteenth century on slavery, having seen its evil in their own slave-owning family in South Carolina. Like Elizabeth Cody Stanton, Lucretia Mott, and many others, the Grimké sisters linked women's rights to their public opposition to slavery and their opposition to alcohol. These women were, to be sure, subject to much abuse for entering the rhetorical arena, but their contributions were so effective and noteworthy that their statements have become part of the rhetorical canon. Excerpts from the work of Maria Stewart, the Grimké sisters, Phoebe Palmer, and Frances Willard appear in Bizzell and Herzberg's *Rhetorical Tradition* even though these works are quite different in nature from the work of Hugh Blair, George Campbell, or Richard Whately – not to mention Cicero, Aristotle, Augustine, or Erasmus. One might argue that Frances Willard's assertion that male ministers are speaking only to men, in *Women in the Pulpit*, is concerned with the rhetorical topic of the audience, but Willard's discussion really focuses on politics, not the construction of discourse. Likewise, the works of Sojourner Truth and Frederick Douglass are not concerned explicitly with rhetorical theory or pedagogy, but they are nonetheless being read into the rhetorical canon because they do reflect ideological and social shifts in rhetorical theory.

Indeed, compared to rhetorical practice at the forefront of social change, what is going on in rhetoric proper has often seemed rather dull. At one point, people interested in the history of rhetoric have generally concluded that there was little of interest or value going on in the nineteenth century. If invention involves essentially the process of adapting pre-existing materials for an audience, and if this process involves following simple notions of form (introduction, body, conclusion; topic sentence and supporting sentences) and correctness, then composing looks much like editing. Alexander Bain's *English Composition and Rhetoric: A Manual* (1866) provided an influential map of the kinds of discourse: description, narration, exposition, and persuasion. But this formula leads to a classificatory or analytical scheme. For A. S. Hill, in *The Principles of Rhetoric*, rhetoric is defined as "the art of efficient communication," and the most potent enemy of efficiency is poor grammar. At the other end of the universe from this outlook, we find Romanticism, which assumed that the writer or speaker would rely upon imagination and spontaneous expression, not training or precepts or even practice. From this perspective, writing can't really be taught. Grammar, editing, usage can be taught. But in that case, it would seem that almost any educated person could teach writing. Thus, at the end of the nineteenth century, "rhetoric" is not exactly the most prestigious subject in the curriculum.

Nan Johnson's *Nineteenth-Century Rhetoric in North America* is a good starting point for understanding this still-neglected period. Thomas Miller's *The Formation of College English: Rhetoric and Belles Lettres* is essential (and engaging) reading for this period also. Winifred Bryan Horner's *Nineteenth-Century Scottish Rhetoric: The American Connection* and Henry Hubert's *Harmonious Perfection: The Development of English Studies in Nineteenth-Century Anglo-Canadian Colleges* provide different national perspectives. Lucille Schultz's *The Young Composers: Composition's Beginnings in Nineteenth-Century Schools* and S. Michael Halloran's "From Rhetoric to Composition: The Teaching of Writing in America to 1900," in Murphy's *Short History*, focus on writing pedagogy. A valuable collection of primary documents has been assembled by Mariolina Salvatori in *Pedagogy 1819–1929: Disturbing History*. Much good work has recently been done on women, race, and rhetoric: see especially the collection of essays edited by Molly Meijer Wertheimer, *Listening to Their Voices: The Rhetorical Activities of Historical Women*, in addition to Carol Mattingly's *Well-Tempered Women: Nineteenth-Century Temperance Rhetoric*, and Shirley Wilson Logan's *"We Are Coming": The Persuasive Discourse of Nineteenth-Century Black Women*.

Twentieth- and Twenty-First Century Rhetoric and Composition. The most notable historical development in this period is the invention of a robust academic discipline. Over the past decade, only British literature as a field offered more jobs than Composition and Rhetoric in the Modern Language Association's

Joblist. According to David Russell, in the field of Composition and Rhetoric, "There was a great deal of excellent historical research published from 1984 to 2003 – by far more than in any other profession I know of" ("Historical Studies" 267). These innovative and influential historical studies include work by Susan Miller, Robert Connors, James Murphy, Sharon Crowley, Susan Jarratt, George Kennedy, Thomas Miller, and many other scholars. Theoretical work in Rhetoric and Composition has achieved an impressive level of sophistication, accessing theory from other disciplines (literary criticism, philosophy, history, anthropology) and recovering theorists from earlier times (I. A. Richards, Kenneth Burke, Nietzsche, the Sophists). Quantitative research, although perhaps not currently in vogue, has advanced and challenged what we believe that we know, and reports from all sorts of classrooms have enlarged the repertoire of teachers all over the world. Although the teaching of writing as a distinct discipline remains largely an enterprise of the United States, Composition is making inroads in Canada, Australia, the United Kingdom, New Zealand, and elsewhere.

Still, Composition continues to be seen generally as a preliminary study, preparatory to something else. English A was the first course required of all students at Harvard in 1872, and First-Year Composition (or First-Year Writing, or First-Year English, or Freshman Composition, etc.) has continued to be a mandatory course at most institutions. In the nineteenth century, writing was taught in the elementary or middle school grades, focusing on penmanship, copying other texts, but evolving into composing, as students wrote about their summer vacations and their opinions about all sorts of things. This preparatory status of writing instruction no doubt has something to do with the struggles of Composition to gain academic respect. Graduate students, faculty spouses, junior faculty, part-time faculty – these people could be assigned to teach writing, leaving the senior faculty available to teach subjects more suited to their accomplishments. In the very first issue of the *Publications of the Modern Language Association*, in 1886, James Morgan Hart considers what should be done with logic, rhetoric, and linguistics in "The College Course in English Literature." So that the course can focus on literature, Hart suggests that logic and rhetoric be shipped to the department of Philosophy. Logic has been embraced by Philosophy: Whitehead and Russell's *Principia Mathematica* in 1910 "sent a clear signal to all liberal arts teachers that they were no longer experts in logic," as James Kinneavy puts it (188 in Horner and Borton, *Present State*).

In 1914, Speech teachers dramatically walked out of the National Council of Teachers of English, providing a home outside of the English department for rhetoric. Given the task of teaching students how to write logically and persuasively, typically without being trained in logic or rhetoric, writing teachers surprisingly did not form the Conference on College Composition and Communication until 1949; even more surprising perhaps, the 4Cs did not get much traction until a few decades later. In 1963, the NCTE issued an important report on the state of knowledge in composition. In 1965, with *Classical Rhetoric for the Modern Student*, Edward Corbett displayed the value of serious historical scholarship. In 1966, the Dartmouth Conference brought a remarkable group of thinkers together. Donald Murray published *A Writer Teaches Writing* in 1968; Janet Emig's *Composing Processes of Twelfth Graders* appeared in 1971. These events and many others resulted in the emergence in the 1970s of Composition as a profession.

The recovery of classical rhetoric, sparked most notably by Corbett, as well as the ongoing discovery of writing pedagogy's history, played a key role in the professionalization of Composition and Rhetoric. Arguably the most important idea driving the field is the notion that writing is a process, amenable to intervention, practice, explicit strategies. Classical rhetoric's canon, featuring invention and arrangement, tended to expose the narrowness of Current-Traditional Rhetoric's focus on grammar and style. As a teachable process, writing is a crucial part of education, allowing students to convey their insights. But Peter Elbow, Donald Murray, Ken Macrorie, and many others also realized that writing was also a means of discovery, a way of learning, as writers come to ideas and understandings by means of the process. Indeed, such perception, dynamic and constructed by language, is the nature of what we can know, according to a wide variety of philosophical and theoretical projects. For Kenneth Burke, Richard Weaver, Chaim Perelman (with Lucie Olbrechts-Tyteca), Wayne Booth, Stanley Fish, Richard Rorty, and many others, rhetoric is pervasive. In *The New Rhetoric* (1958), Perelman for instance argued that even science is based on argument and persuasion. All discourse is rhetorical. Terry Eagleton draws the logical conclusion for literary theory, calling for a criticism that is fundamentally rhetorical, addressing "the wider social relations between writers and readers, orators and audiences," embedded in their social contexts. Literary study that is aesthetic, that contemplates artistic form, is ignoring the power of literature – how it is "constructed in order to achieve certain effects" (205–6).

If everything is rhetorical, then where does this new field end? Here is James Kinneavy's startling declaration of what he will *not* consider in his overview of "Contemporary Rhetoric" in *The Present State of Scholarship in Historical and Contemporary Rhetoric*, given rhetoric's expanse:

> Thus, I will not consider some of the very legitimate areas of rhetoric: marketing, managerial rhetoric, discussion and debating techniques, interviewing, oral interpretation, film and radio and television production (as such), general semantics and modern linguistic semantics, narrative theory, theory of description, axiology, logic, and the philosophy of science. Finally, entire areas of modern psychology, such as learning theory and cognitive science, are also excluded. (190)

The topics that Kinneavy does cover – and these sections are in fact written by his students – suggest the challenge of contending with such a sprawling field: reference works (a resource, not a topic of course); situational context; communication theory, hermeneutics, and pragmatics; argumentation, informal logic, and the rhetoric of science; dialectic, exploration, and epistemology; technical writing, journalism, and information theory; propaganda, political rhetoric, and commercial advertising; religious oratory; rhetorical criticism; women's studies/gender studies; self-expression; mass media and small group media; semiotics and semiology; rhetoric as metaphor; computers and rhetoric; and rhetoric and the teaching of composition. The contrast in ambition and reach in the field of Composition and Rhetoric is indeed striking: on the one hand, we simply want to teach writing effectively; on the other hand, a vast galaxy of knowledge (but not the whole universe) is our purview. Even what Kinneavy has omitted, such as learning theory, has actually played an important role in composition's development. The whole language movement, for example, which evolved from the learning theories of Dewey, Piaget, and Vygotsky, has influenced the teaching of writing, especially in the National Writing Project and the work of James Britton, Alvina Burrows, and others.

The teaching of writing is itself a rhetorical site, a canvas for social interests and issues. Does the gender, race, sexual orientation, or disability of the student or teacher matter? In what ways? Some especially interesting archival work by JoAnn Campbell has identified some shrewd ways that women students at Radcliff, Mount Holyoke, Wellesley, and elsewhere resisted the patriarchal rhetorical structures of their male teachers. Related work by Sandra Harmon, Heidemarie Weidner, Vickie Ricks, and others has enlarged our understanding of how women have learned to write. Shirley Wilson Logan, J. J. Royster and J. C. Williams, Keith Gilyard, Scott Zaluda, Devon Mihesuah, and others have extended our awareness to the instruction of people of color. This recovery work is an ongoing project, with rich archives waiting to be inspected. In *A Group of Their Own: College Writing Courses and American Women Writers, 1880–1940*, Katherine Adams's survey of various famous women writers and their experiences with composition courses offers one instance of the kind of engagingly imaginative history that can be written. This history helps us to understand where we are and how we arrived here. On the role of theory in understanding where here is, see Raúl Sánchez's *The Function of Theory in Composition Studies*. Where Rhetoric and Composition is going – that will be shaped by forces too varied and complex and unthought of to predict, I suspect; but computer technology, which to this point seems to have made a rather modest contribution, seems likely to be a driving force in the future, as the work of Cynthia Selfe and others indicates.

James Berlin's *Rhetoric and Reality: Writing Instruction in American Colleges, 1900–1985* offered the first history of college composition in the twentieth century. Although his classificatory scheme has proved controversial, it is nonetheless a useful starting point. Bizzell and Herzberg's "Introduction" to the "Modern and Postmodern" readings in their *Rhetorical Tradition* is also a good orientation, in addition to Vincent Caseregola and Julie Farrar's "Twentieth-Century Rhetoric" in Theresa Enos's *Encyclopedia*, and Karlyn Kohrs Campbell's "Modern Rhetoric" in Sloane's *Encyclopedia*. Robert Connors's essential historical work has been conveniently collected in *Selected Essays of Robert J. Connors*, edited by Lisa Ede and Andrea A. Lunsford. John Brereton's collection of portraits of writing teachers in *Traditions of Inquiry* is fascinating, and Brereton's fine collection of primary sources, *The Origins of Composition Studies in the American College, 1875–1925*, is also interesting and revealing. On the contributions of women in particular to the early twentieth-century history, see for instance Joy Ritchie and Kathleen Boardman's "Feminism in Composition: Inclusion, Metonymy, and Disruption." Joseph Harris provides a detailed history of the latter part of the century in *A Teaching Subject: Composition Since 1966*. Richard Ohmann, in "Professionalizing Politics," revisits his classic 1976 study, *English in America: A Radical View of the Profession*, in Mary Rosner et al.'s useful essay collection entitled *History, Reflection, and Narrative: The Professionalization of Composition, 1963–1983*. For eclectic, opinionated, wide-ranging histories, see Susan Miller's

Trust in Texts: A Different History of Rhetoric and Byron Hawk's *A Counter-History of Composition: Toward Methodologies of Complexity.*

Prepared with this map of resources, let's turn now to the adventure itself: the classroom.

RECOMMENDATIONS FOR
FURTHER READING: MEMORY

Conley, Thomas. *Rhetoric in the European Tradition.* University of Chicago Press, 1990.

Connors, Robert J. *Composition-Rhetoric: Backgrounds, Theory, and Pedagogy.* University of Pittsburgh Press, 1997.

Hawk, Byron. *A Counter-History of Composition: Toward Methodologies of Complexity.* University of Chicago Press, 2007.

Miller, Thomas. *The Formation of College English: Rhetoric and Belles Lettres in the British Cultural Provinces.* University of Pittsburgh Press, 1997.

Yates, Frances. *The Art of Memory.* University of Chicago Press, 1966.

The problem: Do you know enough to teach?

6 Delivery

The teacher who has not a passion and an aptitude for imparting instruction in English, who does not feel that it is the great thing in life to live for, and a thing, if necessary, to die for, who does not realize at every moment of his classroom work that he is performing the special function for which he was foreordained from the foundation of the world – such a teacher cannot profit greatly by any course of training, however ingeniously devised or however thoroughly applied.

Fred Newton Scott (1908)

This chapter deals with "delivery" in three senses: (1) the fifth canon of rhetoric, entailing advice on how to deliver a speech, after one has invented, arranged, styled, and memorized it; (2) the presentation of any text or communication, including everything from the font and paper used to the way a website is organized; and (3) the pedagogy involved in implementing a course in rhetoric and composition. My emphasis will be on the third meaning here, but the two preceding ones are not unrelated to the challenge of delivering Composition and Rhetoric courses most effectively.

ELOCUTION

Tony Bennett, as much as anyone who has ever sung, knows how to deliver a song. Most famous for "I Left My Heart in San Francisco," he makes any song his own, controlling the pitch, volume, timbre, and phrasing of every note beautifully. But consider the surprising focus of Ben Ratliff's remarkable review of a Bennett concert performed in December, 2008, when he was 82 years old:[1]

Near the beginning of "I Left My Heart in San Francisco," delivering the line "the glory that was Rome is of another day," he folded his arms as if about to deliver a history lecture. This is the moment, the motion implied, where you start trusting the protagonist of this song. And in Alan and Marilyn Bergman's and Michel Legrand's "How Do You Keep the Music Playing?," as he sang the counterintuitive line, "the more I love, the more that I'm afraid," he did something so quickly it was nearly subliminal. It was a slight shoulder shrug; a half-swivel of the wrists so that the left thumb is pointed to 10 o'clock and the right thumb to 2 o'clock; eyebrows raised and eyes looking downward. It meant: this might be hard to understand, but stay with me.

Ratliff aims to expand our appreciation of Bennett's artistry by drawing attention to physical aspects of his delivery that some in the audience might not have thought of as part of the performance or even consciously noted. For Bennett, Ratliff tells us, delivering the song includes more than the voice. Did Bennett learn these gestures? Invent them himself? Are they unconscious, intuitive, or carefully choreographed? What if an aspiring singer were to use Ratliff's analysis to guide his own performance? Would that be silly or shrewd?

For a popular group of rhetoricians in the late eighteenth and early nineteenth centuries, it seemed clear that explicit guidance on voice and even gesture would be quite valuable. Not only *could* one learn how to deliver a speech, but cultivating such ability was crucially important. In William Scott's popular 1779 *Lessons in Elocution*, a speaker is instructed to begin "by resting the entire weight of his body on the right leg; the other just touching the ground ... the right arm must be held out with the palm open in a 45 degree angle."[2] Scott proceeds to describe the position of every limb and joint, every facial expression, every inflection, tone, and tempo of the voice. Similarly, Gilbert Austin's *Chironomia* (1806) presents a set of symbols that can be used to mark a text for delivery, showing where to speak slowly and softly, where to be loud and slow, where to pause, even where to whisper. Austin was not the first to propose such a system, and although this kind of guidance might seem absurd, Jay Fliegelman has in fact convincingly argued that Thomas Jefferson used such a system in marking up his manuscript of *The Declaration of Independence*. Jefferson, a notoriously poor orator, nonetheless was producing a document, Fliegelman argues, that was meant to be read aloud, and Jefferson in his draft was thinking of controlling the way that it would be read. Like other Elocutionists, Austin even provides instructions – shades of Tony Bennett – on the positions of the hands "used by ancient Orators." How in the world, you might ask, could these Enlightenment rhetoricians purport to know how ancient orators deployed their hands?

In fact, Quintilian does discuss delivery in considerable detail, including the use of the hands, and he was not alone in this level of attention.[3] Demosthenes, contemporary of Aristotle, was reported by Cicero and others to have said that the three most important aspects of a speech are delivery, delivery, and delivery. Theophrastus who followed Aristotle as leader of the Peripatetic School, wrote a treatise *On Delivery*, which is now lost, but which apparently influenced the *Rhetorica ad Herennium*'s extensive treatment of the fifth canon. As Cicero puts it, all the parts of oratory "succeed according as they are delivered. Delivery ... has the sole and supreme power in oratory; without it, a speaker of the highest mental capacity can be held in no esteem; while one of moderate abilities, with this qualification, may surpass even those of the highest talent" (*De Oratore or Cicero on Oratory and Orators* 3.213). Thus, there is plenty of ancient precedent for James Burgh's efforts in 1764 in *The Art of Speaking ... in which are given Rules for expressing properly the principal passions and Humours, which occur in Reading or Public Speaking.* Burgh assumes with his Elocutionist contemporaries that there is a grammar of emotions in which particular emotions are displayed in particular ways, and that speakers should embody the emotions they are attempting to convey. In *De oratore*, Cicero observes that "every emotion of the mind has from nature its own peculiar look, tone, and gesture" (396). And here is how Burgh, obviously following

Cicero's lead, says the speaker should compose himself in order to display and convey "moderate love":

> Love, (successful) lights up the *countenance* into *smiles*. The *forehead* is *smoothed*, and enlarged; the *eyebrows* are *arched*; the *mouth* a little *open*, and *smiling*; the *eyes languishing*, and *half shut*.... The *countenance* assumes the *eager* and *wishful* look of *desire*. The *accents* are *soft* and *winning* ... both *hands pressed* to the *bosom*. *Love* unsuccessful, adds an air of *anxiety*, and *melancholy*. (qtd. Fliegelman 31)

Why did the high point of pedagogical confidence and specificity in teaching delivery, reviving and even extending this ancient canon, as exemplified by Burgh, Scott, Austin, and others, occur in the late eighteenth and early nineteenth centuries? The scientific revolution was in the process of devaluing or at least complementing the commonplace knowledge of tradition and authority. Instead of words, the quest for knowledge focused upon things, upon empirical observations and descriptive explanations. Invention thus became an activity that was essentially outside of rhetoric. To find material about children, for instance, one would study children – and not the collected wisdom of the ancients regarding children. Similarly, whereas the classical tradition had provided formal patterns of arrangement, applicable to any situation, the new science seemed to many people to suggest that arrangement should instead be directed by the structure of the subject, or the structure of the audience's expectations – or just about anything other than the format for a classical oration. For John Locke, one of the guiding intellectual lights of the Enlightenment, eloquent style was just an obstruction to understanding, as we have seen. A clear and simple style would allow words to reveal things most transparently. Style was grammar. There were certainly great speeches made in the eighteenth century, but with the rapid expansion of print, the growing accessibility of paper, great powers of memory were not widely cultivated. Thus Rhetoric was left with the mechanics of delivering a speech – how to pitch the voice, how to move the hands, what postures to assume, and the like.

The most famous and influential of these rhetoricians to focus upon delivery was Thomas Sheridan, who started his career as an actor, but in 1756 began to focus his attention on a series of wildly popular lectures. In his *Lectures on Elocution*, published in 1762, Sheridan stressed a "natural" tone, standard grammar, conventional gestures, aiming for a delivery that supported and did not distract from the message. But Sheridan's driving idea, placing elocution at the center of educational reform, can be discerned in the amazing title of the book he published in 1756: *British Education: Or, The Source of the Disorders of Great Britain. Being an Essay towards proving, that the Immorality, Ignorance, and false Taste, which so generally prevail, are the natural and necessary Consequences of the present defective System of Education. With an attempt to shew, that a revival of the Art of Speaking, and the Study of Our Own Language, might contribute, in a great measure, to the Cure of those Evils.*[4] Sheridan's startling insight, that reviving the art of speaking might reform morality, dispel ignorance, and promote good taste, was in fact already circulating in the eighteenth century. His godfather, Jonathan Swift, had much earlier proposed "fixing" the English language in an essay published in 1712. Samuel Johnson had embarked on his great *Dictionary* project in 1747 with precisely that aim of stabilizing and correcting the language. Indeed, the notion that the decay of language skills is related to – indeed, is contributing to or even causing – educational and social and moral and religious and artistic decay is an idea that has bubbled up again and again in modern American culture, yielding the back-to-basics movement, entrance and exit exams, required writing courses, and much else as we have seen in Chapter 4 above on "Style." In Sheridan's career, I think we see the crossing of two conflicting views of delivery: that it is just acting, an extension of Sheridan's theatrical expertise; and that it is foundational, with rhetoric as the focus of education, and delivery at the center of that focus.

These diverging views of delivery have persisted in the modern development of the field of Speech, becoming Speech Communication, then Communication, then Communication Studies. Not surprisingly, with the emergence of Romanticism, training in oratory during the latter part of the nineteenth century was generally neglected, although student oratorical clubs were popular. But by the early twentieth century, teachers who were interested in oral training began to break away from English departments, forging a new discipline that divided along the fault lines of writing versus speaking, literature versus rhetoric. The official fracture came in 1914 at a meeting of the Oral English section of the National Council of Teachers of English, when a relatively small minority of a small group, seventeen of more than 100 members, voted to form a separate body dedicated to public speaking.[5]

These new units generally concentrated at first on the practical aspects of oratory – how to construct a speech, how to speak clearly, how to reach different audiences, and so forth. Yet even by the 1920s, the field was already evolving in the two different directions epitomized in Sheridan's career: The Midwestern School advocated dealing with every aspect of speech in the largest sense, from argumentation to ethics to acting to television, and much more. To address this universe of communication, the Midwestern School believed that scientific, empirical studies would reveal guiding principles and behaviors. The Cornell School, however, focused on public speaking as an art, questioning the practicality and feasibility of studying every kind of communication scientifically. The Midwestern School struggled to define and master its turf: Why, for instance, should the study of argumentation or television or journalism be limited to what is spoken? And if Speech includes writing, why is it separated from Composition? Ambition threatened to dissolve the discipline's borders. The Cornell School, however, lacking imperial designs, struggled to hold onto its turf, as business and education schools attempted to take over business and educational communication. Thus, on the one hand, in the 1930s

and 1940s diction was increasingly stressed in some Speech departments in the United States, returning in a sense to the concerns
of the Elocutionists. Instead of Scottish or lower-class accents, the
Delsarte system, developed to train actors and adopted by Speech
teachers, sought to banish Southern accents and other aberrations
from the preferred mid-Atlantic dialect. This restricted view of
Speech, extending the Cornell or Elocutionary approach, stood in
stark contrast to the new field of Communication with its virtually unlimited ambition, extending the Midwestern vision. Speech,
or Speech Communication, or Communication, or Communication
Studies, continues to debate whether it is an art or a science-based
field, whether it focuses on public speaking or all sorts of communi-
cations, including even nonverbal.

These divergent views of delivery are arguably inherent in its
conception. The Latin term for the fifth canon, *actio*, is related to
the English word for "actor," and it refers to the action or plot of a
play, but it also refers to the action of a magistrate. It is an intriguing conjunction, linking the judiciary and the theatre, exposing
the idea that civilization and order are maintained by a performance, by the theatre that is the legal system. The Greek term for the
fifth canon is ὑπόκρισις (*hypokrisis*), a term that could be applied
to any public performance. But *hypokrisis* is related to *hypokrites*,
which is concerned specifically with the performance of an actor,
and the theatrical term over time apparently tainted the neutral
term, yielding eventually our term *hypocrisy*. In the fourth century BCE, Demosthenes derisively applied the term *hypokrites* to
Aeschines, his political rival, who had in fact been an actor before
becoming a politician. For a politician, the charge of insincerity,
of hypocrisy, is especially serious: how can the public trust the
politician who is an adept actor? What does he or she really mean
or stand for? Although Ronald Reagan was sometimes ridiculed
for being an actor pretending to be President, Reagan's ability to
project sincerity was especially impressive. George W. Bush may
have been appealing to some voters precisely because he was rather

inarticulate: he seemed trustworthy because he wasn't a smooth talker.

Although some might question the ethics of pretending to be someone we aren't, Martin Jacobi has even argued that practicing delivery in itself will improve the ethics and values of students in several ways. Expounding on Quintilian's assertion that the practice of rhetoric leads to the improvement of one's character (an assertion that may seem odd today), Jacobi notes that speakers will want to present themselves as virtuous, because their audience will be more willing to be persuaded. And in presenting themselves as trust-worthy and virtuous, students get to see how "the good has the nat-ural advantage and attraction," as Jacobi says, referencing Aristotle (25). At the very least, as Plato contends, it's helpful to know what the truth is if the speaker wishes to lie.

There are some ironies, if not absurdities, apparent here, and the fifth canon has indeed proved to be especially problematic. The elocutionists repeatedly stressed the importance of being "natural" in delivery at the same time that they were giving such explicit and detailed instructions on how to perform. Such a paradox, in which the most effective artfulness appears to be artless, arguably extends to all aspects of rhetoric. In other words, the same questions that apply to all the other offices of rhetoric certainly apply also to deliv-ery: Is it necessary or possible to teach people to be natural? How? Can delivery be taught at all? Delivery in the classical sense involves the body as an instrument, and Cicero links the tones of speaking to musical chords; but some people sing beautifully without training, while others have poor equipment to work with, and some are tone deaf altogether. The same thing would appear to be true of oratorical delivery – and of invention, arrangement, style, and memory. Some people are smarter, better read, more attractive, more engaging, more appealing than other people, but that does not mean that teaching delivery is futile.

These issues apply of course to the particular kind of deliv-ery that teachers perform. Are good teachers just born, or are they trained? Should an inexperienced teacher just be "natural," letting his or her own personality lead them to an effective way of teaching? Or should the neophyte teacher, in the spirit of the Elocutionists, be given detailed and explicit guidance – a syllabus to follow, discussion questions to use, rubrics for marking papers, advice on how to move one's hands? The last thing most inexperienced teachers want to convey to their students is their lack of experience: a teacher does not want to appear to be playing the role of a teacher, pretending. And yet, what we learn from the history of delivery is that a speaker, including a teacher, can appear most "natural," comfortable, in control, effective, by studying the art and (for many people) working against or supplementing their "natural" abilities. We do in fact assume a role when we teach, or speak, or perform in any way.

Teachers can learn on the job, to be sure. The training for most new writing teachers in my generation consisted of receiving a copy of a textbook and a sample syllabus prior to the first class. But self-taught swimmers, tennis players, actors, salesmen, teachers, and neurosurgeons probably are not as effective as they might have been with some guidance. Demosthenes, according to legend, filled his mouth with pebbles and practiced speaking at the shoreline above the roar of the breaking waves. But Demosthenes was an uncommon orator, and even he had his mentors. At the least, if the training is any good, then teachers can learn more efficiently what their options are.

Thus, in the spirit of the fifth canon of rhetoric, and continuing to draw on that tradition, let's proceed to see what pedagogical advice can be given in Composition and Rhetoric.

PEDAGOGY

Teaching begins, on the one hand, with an overarching philosophy and goal, and on the other hand, teaching begins with a series of statements, responses, interactions, questions, and more. We can think about teaching, in other words, from the top down, a satellite view of the terrain covered by a course; or from the bottom up, a step-by-step description of everything from the syllabus and writing assignments to the raised eyebrow at a question that suggests the student hasn't done the assigned reading. Which comes first – the individual bits of teaching or the guiding principles? How will you know what to say and do on the first day of class if you don't have a theory to drive your practice? But how can you evolve a philosophy without an understanding of the activities that are possible? Like writing an essay – you can't write the first sentence without knowing what you're going to say, but you can't discover what you're going to say without writing the first and subsequent sentences – teaching is an impossible chicken-and-egg dilemma. It's a small miracle whenever it works.

What overarching philosophy of writing instruction will guide your teaching? What exactly are you going to do during the first ten minutes of the first class? And then? First let's examine teaching a Composition and Rhetoric course from the top down, surveying the range of theories that might drive the course. Then we'll consider the individual pieces of the course, looking from the bottom up.

A classic and still-useful survey of the theories available is James Berlin's "Contemporary Composition: The Major Pedagogical Theories," published in 1982, the same year that Maxine Hairston was describing the discipline's paradigm shift from product- to process-oriented instruction. Berlin noted that every approach to the teaching of writing conceptualized the writing process in some way, and so it wasn't very useful to distinguish writing pedagogy simply in terms of "process" versus "product," the usual dichotomy. Berlin suggested that we think in terms of how different approaches view the world, language, rhetoric, and truth. Four contrasting epistemologies – Aristotelian, Current-Traditional, Neo-Platonic, and Epistemic – generate different views of the writing process, Berlin argued. The world, according to the Aristotelian and the Current-Traditional perspectives, exists independently of us and is perceived by our senses. This is the commonsense, ordinary view of the world, but it's not the only way to think about things. From a Neo-Platonic point of view, the world is always in flux, and our perceptions of it are unreliable. And from an Epistemic vantage point, there is a gap between the mind and the world, and therefore the external world is necessarily constructed by the perceiver using contextual, social, and relational frames.

How do different approaches view the nature of truth? The Aristotelian approach, Berlin says, sees truth as the result of mental operations performed upon the sense data we receive. These logical operations conform to the mind and to the universe: language and thinking are suited to the world we inhabit. Words correspond to reality when used properly. The Current-Traditional stance also sees truth as the result of mental operations, but with a striking difference, assuming that we should rely upon observation, not logic; induction, not deduction. The Neo-Platonic view sees truth as the result of internal apprehension: the individual soul grasps it. Thus, truth can be apprehended but it can't be communicated fully to others. They must see the truth for themselves. And the Epistemic view sees truth as something that is contingent and constructed: the truth is a transaction between sense data and mental structures. As such, the truth is subject to social influences, and so an individual's perceptions should be validated by others. Truth, in other words, is a kind of community project, from the Epistemic perspective.

If you believe that rhetoric deals with the probable – with law, politics, public behavior; if you think rhetoric is concerned primarily with finding arguments – rational and emotional – to persuade an audience, then you're an Aristotelian, in Berlin's schema. If you see rhetoric as concerned with all discourse and how to adapt a pre-existing message to an audience, then your outlook is Current-Traditional, according to Berlin. If you think rhetoric shapes community by struggling for one version of reality versus another, then your vantage point is Epistemic: rhetoric is crucial because it is "at the center of the discovery of truth." The nature of language varies with the different approaches also: the word stands for something, apart from its meaning within a sentence (Aristotelian); the word corresponds with reality, if we use it carefully (Current-Traditional);

the word is inadequate for conveying reality, but it can inspire others to move toward some insight (Neo-Platonic); the word creates the world, determining what shape it can take (Epistemic).

Does it matter where, philosophically, the writing teacher stands with regard to the world, truth, rhetoric, and language? Berlin's framework allows teachers to think about the assumptions underlying their practices, to consider whether their courses are philosophically coherent, to think about the instruction we are providing in relation to what we are expecting from students. To take an obvious example, a teacher might discover that the course's activities are focused upon an Aristotelian approach, stressing logic and reasoning, but the work is being judged by Epistemic standards, by how the writing constructs and addresses a particular context and community. Or, perhaps some aspects of the course proceed from Current-Traditional assumptions (stressing correctness and clarity), and other parts of the course might be based on Neo-Platonic assumptions (stressing inspiration and imagination).

At the same time, some limitations to Berlin's framework have been manifest: Berlin's advocacy of the Epistemic approach raised the possibility that the other approaches were in a sense foils for his case. Consider by way of contrast how Timothy Donovan and Ben McClelland, in 1980, divided up the field in their collection of essays, *Eight Approaches to Teaching Composition*. Donovan and McClelland's contributors divided the field into pure process, prose models, experiential, rhetorical, epistemic, basic, conferencing, and cross-disciplinary. Although these categories lacked the philosophical neatness of Berlin's schema, they did capture overlooked aspects of pedagogical practice: conferencing, for instance, might be seen as a distinctive approach or as an activity within any number of different philosophies. In 1986, Lester Faigley argued that the competing theories of process should be seen as expressive, cognitive, social, and Marxist. William Woods argued that the field should be divided into "student-centered" and "discipline-centered" pedagogies, with the latter aiming to socialize students, giving them the skills and values of academia, and the former aiming to elicit and refine the talent and ability inherent within the students.

In 2001, Gary Tate, Amy Rupiper, and Kurt Schick offered *A Guide to Composition Pedagogies*, a collection of essays by accomplished figures that covered the following: "Process Pedagogy," "Expressive Pedagogy: Practice/Theory, Theory/Practice," "Rhetorical Pedagogy," "Collaborative Pedagogy," "Cultural Studies and Composition," "Critical Pedagogy: Dreaming of Democracy," "Feminist Pedagogy," "Community-Service Pedagogy," "The Pedagogy of Writing Across the Curriculum," "Writing Center Pedagogy," "On the Academic Margins: Basic Writing Pedagogy," and "Technology and the Teaching of Writing." This is a valuable volume: the essays by Ann George (on critical pedagogy) and Susan Jarratt (on feminist composition), for instance, are superb, still essential reading. But as a way of organizing the field and displaying the different pedagogies available, the categories seem a bit like those in Jorge Luis Borges's famous story, "The Analytical Language of John Wilkins," which wonderfully divides the creatures of the earth into "those that belong to the Emperor, embalmed ones, those that are trained, suckling pigs, mermaids, fabulous ones, stray dogs, those included in the present classification, those that tremble as if they were mad, innumerable ones, those drawn with a very fine camelhair brush, others, those that have just broken a flower vase, those that from a long way off look like flies."

But Tate, Rupiper, and Schick are able to divide composition pedagogies in an overlapping and ambiguously related manner because such a consensus among composition specialists has emerged about how to teach writing. Since the 1980s compositionists have widely assumed that writing courses should focus on writing, not grammar quizzes or the analysis of model readings or exercises; that students should receive feedback on their drafts and have the opportunity to revise (writing is re-writing); that this feedback can usefully extend beyond the teacher to include the students' peers; that this feedback should be constructive; that invention is important for all writers, including students; that writing is a powerful learning tool; and much else. So does the writing teacher really face any substantial options, beyond, say, what sort of sartorial image to project? If there is extensive agreement about pedagogical theory, there is nonetheless considerable diversity about the goal of process teaching, and the resulting implementation of that theory. There are theories, in other words, that are based not upon epistemology, but are driven instead by the social purpose of writing instruction, by politics.

Paulo Freire's *Pedagogy of the Oppressed* has been an especially powerful theoretical model for Composition and Rhetoric. Freire's work was first published in Portuguese in the revolutionary year of 1968, and in English in 1969, but the English translation published by Continuum in 1982 (a busy year!) provided widespread access to his work. Freire argued that educators must oppose the "banking concept" of education with a "problem-posing" approach. In the banking theory of education, teachers deposit the oppressor's knowledge to ensure that students remain "docile, unthreatening servants of the state." As Freire puts it:

> Banking education resists dialogue; problem-posing education regards dialogue as indispensable.... Banking education treats students as objects of assistance; problem-posing education makes them critical thinkers. Banking education inhibits creativity and domesticates.... Problem-posing education bases itself on creativity and stimulates true reflection and action upon reality. (71)

Even though Freire's pedagogy was designed to serve poor and illiterate Brazilians, his work has been embraced by many developed-world writing teachers, especially in the United States, because it connected the classroom to society and progressive change. For Jane Tompkins, Freire offered "a way to make teaching more enjoyable and less anxiety-producing," authorizing a liberatory classroom practice, consistent with her political beliefs. For bell hooks, in *Teaching* to *Transgress*, Freire inspires teachers to move "against and beyond boundaries" and work for radical change. As Richard Miller puts it, "Freire has given teachers a way to see themselves as something other than the mindless functionaries of the state apparatus responsible for tidying the prose of the next generation of bureaucrats" ("Arts of Complicity" 11). It seems safe to say that very few people who have gotten advanced degrees in the humanities really wanted to be bankers; we want to be problem-posers, thinkers, life-long learners ourselves. And it is easy to see how process writing teachers, open to the idea that students are teaching, and teachers are learning, would find Freire's philosophy especially inviting. Ira Shor, Patricia Bizzell, Eleanor Kutz and Hephzibah Roskelly, among others, have advocated importing Freire's ideas into the classroom.

However, there are some worrisome implications with regard to incorporating Freire into our theories of Composition, as Peter Elbow, James Berlin, Peter North, and others have pointed out. Freire insists that the teacher, "together with the students," must create "the conditions under which knowledge at the level of *doxa* is superseded by true knowledge, at the level of the *logos*" (68). How can the teacher be a problem-poser if there is some "true knowledge" that the students and teachers are expected to gain? If the teacher has the answer – and Freire certainly believes that he does: resist the oppressor: revolution – then there is in a sense only the illusion of collaboratively posing and pursuing a problem. Freire even asserts that those who pull back from his pedagogy do so only because they realize "if their analysis of the situation goes any deeper," then they will have to agree with him or "reaffirm" their myths. Maxine Hairston was an early critic of "liberation" politics in the classroom, arguing that "we shouldn't even have to mention our anger about racism and sexism in our society – that's given" ("Diversity" 187). The classroom, Hairston maintained, is not the place for politics, progressive or otherwise. Richard Miller, who reports that he was "swept away by Freire's vision" early in his career, does acknowledge that his students "resisted the 'politicization' of the classroom," and the quality of their work seemed little different from the work in other "more traditional" classrooms (11).

Still, James Berlin's assertion that "a way of teaching is never innocent" is difficult to dismiss ("Rhetoric and Ideology" 492), and many teachers have decided to make explicit the political contexts of their teaching. Donald Lazare, for instance, attacks "the present, generally unquestioned (and even unconscious) imposition of capitalist, white-male, heterosexual ideology that pervades American education" (190). Lazare is writing in 1995, and I would like to think that his assessment would be more positive today. Certainly, many people in Composition see the leading edge for social change going through writing classrooms. Susan Jarratt and others have in fact argued that certain standard practices in Composition and Rhetoric "are especially useful for advancing ... feminist goals" (Tate *et al.*, *Guide* 124) – collaboration and revision, for instance. Here's Jarratt:

> As Lisa Ede and Andrea Lunsford explain in *Singular Texts/ Plural Authors*, writing collaboratively challenges the notion of an isolated and autonomous self – a masculinist model – and replaces it with a multivocal, relational writing process. Revision, as well, has radical feminist potential as yet little recognized ...

Is it a caricature to say that the "isolated and autonomous self" is "a masculinist model"? What do we do with all the emphasis on "teamwork" that pervades male-dominated sports? When a woman makes an independent and innovative accomplishment, is she behaving in a masculinist fashion?

Even for teachers who might agree writing courses should be about writing, not politics of any kind, the fact remains that our lives are inescapably political. In a culture that is awakened to feminist issues, how can students write about almost anything without raising such concerns in some way? Theory becomes practice, of course, and the questions of what students should write about, what they should read, what is the purpose of talking about their writing and reading – these questions and other practical, day-to-day matters become inescapable and bound up with our largest philosophical issues. Writing pedagogy arguably begins (and I'm not kidding here) with your answer to the question of the meaning of life. After all, what are we here for? Composition and Rhetoric asks the teacher to confront his or her role in engaging with the political ideas of students in ways that other disciplines do not.

Consider Karen Kopelson's essay, "Of Ambiguity and Erasure: The Perils of Performative Pedagogy," in which Kopelson assumes that her pedagogical goals include advancing a political agenda. "The question," Kopelson says, "the dilemma, is how to advocate those political positions to which we are committed" when students are resistant to them (564). Kopelson is speaking in particular about her status as a lesbian, which she believes is obvious since she is, in her own view, "pretty much a walking stereotype" (563). "We know," Kopelson notes, "that advocating particular political positions in the classroom becomes much more highly charged and fraught with risk when we are going to be read as occupying somehow 'corresponding' identity positions, and thus as advancing political/pedagogical 'agendas' based on or arising from those identity positions" (564). Kopelson agrees with the "performative pedagogy" of Susan Talburt and others, which strategically presents an ambiguous identity, allowing straight students to think "perhaps" she is straight. In her fascinating essay, Kopelson reveals that her efforts to enact a "productively indeterminate" teacher identity actually resulted in at least some of her students not only being completely unaware of her status, but also even having trouble believing, when she comes out after the course, that she is, as one student puts it, "an actual lesbian." Another student is positively stunned when she tells him she is a feminist. He would never have guessed, apparently, even though they read Atwood's *Handmaid's Tale* and Octavia Butler's *Kindred*. While some teachers would find that impartiality ideal, Kopelson does not: "I meant to perform my 'savvy' neutrality – especially in this particular writing course, which had been focused on gender and sexuality issues. I did not, however, mean to *disappear*" (566).

There are at least two issues involved here for anyone teaching writing: First, will your course use politics to teach writing, or use writing instruction to teach politics? Although we may see that writing is unavoidably entangled in social awareness, the commitment to advancing any position arguably usually exceeds the course description. Would we be comfortable with a Geology course that discusses natural gas and oil deposits from the point of view that they should be exploited aggressively, without regard to the environmental consequences, because God obviously placed those resources there for mankind to use? What does academic freedom allow? Academic freedom doesn't allow a Geology professor to teach Shakespeare's tragedies in Geology 101. Nor should it address theology, in my opinion. By the same token, a course in writing should deal with writing. Students should learn how to use political materials, how to address political audiences, how to make political arguments, and how to resist them, but in general they shouldn't be taught which side of a political debate to be on. Still, I have had a student who turned in an essay about torturing rabbits, which turned out to be a failed satire. Had he been serious, I would have been comfortable asking him to write on another topic and consider seeking some counseling. But within a rather broad range, I think we are better off if we pose the right problems and give students the right tools, trusting them to find the right sides for themselves.

Second, advancing a political position unavoidably places students in an awkward position. Of course, life itself is sometimes awkward, but consider: Do the students echo the teacher's position if it is different from their own, or do they risk expressing their authentic views? If they disagree with the teacher, and the teacher criticizes their writing, how can they determine that it's not their politics that's really at fault? After deciding several hundred grade appeals, I can assure you that sometimes teachers do lose their bearings when a student voices opinions that offend them, but even more often, in my experience, students believe that they're not being treated fairly, when really in truth they are. Teachers, to be sure, are sometimes not as good at acting as they believe they are; students may well know where their teacher is coming from despite any efforts to display neutrality. But by working to convince students that their logic and expression counts, not their political values, teachers actually have the best chance, I believe, to influence their students, showing them how to think and write. Thus, Freire's problem-posing stance, without the commitment to a particular solution to the problem, seems especially appropriate.

ACTIO

Let's now consider pedagogy from the bottom up, thinking not in terms of overarching theories, but rather particular activities and policies – the equivalent of the hand gestures and stances of delivering a writing course, the actual performance, which classical rhetoric calls *"actio."* I'll arrange this discussion chronologically in terms of a checklist.

First contact

1. Constructing yourself and your syllabus: course description, grades, writing assignments, readings, activities

Whether you write it, or it's given to you, the syllabus is the governing document, the Declaration of Independence and the Constitution in a sense, for your class (supplemented of course by the policies of the institution). This document provides the framework for what you're going to do, setting the tone and suggesting what to expect. If the tone of your syllabus, which I will assume includes a statement of your course policies, implies that you have low expectations or that you aren't really happy to be teaching the course or that you are a humorless dullard, then the course is off to a bad start. You want to suggest that the course is going to be engaging, challenging, fair, and useful. You need to think of the syllabus in terms of a contract – not only what you are requiring of the students, but also what they may expect from you. So it's a good idea to have a sentence some-where indicating that the assignments and due dates are tentative and subject to change, and that adjustments, if needed, will be made by announcements in class and/or the circulation or posting of a new syllabus. And what else ought to be in the syllabus that should be distributed to students on the first day of class?

Like any official document, it has a title: the name of the course and its unique designation, including its location. (Find the classroom before the first day. Obviously you'll want to arrive early to class, especially on the first day, and the classroom might not be where you think it is.) The document has an author, or at least an exe-cutor, and that's you. First-time teachers understandably often worry about many things, including what their students should call them (which is related to what they're going to call their students), how to dress, whether to stand at the front of the room or move around, lecture or discuss or both, and much more. Here's James Lang in his helpful and engaging book, *On Course: A Week-By-Week Guide to Your First Semester of College Teaching*, describing his first class meeting:

> Concerned about the fact that I was probably only three years older than the students I would find in the class, I decided to forget about trying to impress them with my authority, and to try instead to seem like one of them – so I was wearing sandals, a pair of navy-blue khakis that I had cut raggedly into shorts, and a white T-shirt. I was nervous, so I kept it short. I gave them the syllabus and the first assignment sheet for the course, read through both documents, and then let the students go. (21)

Lang humorously invites his readers to send him a postcard listing all of the bad decisions here to be eligible for a drawing for a free lunch. It's a smorgasbord of bad ideas.

Some academics might ridicule even considering such issues – what students should call you, what you should wear, what you should call them – but in terms of the rhetorical situation of delivering the class most effectively, it seems unrealistic to ignore them or pretend they don't matter. If you try to blend in with the students for instance, sartorially, authoritatively, even nominally, then you're being disingenuous. You can't be one of the students and teach the class. They know that, although they may be willing to pretend along with you that they don't. In truth, you have to assume the teacher's role. But that doesn't mean that there should be a dress code and formal titles. I know one superb teacher who gets his students to tackle the most demanding philosophical and theoretical issues, who has undergraduates devouring Derrida, Lyotard, Foucault, Heidegger – and he wears jeans and T-shirts (sometimes with holes, not exactly crisply pressed). I don't know whether he chews tobacco in his classroom, but he carries a little spit cup into faculty meetings. I don't know of anyone else who could pull off what he does, but he's undeniably brilliant, serious, scholarly, brash, energetic, witty. Perhaps his personal presentation disarms his students, allowing him to slip in under the radar the most rigorous and demanding reading lists and assignments imaginable. His students call him by his first name, at least until they evolve an affectionate nickname. I know someone else who wears French-cuffed shirts, bow-ties, calls his students by their last names, preceded by "Mr." or "Ms." – and he doesn't have to say to the students, please call me "Professor Lincoln" (not his name, by the way). The question is not which strategy is better – formal, informal, a contradictory mixture? The question is – what will work best for you?

I think that students should view every class as an important professional event. I dress up, collared shirt and tie, jacket, nice pants, real shoes; and I try to project the sense that I'm really excited about the course, but I'm also very serious. I use humor as a tool, but I don't see my job as entertaining the students. I want to be seen as concerned about my students, reasonable, but absolutely dedicated to their maximal intellectual advancement. When I was younger, when students might have called me by my first name, they never did: I was "Mr. Lynn," then "Dr. Lynn," in part because I had on a tie, and because they were "Mr. Smith," "Ms. Rogers," etc. I've found that this sort of surface formality works for me, allowing me, for instance, to kid my students gently without seeming too familiar, I think. If you don't put your first name on the syllabus, you're suggesting that you want to be called by your last name. Or, if you tell students how to pronounce your last name, that too is a hint. If you're not a professor, then don't list yourself as "Professor" on the syllabus. If students refer to you as "Dr. Frankenstein," and your last name is indeed Frankenstein but you don't have a doctorate, do correct them. By the same token, although the practice may be different at your school (especially if it's in the Ivy League), I think it's okay gently to correct students who call you "Ms." or "Mr." and you do have a doctorate. It's an appropriate recognition.

One approach to sartorial self-delivery is to consider how you would dress for an interview to get the job that you have. You probably won't go wrong wearing that, even if all your colleagues wear stained and wrinkled overalls. Any tie that is a "conversation starter" is no doubt a bad idea. It's a mistake to wear anything in the classroom that might reasonably make your students uncomfortable, whether it's a political campaign button (more on this in a moment) or funny T-shirt, unusual piercings, exposed tattoos, cleavage, chest hair, dark sunglasses, Chicago Cubs baseball hat. Students, to be sure, in my experience generally exhibit considerable tolerance, especially if the teacher is dedicated and capable. But there's no reason to make your appearance an obstacle to overcome.

Likewise, the presentation of your syllabus should be a reflection of the classroom environment that you expect. Here are some things to avoid: lavender paper, onionskin paper, textured paper, any other kind of odd paper, weird fonts, grammatical errors, missing words, punctuation errors. Your syllabus is a piece of writing: it should represent your best rhetorical efforts. So what information should be conveyed? After the name of the course, the time and place of meeting, and your name, you want a course description, a brief explanation of what will be in the course and what students will come away with. Books and articles often begin with a quotation, and thinking of your syllabus as a piece of writing, you might use a quotation to lead into the course description. Whenever I teach a course in the history of rhetoric, I use this quotation from C. S. Lewis as the epigraph for my syllabus: "Rhetoric is the greatest barrier between us and our ancestors." Lewis's observation asserts the importance of the course: if you want to connect to the past, you've got to understand rhetoric. Imagine how the following three quotations would grab students' attention, and would frame students' expectations differently:

> I try to leave out the parts that people skip.
>
> Elmore Leonard

> If there's a book you really want to read, but it hasn't been written yet, then you must write it.
>
> Toni Morrison

> The act of putting pen to paper encourages pause for thought, this in turn makes us think more deeply about life, which helps us regain our equilibrium.
>
> Norbet Platt

Here's an example of how a syllabus might begin:

Composition and Rhetoric: English 101 (049)
MWF 10:10–11:00, Gambrell Hall 410
Ms. Anna Williams

"Writing became such a process of discovery that I couldn't wait to get to work in the morning: I wanted to know what I was going to say." – Sharon O'Brien

Course Description
English 101 is designed to offer you structured, sustained practice in critical reading, analysis and composing. During the semester, you will read a range of challenging, linguistically rich texts in a variety of genres – which could include academic, literary,

rhetorical, cultural, and multimedia works – and write expository and analytical essays in response to them. Through these
reading and writing assignments, you will explore the intercon-
nectedness of reading and writing, and you will learn how to use
both reading and writing as venues for inquiry, learning, thinking, interpretation, and communication. The course will provide
instruction and individualized feedback to help you advance as a
careful, thoughtful reader and as an effective writer.[6]

You may want to call the "course description" something
livelier, and you also may want to use a different heading for the
necessary information about where your office is located, when you
plan to be there, how to get in touch with you (other than by coming by during your office hours), which for most people is an email
address and/or a mailbox in the department, and when it's okay to
call you at home, if it ever is. I always include my at-home number
with guidance about when it's too late to call, and students have
rarely called me and never after-hours. Including that information
does send the message that you want to be available, but if you're
uncomfortable about giving out your home and/or cell phone numbers, then don't. You can demonstrate your interest in your students
in many other ways.

You'll want to give students a sense up front what the course
assignments will be. Again, this may not be something that you'll
have to decide if there is a standard syllabus, but if it's up to you,
how many writing assignments will you have, and what will they
be? If we agree that the more students write, the more opportunities
they have to improve (within reason, of course; we don't want them
to flunk their other courses or collapse walking to class), then what
is the maximum amount of writing that can satisfyingly (not puni-
tively) be assigned in a semester? Here's what I have found works
well: a one-to-two page assignment due every week, replaced every
fourth week by a revision of one of the three preceding papers; and at

the end, a final revision of one paper. This sounds like an incredible amount of writing: In other words, in a fifteen-week course, students will have an original paper due (skipping the first week) at the end of weeks 2, 3, 4, 6, 7, 8, 10, 11, and 12. Revisions of selected papers will be due at the end of weeks 5, 9, and 13, with an additional revision of a selected paper due at the end of week 14. This plan gives you a week's cushion, which can be a week to review for the final exam if you're able to keep up (and yes, you should definitely give a final exam, as I'll explain below).

Here are some things that I like about this plan:

- Students don't have to revise every essay. They can decide, in consultation with their teacher or peers, which pieces are most promising, which revisions would teach them the most.
- The essays are relatively short, discouraging padding, encouraging substance.
- With weekly essays, students get lots of experience developing a topic. They get to experience the writing process multiple times.
- Students have more chances to benefit from feedback. They have more grades to average, reducing the exposure for any particular essay, thus encouraging an essential behavior in writing growth: risk taking.
- They also have more chances to comment on their classmates' work.

The drawback to this plan, however, is obvious: How will the teacher survive? Nine essays? Three revisions? My sense is that the average number of essays for writing courses in college is four to six. But here's how this works: First, we're talking only nine to eighteen original pages, plus another three to six revised pages. For each student, then, it's the equivalent of a major research paper. Still, this is a lot of material for the teacher to read carefully and comment upon thoroughly. Fortunately, research on the efficacy of teacher responses shows us that students can make use of a limited number of comments, and further that positive encouragements should substantially outnumber negative comments. Although it may be satisfying for the teacher to mark every error, missed opportunity, weakness, and virtue, all that investment of time is misdirected. It requires, to be sure, great discipline to focus on a few areas for improvement, commend some good things about an essay, and return the paper. But by limiting your comments to what the student can understand and deal with, you'll be doing a better job, working smarter, not harder.

For this strategy to work, it's important for your students to understand what you're doing – to explain in your syllabus, and revisit periodically, that you will not be marking every error, any more than you'll be marking everything that's correct! Instead, you'll be intervening selectively. If you mark a particular kind of punctuation error, for instance, the student should recognize that there may be other instances of the same or similar errors. To underscore this point, I may annotate a student's paper until I think there is enough for the student to work with, and then I'll draw a line across the page at that point, indicating that my comments end at that point.

In addition to understanding how their teacher will respond to their work, students also should know how their grades will be determined. Many writing teachers believe it's counterproductive to put grades on individual papers: students certainly will pay more attention to your comments in the absence of a grade. If the grade is good, they may assume they don't need to read your comments carefully since obviously they did well. If the grade is bad, they may not read your comments carefully because they're dispirited or because they assume you're not very astute, having failed to appreciate their performance. A portfolio approach to grades, adapted from the fine arts, allows teachers to assign a grade at the end of the course. The teacher's roles as coach and judge, as Peter Elbow has noted, are contradictory, and the portfolio approach to grading allows the teacher to focus on coaching during the course. For some students, however, the absence of grades is stressful and distracting, and these students should be encouraged to ask the teacher how they're doing so far, I think. And it seems only fair that students who are doing poorly should be made aware of their situation.

If you do decide to go with a portfolio system, your syllabus should spell out how portfolios will be evaluated. Will you read through the entire folder and then give an impressionistic, holistic grade? What will your impression be based upon? Will you grade each piece of work, then calculate an average? Will later work count more than earlier? Will you allow students to select some essays out, so that you're only grading what they see as their best work? Many departments and programs have guidelines for grades that are available to students, rubrics that indicate the features of work that should receive an A, B, C, D, and F. You'll find, as you might expect, considerable consistency in these standards. Sometime in the 1980s, I adapted the grading criteria that John Trimble was using at the University of Texas (with his permission, of course), and those criteria have been revised and tweaked over the years. Here are the standards used at the University of South Carolina for an "A" and a "C" paper, which are very similar to the standards at many colleges and universities. (The standards for other grades are available at the First-Year English Program's website.)

The "A" Paper

The "A" paper surpasses requirements of the assignment in a fresh and sophisticated manner, using precise and effective language that helps the audience understand and engage in the issue at hand. The paper effectively meets the needs of the rhetorical situation in terms of establishing the writer's stance, attention to audience, purpose for writing, and sensitivity to context. When appropriate to the assignment, the writer demonstrates expertise in employing the artistic appeals of ethos, logos, and pathos appropriately. If revision is required, the writer does more than correct surface errors in an effort to improve the content and presentation of the essay.

The topic itself is clearly defined, focused, and supported. The essay has a clear and provocative thesis that is supported with specific and appropriate evidence, examples, and details. Any outside sources of information are used carefully and cited appropriately. The essay demonstrates good judgment and an awareness of the topic's complexities.

The organization is appropriate for the purpose and subject of the paper. The introduction establishes a context, purpose, and audience for writing and contains a focused thesis statement. The subsequent paragraphs are controlled by explicit or implicit topic sentences; they are well developed; and they progress logically toward the conclusion. (If appropriate, headings and subheadings are used.) The conclusion moves beyond a mere restatement of the introduction, offering implications for or the significance of the topic.

The prose is clear, readable, and sometimes memorable. It contains few if any errors in grammar or usage, and none of these undermines the effectiveness of the paper. The essay shows proficiency with style (subordination, variation of sentence and paragraph lengths, interesting vocabulary, figurative language) and creativity in presentation.

The "C" Paper

The "C" paper attempts to follow the assignment and demonstrates some sense of audience and purpose. But the essay as a whole fails to fulfill expectations because of flaws in design and/or execution. The paper shows minimal improvement on revision.

The topic is defined only generally; the thesis statement is merely adequate (it may be too broad, for example); and the supporting evidence, while gathered and used responsibly, is, nevertheless, often obvious and easily accessible. The writer demonstrates little awareness of the topic's complexity or other points of view, leaving the paper with minor imperfections or inconsistencies in development, organization, and reasoning.

The organization is fairly clear. The reader could outline the presentation, despite the occasional lack of topic sentences. Paragraphs have adequate development and are divided appropriately. Transitions are present, but they are mechanical.

The expression is competent. Sentence structure is unsophisticated, relying on simple and compound sentences. Word choice is correct though limited. The paper contains errors in spelling, usage, and/or punctuation, though these do not affect the audience's ability to understand the essay. The paper may contain inflated language, wordy structures, and clichés.

Although these descriptions are lucid and detailed, most students really need some examples to get a sense for example of how a "clear and provocative thesis" differs from a "merely adequate one." So a useful activity early in the semester, perhaps even on the first day, involves simply reading and discussing sample student papers. You'll want to do this in an atmosphere of encouragement and constructive criticism, so when you're talking about a "C" paper, the point is not to ridicule or criticize, but to identify how it could be better. It's especially effective, therefore, if you can also circulate an improved revision of that paper. Obviously, if you're a new teacher, you'll have to rely on your colleagues for illustrations. You'll want to establish a network of people who will help you (ask: most people are happy to be considered experts) and a file of illustrations as you go along. Student papers that you circulate should have the name and identifying information removed. Should you have the permission of the students to use their work, even if it isn't attributed? Is it even fair to use their work with their permission?

Your syllabus is a good place to address this issue, followed up by a class discussion, indicating to your students that informed writing classrooms today are collaborative enterprises, that they will be reading the work of their classmates and sharing their own work in a mutually supportive and beneficial environment. The students should know that this collaboration will include using their work as illustrations or examples, and they should be reassured that their work will be treated respectfully. At the same time, the students should realize how a writing workshop works: in particular, it's important for all the participants to provide honest and sincere feedback that is designed to improve the piece of writing and the writer, while at the same time being tactful and supportive. Students, especially in the most introductory classes, may wonder whether they really can contribute anything to the discussion of a piece of writing. What do they know? And of course what they know is how the work affects them, what they notice, what is clear, what isn't, what's interesting, what's boring. Students' responses over the course of a semester should become more informed and sophisticated, but even at the outset, they can provide valuable insights for their classmates. As they read each others' work, they will inevitably gain some sense of quality, of what makes for a better piece of writing.

For some teachers, either the system they're in or their own constitution really limits their ability or willingness to leave grades off of individual papers, and so some sort of middle ground might be desired. For instance, I've often used a grading system that places papers into Inferno, Purgatory, or Paradise, with three levels for each category. Thus, Inferno 3 is the worst possible paper, and Paradise 1 is the best. This system doesn't map onto the A/B/C system exactly, but it does give students a definite indication of where their paper ranks, relatively speaking. They don't know exactly what Purgatory 3 translates into (and I try to resist providing that, unless I think it would be useful for the student to know), but they know it could have been worse and needs to be better. For revising, their concrete goal is to move the paper toward Paradise. In some classes, I've allowed students unlimited revisions, and when I've had the time to do that, it has been quite satisfying to watch their papers work their way up the scale.

Whether you have writing assignments due every week, or every third week, or every class meeting will obviously influence the kinds of assignments that you give. Again, you may be given the assignments, or you may have complete freedom to invent them. The assignments, I'm convinced, matter much less than we think. I've seen wonderful writing emerge from what might seem like a silly assignment: the teacher picks up a fallen leaf for each student on the way to class, hands them out, then says "Write two pages about your leaf." For what audience? For what purpose? "You can work that out," the teacher said, with an excited smile. "I have great faith in you to do some excellent work." I've also seen terrific writing come out of lengthy, brilliant, step-by-step directions, leading the students through an analysis of a particular audience, a particular task, particular materials. Themed classes can be quite enriching: Writing about the Environment, The Meaning of Life, Detective Stories. Some teachers prefer to let students evolve their own topics, and if you're careful to work with the students enough to preclude the powerful temptations to borrow writing, this open-endedness can work beautifully.

There are of course theoretical frameworks that can guide the kinds of assignments you give. James Kinneavy's aims and modes, for instance, have been used in many places to provide a structure for syllabi. If you assign an expressive essay, a persuasive essay, a referential essay, and a literary essay, your students will have gotten some experience with all four aims. To cover the modes, you need to assign a description, a narration, a process, and an evaluation. In Kinneavy's model, these aims and modes cover the kinds of writing students might do. Personally, I like to give students a variety, including a few entirely open-ended assignments, some vague prompts (write a letter to the editor of your hometown newspaper; write a letter to your senator), and some detailed assignments that require following directions (read three recent articles about the fence on the Mexican border and consider in an article for the student newspaper how effective you believe it will be; go to Trinity Cathedral's graveyard, pick a person who is buried there, and write an obituary for that person: no other research, besides visiting the graveyard, is permitted for this first draft).

The kinds of writing assignments that work best, according to the research surveyed by George Hillocks (*Research*), are those that are "environmental" in Hillocks's special sense: they immerse the student in a context and require the analysis of information and the shaping of the essay for a particular audience. Such essays are "real-world" assignments – except the world may be invented: that is, students may be given information about a community (population, economy, climate, etc.) and given a particular problem to address for an audience in that imaginary community. What students lose as assignments become more specific is the opportunity to imagine and create their audience and purpose. What they gain with more specific assignments is the ability to follow directions, to perform within specified parameters. Thus, although some readers may find my agreeableness appalling, I truly don't think it matters greatly what students are writing about. But, obviously, the course will be more fun if they're engaged and excited about what they're writing – but even then, one could argue that you need to learn how to write about things that aren't always scintillating: that's the way that the real world works. Finally, although I'm sure that a good writing course can be delivered by a talented teacher using only the students' own work as the text in the class, there are very obvious benefits to assigning some exemplary and/or stimulating readings. Students can respond to essays, letters, stories, poems, advertisements, corporate reports, just about anything. If the writing is adroit, students can imitate what works; if it's poor, then they can identify moves to avoid.

What else does your syllabus need to address? Let's turn now to several persistently thorny issues.

2. Constructing yourself, part 2: Determining your policies
on attendance, tardiness, late papers, and participation

What should your policy on attendance be? Some teachers don't take attendance, saying for instance that students are adults and they should be able to decide whether they want to attend. Or they may say that if the classroom activities are interesting and important enough, you don't need to take attendance – the students will be there. Or they may say that taking attendance is distracting, or starts the class on the wrong note, or takes too much time especially in a larger class, or something else. Here's why you should keep track of who's attending: How can you help a student who's struggling if you don't know whether missing classes might be part of the problem? How are we helping to prepare students for their lives and their careers if we don't track attendance? The vast majority of jobs require timely and regular presence. What message are we sending about how much we value the class if we don't even bother to record who's there and who isn't? The semester that I didn't take attendance, I found that for some students the weekends were beginning on Thursday; breaks were beginning a day or two early; and I was constantly having to answer questions from someone who had missed class. Of course you can give quizzes and assign grades to in-class activities, and that will encourage attendance, but go ahead and take the roll: it will help you to learn the students' names, and it will say to them, "I care about whether you're here. You need to be here." At my university, teachers *may* impose a grade penalty after a student has missed over 10 percent of the classes; in our writing program, if the student misses over 25 percent, he or she cannot earn a passing grade. These seem to be reasonable policies. I will always listen to students' explanations, and I tell them on the syllabus that if they are truly sick, I would prefer that they not attend class, especially if they have something contagious. I encourage them to get notes from the health center or their personal physicians documenting their illnesses, just to keep everyone honest. I view missing class because of the flu differently from missing the class because of a hangover. And so I don't understand why some teachers put on their syllabi that they don't have any excused absences, that every absence counts the same. If the student is having her appendix out, you cut her no slack? If she's accepting a Rhodes Scholarship, you're going to count her absent? If the CDC quarantines her because she has an airborne version of Ebola?

If you agree with me that attendance counts, and that as teachers we're smart enough to weigh particular absences, you should know that we've just opened the door to another problem: tardiness. If a student is ten minutes late, and you've marked him or her absent, then you've got to change your roll. But you can, in your syllabus, make it the student's responsibility to tell you, after class, if he or she arrived late, and make sure that you note that on your roster. How late, however, will you allow a student to arrive and still be counted present? Some teachers, determined not to deal with chronic latecomers, include a policy that says if you're five minutes late (or ten, or seven and a half), then you're counted absent. The most rigorous policy I've seen counted anyone absent who wasn't in his or her seat when the teacher started the class – and this guy would lock the door and make late students knock to get in. On the day I observed his class he was, of course, late to class himself (a traffic jam), and his students took great delight in locking him out. This sort of policy is a mistake because the beginning of any class may too easily devolve into an argument over what time it is. The best strategy, I think, is a statement in your syllabus asserting how important it is to be on time, and saying that recurrent lateness may be counted as an absence. If you combine this warning with classes that start on time, and often involve a quiz or other structured activity at the very beginning, then you'll find usually that lateness isn't a problem. And if it is, talk with the student: you never know what's going on in their lives. Although you can't fix all their problems (and you should not attempt to do amateur counseling), you may be able to help, or direct them to some help.

I suggest that you handle late papers in a similar fashion to the way that you deal with late people. That is, you need to require that papers be turned in on time, but you also need to be reasonable about exceptions. I've seen syllabi that say silly things like "LATE PAPERS ARE NOT ACCEPTED!" or "Late papers will be downgraded one letter grade for every day, including weekend days. No exceptions." This position seems absurdly harsh. The golden rule works well in this and many other things. If your grandmother died, you'd appreciate a little extra time to get your paper done. Sometimes, to be sure, students are late because they are lazy or undisciplined, and some nudging is in order, but sometimes papers are late because the student is trying very hard, or has a real problem, or the teacher's preparation for the assignment was lousy.

You'll want to indicate the weighting of the different items in the course that are graded. How much will the papers count, the quizzes, the homework? Although some teachers include effort and improvement in their grading scales, the only ethical and responsible basis for grading, I believe, is the work that students produce. It is more than difficult enough to try to evaluate fairly and consistently the work that students turn in. Assessing effort and improvement may sometimes seem easy enough, but it is impossible ultimately to establish reliable baselines that would indicate how much a student is trying or improving. We could easily wind up rewarding students for intentionally performing poorly at the outset of courses. The tangible end, the objective that can be graded, must be a series of finished manuscripts, reflecting (we hope) what the student has learned. So, I would submit, the end in mind when teaching writing is this: guiding students to demonstrate that they have learned to write effectively.

Does this mean that teachers shouldn't assign some percentage of the grade to "Classroom participation"? It is daunting, even for experienced teachers, to contemplate a classroom in which students stare silently while the teacher flails away at an inert discussion. But classroom participation, like effort or improvement, is a problematic metric. For most teachers, it's too distracting and bothersome to track who is talking how many times, and how informed or relevant or intelligent their comments are. The alternative is an impressionistic grade, which may seem fine until the "participation" grade is the difference between one letter and another, or even passing and failing – can the impression then be explained and defended? Students may believe that good class participation involves speaking up and anticipating or agreeing with the teacher's viewpoints; bad participation is keeping quiet or disagreeing. In the best of all worlds, we have a harmonious and talkative class; and in our world of *hypokrisis* and *hypokrites*, some students will find themselves choosing between an authentic or hypocritical role.

3. Conducting the first class

You have your costume for the first day ready, your syllabus written. How will you deliver the first class meeting?

First, it's okay to be a little nervous. Think of the adrenalin as an energy boost. Do resolve to enjoy yourself and have a good time. If you are miserable, your students will be also. Begin with a smile and maintain eye contact with your students. Introduce yourself, take the roll, distribute your syllabus and begin talking about the course. Some teachers like to use some ice-breaking games or activities, but these seem hokey to me, and the activities of the class itself will break the ice soon enough. I do like to have the students introduce themselves – their names, hometowns, majors. After you've discussed the course, and fielded any questions (it's okay if there aren't any), I suggest circulating some writing – some exemplary passages or brief essays, by students or professionals or both. I'd accentuate the positive in this discussion, letting the students know what you like, and essentially celebrating the samples as good writing. Ask the students to ruin a few sentences in your samples: that is, revise them so that they're worse. This is usually entertaining; students enjoy it; and it's interesting to compare the revision to the original. By seeing exactly how the passage was ruined, you can get a better sense perhaps of what was good about it in the first place.

Finally, it's a good idea to collect a sample of their writing, giving yourself some idea of just what you're working with, as well as some material potentially for the following class. I like to ask students to write about their experiences in previous writing classes and their expectations for the course. I often discover useful things.

4. *Conducting the rest of the classes: The rhythm*

Let's look at the sequence of assigning, working toward, receiving, commenting upon, and returning student papers. Whatever the assignment, even if it's "Write one or two pages about any topic of interest to you," I suggest that you make the assignment in writing: people have an amazing capacity to misunderstand things they hear, from the due date to the length to the assignment itself. There are advantages to giving out all the assignments at the beginning of the year (students know what's ahead) or one by one (you can make adjustments as you go along without making changes). Let's pretend that you are asking for weekly papers, and the first assignment is for a one-page description of their dorm room or apartment. If you don't provide guidance on the purpose and the audience, then you'll probably get a wide range of papers, ranging from emotional rants to precise descriptions. Allowing students that freedom to evolve a purpose and an audience is certainly worthwhile, encouraging their creativity. But you may want to be more specific, offering practice in following directions, and so they might imagine they're writing a letter to a board of trustees member who has asked for candid assessment of where students are actually living (an evaluative description); or perhaps they should imagine that they've been hired by a new magazine called *Interior Design* to write about how students decorate their spaces; or they should write essays for a general audience about how their living spaces reflect and/or do not reflect their personalities. Such an obvious topic can be shaped in many ways, of course.

Here's one sample assignment. I've tried to make it an interesting piece of writing, illustrating the richness and precision that I'm trying to encourage. I've tried to give it an engaging title and epigraph, and I've offered some priming questions. It identifies an audience and a complex purpose. I borrowed it from John Trimble, and

I've used it for many years as the initial essay in a writing course. It works nicely. But there are at least eight million other ways to begin a course.

The Inky Past: You and English

"'Whom are you?' said he, for he had been to night school." – George Ade

You've been sitting in English classes for years. What have you been doing – thinking, learning, failing (or refusing) to learn? To help me understand just who it is I'm teaching – where you are as a writer, how you got there, your present trajectory – and to clarify for yourself and your classmates where you're coming from, give us an account of your experience with that multi-headed creature, your past English classes. Make your recollection as honest as you can. Rainbows or sewer rats, paint it the way you see it.

Here are some questions that might be helpful to get you started:

- Can you recall two or three specific instances that seem to crystallize what you enjoyed most or least in those classes?
- Can you recreate for us two or three specific teachers who remain memorable to you?
- Can you recall how you reacted to formal grammar instruction, or comments on your papers, or some in-class activity?
- Can you recall any specific papers that you wrote? What did you think of them? What do you think now?
- Can you think of any writing taboos that you've been taught? Are there things that bug you? Or that bugged your teachers?
- Do you find yourself writing today with one of your previous teachers looking over your shoulder? Who is your imaginary audience for what you write?

> Chock this essay full of details. We don't want empty
> generalizations. And have fun. We want to have fun reading it.
> Length: one or two pages.

Before giving out an assignment, you should try it out yourself. You'll be amazed by how useful this is. But if you absolutely
don't have time to complete the assignment, then you should at
least begin it. Trying out your own assignment is extremely valuable
class preparation – it's a good investment of your time. You need to
understand from the inside what is involved in doing the assignment. Even if you're using a portfolio grading system, and you're not
going to grade individual papers, you need to have a clear sense of
what's involved in a successful paper. Such an awareness will allow
you to work much more effectively with your students as they work
through the process of writing their papers. So the first day of this
paper cycle – let's say it's a Monday – you'll discuss the assignment;
perhaps talk about some assigned reading that is relevant to the
assignment, pointing out strong features the students can adapt; and
get the students started on their drafts. One way to get them started
is to have them write for 5 minutes, then share what they've written with a couple of classmates and gather some feedback. As the
students are discussing, you can move about the room, answering
questions, reading a few of the responses, listening in.

For Wednesday, you could require the students to bring a draft
to class (thus avoiding last-minute rush writing). Students might
have a choice of reading aloud a few sentences that they like, a few
sentences that they're struggling with, or sentences they'd like some
feedback on. Students could talk about their problems with the
assignment. You could again share exemplary passages, offer some
tips on writing, discuss editing and some specific things that students should look for. On Friday, students could read each others'
work, writing comments (with a signature at the end), using different colors of ink to help you sort out who's saying what. You might

ask the students to bring two copies of their papers – one for marking up by their classmates, and one for you to mark, although frankly I find it useful to see what their peer editors are saying. Most students will tend, especially at first, to offer superficial and polite comments. They'll feel inadequate to the job of evaluating someone else's writing. You'll have to encourage them to accentuate the positive but to offer genuinely useful comments by being honest. They are, after all, as much of a reader as anyone else: their opinions are valuable. Sometimes their responses will be eccentric, even silly, but over time the wealth of response is helpful. It's a good investment of time to look at some samples of edited papers, with a variety of responses. And it's also useful to encourage students to use the standard proofreader's marks (most dictionaries feature these). Even simple comments can be quite useful: "Don't quite follow this." "I like this sentence." "Hey, nice image." "Check the punctuation here. Looks wrong to me." "This is good. Talk some more about this." For each paper, you might encourage students to look especially for particular features: effective verbs, or a particular convention of punctuation, or logical assumptions, or figurative language. Before the class ends, you might allow the authors to see the comments on their papers, writing a response to the comments, before turning in the papers to you.

It's crucial for students to double-space, allowing room for editing. It's also important for them to observe a certain decorum. If it couldn't appear on prime-time television, I say, then it's too racy for the classroom (and "Saturday Night Live" is not prime-time). If you teach long enough, you will encounter students who want to push the envelope's edge, who want to shock their classmates. If you discuss the ground rules beforehand, you can limit this likelihood, but if students do still turn in something that makes their classmates uncomfortable, you can simply ask them to provide another essay, more consistent with the standards of the course. Most students, rather than have to do more writing, will reign in their countercultural streak to some degree.

If this plan sounds easy enough, teaching writing is often indeed a lot of fun. It's amazing to me that everyone doesn't want to do it. There is some effort involved, and when you get home with the students' papers, and they're piled on your desk, it can seem an awful lot like work. The advice that you give your students should work for you too: don't procrastinate; don't try to comment on all the papers at once in a rush the night before you're going to return them. And don't try to comment on everything. Focus on a few problems, some good points, and write a brief summary guiding future work. As you're reading the papers, collect sentences and comments that you can usefully discuss with your students. Again, I'd emphasize the positive, looking for exceptionally good sentences and insightful comments. Even if you astutely identify what's wrong, students still may not have a clear idea of what's right. If we focus on examples of what we're looking for, they'll be much more likely to get it.

There are some papers, however, that even if you are determined to focus your comments, and be constructive, you'll find baffling. No matter how securely you are inhabiting whatever pedagogical theory you choose, there are papers that seem to defy useful feedback. Here for example is the first paragraph (truly it is) of a paper turned in to a teacher under my supervision some years ago:

> William Faulkner spent most of his life in Oxford, Mississippi, where he not received any of their mail. Faulkner in his fiction imagines a Mississippi county Sarttories and the aristocratic Compsons, and the white trash, dollar grabbing Snopses, from the Civil War to modern times.

What would you say to this student? The teacher wrote in one margin, "I do not follow your ideas here," and in the other margin "What's your thesis?", and circled "their" in the first sentence and "Sarttories" in the second. Although it's hard to fault an inexperienced teacher confronting this train wreck of an opening paragraph, it's also hard to imagine that the student found these comments helpful. What should the teacher say? What is going on in this paragraph? The student, it appears, has found something about Faulkner's mail delivery interesting, although it's not clear what: he lived in Oxford, but he received his mail elsewhere? The second sentence may seem totally unrelated to the first, but we can speculate that the student believes he should begin with some biographical comments about Faulkner – a sweepingly authoritative reference to his work. At this point, however, I think it's impossible to know what to say to the student, and if I were responding to this paper, I wouldn't write anything yet. All too often, I think teachers just go through a paper saying whatever occurs to them as they move through it. Let's read on and see if we can get some sense of what the student is trying to accomplish.

Here's the first part of the second paragraph, scrupulously uncorrected:

> In most of William Faulkners work, he usually has a rich family such as the Snopses or the Compsons and they always have had a negro maid or housewife. In his works Spootted Horses and That Evening Shade, he has to women that are very cute, and attractive, and both women are pregant and the really do not know whp the father of the fetus is. One could probably imagine that William Faulkner is or has had many problem with women or in his marriage.

The teacher has carefully marked the missing apostrophe, comma, and capitalization in the first sentence. He has underlined "always" and asked "how do you know?" in the margin. And he has circled "Spootted," "Shade" (the title is "That Evening Sun"), "pregant," "the" (instead of "they"), the space after "problem" (where an "s" should be), and "whp" (for "who"). And he's written "irrelevant" in the margin. Although the student may well learn that he needs to proofread – surely most of these are careless errors – again, this seems to be applying band-aids to an internal hemorrhaging case. So I still would not write anything yet, but I'm beginning to think that student does have an interest, a topic, perhaps even something to say.

The second paragraph continues:

> Faulkner also has incidents in his stories of physiccal abuse to
> women. There is a scene were Henry Armstead smacks his wife
> because she is not strong enough to handle wild horses that have
> not yet been tamed, but Mrs. Armstead like most women in our
> society had enough courage to get back up and try to help her
> husband again. In return, the horses baracade out of the stable
> and tramples over him and break his leg. In another scene we can
> also see that Nancy is beaten and kicked by Mr. Stovall. Let it
> be known that Stovall is a deacon in the church, and cashier at
> the bank. Nancy said something smart and Mr. Stovall knocks
> her down and kicks most of her teeth out. Nancy goes to jail and
> again is beaten up by the jailor.

The teacher has put a great deal of effort into marking this paper, and
the corrections to this passage are numerous. The teacher's handwriting is getting larger, and exclamation points are frequent. The
comments range from what seems to be pretty important, such as
subject-verb agreement, to what seems (in light of all the problems
here) a bit trivial, such as changing the assertion that "most" of
Nancy's teeth were knocked out to "some." The teacher circles the
"lor" part of "jailor," suggesting I suppose that it should be spelled
"jailer," and he also strikes through "that have not yet been tamed"
with reference to the wild horses – which one could argue is not
redundant, that "wild horses that have not yet been tamed" actually
makes perfect sense. The problems are indeed bewildering, but it's
hard to imagine what the student will do in response to all these
comments.

The paper has another long paragraph that also deals with
women who are abused in Faulkner's stories, which is also annotated
fairly heavily by the teacher, followed by this closing paragraph:

> In conclusion, William Faulkner had a private life was a long and
> constant struggle to stay solvent even after fame came to him.

> Although we think of Faulkner as a novelist, he wrote nearly a
> hundred short stories. Fourty-two of the best are available in his
> Collected Stories. Two of the best works from Faulkner to me are
> A Rose for Emily and Barn Burning.

The teacher has added a comma following "In conclusion" and then
simply marked through this closing paragraph with three diagonal
lines, ending with this comment: "I wish I could say something good
about this paper, Ken, but I can't. It has no point; it's poorly written."
The teacher is being honest, and he has certainly put considerable
effort into marking this paper. But imagine that you are the student
who submitted this paper. Now what? Do you have any idea how to
make the paper better, or any reason to think that you can make it
better? Do you want to read more Faulkner, or write more essays, or
work on revising this one? Should you just leave school now? At the
very least, I'd think you'd check to see what time the bars open. The
student does have lots of problems marked, but these are just identified: the student is going to have to figure out how to correct every
one of these myriad problems, if they're going to be corrected. I'm
certainly not arguing that the student doesn't need to understand all
the errors presented in this paper. But isn't it unreasonable to think
that any student, except perhaps a most extraordinary one, would
not be overwhelmed by all these marks? Even more troubling: are
these surface errors the most significant problems with the paper?
What could the teacher say that would help this student?

    The most important thing to address, I believe, is helping the
student to figure out what the paper is about, making it coherent,
and getting a thesis articulated. The paper clearly has a beginning
and end that seem oddly disconnected from the body. In our digital
age, I think teachers must always be wary of papers that are being
cut-and-pasted, or adapted, or just lifted from other sources. Is that
what's going on here? The student clearly is deriving information
about Faulkner's mailing address (in the opening paragraph) and his
finances (in the closing paragraph) from some other source, but it's

either an inept source, or he is not following it closely. The two middle paragraphs seem unrelated to the opening and closing, and it is possible that the student is following some source that deals with women in Faulkner, but again, he is not following this source closely if at all – or it is a terrible source. Here's what I think is probably going on (and a brief conversation with the student could confirm this): I think the student doesn't really understand how a beginning and an ending work in an essay. I think he believes that sweeping biographical tidbits, designed to draw the reader in and demonstrate your own expertise, are the way to open and close, and within this sandwich you offer the meat of your argument. This lack of knowledge could be addressed by some in-class analysis of introductions and conclusions, probably better than any comment on this paper. But I think on the paper I'd write, in the margin beside the first sentence of the second paragraph, "I'd start here. This is where your discussion really seems to begin." And beside the closing paragraph, I'd write, "Hmmm. This seems tacked on to me. I'm not sure what it has to do with your subject."

These comments suggest that I believe the student has a subject, and I do: how women are abused in Faulkner. I don't know if he wants to say something about it, other than note that it is a recurrent theme – which is, in itself, a worthwhile thing to do. I could be wrong, but my sense is that this student has engaged substantially and meaningfully with some of Faulkner's works, and this effort is something that should be acknowledged in the teacher's response. I have to wonder what this student has been taught previously and how this student views himself. It would certainly be misleading to ignore all the problems here, just as it is probably useless to mark them all (especially without explanation). So I would focus on two, writing at the end: "There are a distracting number of stylistic problems here. Let's focus on two. Check the subject and verb of every sentence, and correct the ones that don't agree. If you don't find any, come see me, or go to the Writing Center and ask them to help you work on subject-verb agreement. Also, proofread your paper carefully and see how many errors you can find. I'm sure that you know how to spell 'who'; which other errors here are just proofreading errors?"

The most important comment: I would try to say something about the body of the paper that would encourage the student to focus and develop his topic, perhaps like this: "Your focus on women is interesting, and you've got a good eye for significant scenes. What is the idea that connects the evidence that you present here? What do these scenes that you tell us about have in common? In other words, I'm encouraging you to say explicitly what point it is that you're making here." At this point, I've invested perhaps five minutes in reading the paper and about the same amount of time writing these comments. I haven't marked everything. No doubt I've spent considerably less time than the teacher invested, but I think I have a much better chance of improving the student's abilities and getting a better paper in the revision. And I think the student is more likely to approach the next assignment with a more positive attitude and energy.

As you've probably noticed, as we have been pondering what this paper is trying to be about, I've withheld for strategic purposes the assignment for this paper. We should, after all, be able to discern the assignment from the paper itself, if the paper is successfully addressing the assignment, and sometimes we may tend to see what we expect to be there. In this case, consider for a moment how knowing the assignment that was given alters your view of the student's work:

> One of the more phenomenal aspects of our existence is the seeming paradox of everyday life. We often use our senses in ways and means that are totally diametrically opposed to their seeming intent, i.e. viewing music, etc. For your first assignment you are to compose a 2–3 page treatise which legitimizes or deconstructs the startling notion of one of these interrelationships in Faulkner and expresses your preference for (or lack thereof) it.

The statute of limitations is probably up for the crime of writing this assignment, and it is admittedly an extreme example. But I hope it makes a crucial point: no wonder the student isn't sure what to do. The assignment is, at best, very challenging; at worst, it's poorly worded and ill-conceived. I believe the teacher is asking whether there are instances in Faulkner in which the senses are used in unconventional ways. And the student is also being asked to deconstruct or legitimize these instances (whatever that means). But I'm guessing. There is only one example offered, "viewing music," and I'm not sure that I can provide others: smelling words? Eating poetry (I do like Mark Strand's famous poem about that)?

In delivering an assignment, this teacher is clearly trying too hard and is apparently motivated by the desire for glory and adulation. The assignment does sound sort of smart, but it isn't. In marking the paper, the teacher again does too much work (that isn't helpful) and too little work (designed to nurture the student's abilities).

It is, as I acknowledge, an extreme example, but one that conveys the most important lessons I've learned from over thirty years of teaching writing and reading research in Composition and Rhetoric: Give assignments that will inspire and educate your students; mark their papers fairly and constructively in ways that help them. Simple concepts, sometimes hard to apply, to be sure.

This disaster may seem far removed from the intellectual attractions of rhetoric's rich history and the energizing theories and studies of composing and its pedagogy. In closing this chapter and this book, I want to reflect on how these apparently distant universes are connected, and then direct you to some of the many useful resources on the teaching of writing. In thinking about Ken's paper in light of the foregoing chapters, we might imagine how his literacy training differed from the training of someone educated in ancient Greece, Rome, or Elizabethan England. Although we have advanced tremendously technologically, you have to wonder how well Ken would write if he had received extensive training in classical rhetoric, studying and practicing arguments, translating, working with words and more words. What if Ken had some experience working with invention strategies, with structures of arrangement in various genres, with fluency and copiousness of style? What if he had been Hugh Blair's student, inspired to elevate his taste by intensive reading and reflection? Or what if Ken had been taught by Peter Elbow or Ken MacCrorie, or by anyone whose teaching was informed by a process pedagogy? And why do I assume that he wasn't? Because, I suppose, I have faith in what we have learned about Rhetoric and Composition. I don't believe that Ken or his teacher have been accustomed to thinking much about audience – about what the reader knows and assumes and expects; or about ethos – about fashioning and presenting a textual self; or about logical relationships and connections – about sequencing statements into coherent trains of thought. Compare the clarity and adaptability of the writing assignments in the *progymnasmata* to the miasma of this teacher's assignment, which is unfortunately not as unheard-of as we would hope. Although the independence of every teacher inventing his or her own assignments is appealing, there is something to be said for a set of tried-and-true writing assignments. We may look back with pity upon teachers who began every semester by assigning "What I Did on My Summer Vacation," but it was an assignment that every student could say something about. In the long history of Rhetoric and Composition, there is an unwavering focus on students that is quite heartening. In some recent theoretical work, I do worry that students seem to have receded from consideration, but the heritage of this field is a powerful force returning us to that mission: teach students how to express themselves and persuade others. Deliver Rhetoric and Composition.

RECOMMENDATIONS FOR FURTHER READING: DELIVERY

Anson, Chris, Joan Graham, David Jolliffe, Nancy Shapiro, and Carolyn Smith. *Scenarios for Teaching Writing: Contexts for Discussion and Reflective Practice.* Urbana, IL: NCTE, 1993.

Murphy, James, ed. *A Short History of Writing Instruction.* (2nd edn.) Davis, California: Hermagoras Press, 2001.

Tate, Gary, Edward P. J. Corbett, and Nancy Myers. *The Writing Teacher's Sourcebook.* (4th edn.) Oxford University Press, 1999.

Williams, James D. *Preparing to Teach Writing: Research, Theory, and Practice.* (3rd edn.) Maywah, NJ: Erlbaum, 2003.

Yancey, Kathleen Blake, ed. *Delivering College Composition: The Fifth Canon.* Portsmouth, NH: Boynton/Cook, 2006.

Notes

1 THE OPEN HAND

1. See George Kennedy, "A Hoot in the Dark," as well as his *Comparative Rhetoric* for a discussion of the analogues between human and animal rhetoric. Useful histories of rhetoric and its influence include Kennedy's *Classical Rhetoric* and *A New History*; Conley (*Rhetoric*); Peter Dixon; Murphy, *Short History*; Olmsted; and Vickers.

2. For a sense of what we know and how well it is being applied, see Smagorinsky, especially chapter 3 by George Hillocks, "Middle and High School Composition."

3. See Murphy, *Synoptic History* (25). For an ancient source, see Sextus Empiricus, *Against the Rhetoricians* 96–9. Most scholars now doubt the factuality of this story, and some even say (see Rollinson and Geckle 47–8) that "Corax" was nothing more than a nickname for Tisias – an assertion that does clear up some puzzling passages in Plato, Aristotle, Cicero, and Lucian.

4. For discussions of rhetoric's early history, see Kleingunther, Katula, Smith, R. L. Enos ("Ancient Greek" and *Greek Rhetoric*), Schiappa, Thomas Cole, and Kennedy ("Earliest Rhetorical Handbooks").

5. For a more balanced and appreciative view of the sophists, see Sprague, Jarratt (*Rereading*), Ballif, and Vitanza.

6. On Plato's view of poets, language, and truth, see Rucker, Neel, and Cole.

7. For an excellent introduction to Aristotle's life and works, see Barnes 1–26.

8. Barnes (9–15) discusses whether we should think of Aristotle's works as lecture-notes (the common assumption) or as "working drafts" (Barnes' suggestion).

9. Murphy, *Synoptic* (62), translates *antistrophē* as "mirror-image." What exactly is meant by this term has been the subject of much discussion. In Carol Poster's innovative reading, for instance, Aristotle intends for his students to see rhetoric as the counterpart to his *Sophistical Disputations*, intended to show students how to counter fallacious reasoning for a common audience, just as the *Sophistical Disputations* did the same thing for dialectic. In his edition of Aristotle's *Rhetoric*, Kennedy, interestingly, does not use

"counterpart" (the usual translation), or "mirror-image," "correlative," "coordinate," "converse," or any other possible term. Instead, Kennedy simply uses *antistrophos.* See his explanatory note 2 on pp. 28–9.

10. See Robin Smith (in Barnes 27–65) for a nice introduction to Aristotle's logic.

11. Howell's *Logic and Rhetoric* discusses Zeno's analogy (see 4–5, for instance).

12. The bracketed insertions are Kennedy's, and they seem reasonable enough, but they are subject to question since "testing" and "maintaining" an argument is not limited to dialectic, nor is "defend" and "attack" limited to rhetoric.

13. For clarity, I have added the punctuation in brackets. The other insertions are Kennedy's.

14. Vitanza's and Jarratt's comments occur in an "Octalog" panel discussion. See Murphy, "Political" 31.

15. See Murphy, *Short History* 6, and Wright and Halloran, especially 226–9.

16. See Berlin, *Rhetoric and Reality* 35–6.

17. This history of the Boylston professorship is indebted especially to Heinrichs.

18. In addition to Richard Miller, see Berlin and Hobbs in Murphy's *Short History* 250–3.

19. For an overview of the reception, distortion, and continued vitality of writing across the curriculum, see Susan McLeod and Elaine Maimon, "Clearing the Air: WAC Myths and Realities," *College English* 62:5 (May 2000): 573–83. McLeod and Maimon dispel the idea that WAC and WID are just "grammar across the curriculum" (465), as C. H. Knoblauch and Lil Brannon charged in "Writing as Learning through the Curriculum," *College English* 45 (1983): 465–74.

20. The Doctoral Consortium of Rhetoric and Composition Programs currently lists seventy-one members on its website. Information about the founding dates of PhD programs in Rhetoric and Composition is available in Stuart Brown, Rebecca Jackson, and Theresa Enos, "The Arrival of Rhetoric in the Twenty-First Century: The 1999 Survey of Doctoral Programs in Rhetoric," *Rhetoric Review* 18 (Spring 2000): 233–42.

21. For an insightful discussion of "the work" of composition and how it has been perceived and valued, see Bruce Horner, especially 1–29.

22. For an excellent overview of the issues involved, and a "constructive, collegially engaged" (428) proposal for a fusion of literary studies and composition, see Fitts and Lalicker.

2 INVENTION

1. Eleonore Stump's editions of Boethius's *De topicis differentiis* and *In Ciceronis Topica* offer excellent explanatory essays, biographical information, and authoritative translations with notes.

2. Daniel Fogarty coined the term "current-traditional" in 1959 to describe pedagogy focused on the work's formal features. For insightful discussions of the philosophical underpinnings and instructional practices of current-traditional rhetoric, see Connors, "Mechanical Correctness"; Connors, *Composition Rhetoric* 5–6; Young and Liu; Kitzhaber; and Crowley, *The Methodical Memory* on "current-traditional" rhetoric.

3. Nystrand, "Social," discusses process pedagogy and cites Town and Sams (11).

4. Britton's student, Arthur Applebee, later refined the subcategories of each function and renamed them "informational," "personal," and "imaginative."

5. For overviews, see Hayes, Rijlaarsdam and van den Bergh, Hillocks's "Middle," and "Writing," and Durst.

6. See also Murray's "Write Before Writing" and *A Writer Teaches Writing*.

7. On the National Writing Project, see among other sources Hubbard and Power, and Russell.

8. See Gillespie *et al.* for a good introduction to Writing Centers, not only the service but the research they generate.

9. This quotation is from the NWP website, which is also the source for the number of sites.

10. Lindemann says "In many composition textbooks, the only prewriting technique discussed is the formal outline" (110), but mainstream composition textbooks today typically feature a smorgasbord of prewriting strategies.

11. I have altered the formatting of this passage.

12. In conversation with me, May 2008.

13. See, e.g., Rose.

14. See Bandura, and Pajares and Valiente.

15. Ibid.

16. These estimates are reported by Bowers in a classic 1964 study, which found in a sample of 5,000 students from 99 colleges and universities that roughly three-quarters acknowledged cheating. In 2002, Jensen, Arnett, Feldman and Cauffman, found that 90% of the students admitted to plagiarism and related forms of academic dishonesty. For a recent overview, with suggestions on preventing plagiarism, see Tim Roberts.

17. See Olson regarding the related notion that a cliché is situational: what is a cliché for some readers and writers, is in fact a fresh phrasing for another.

18. See Mooney. In an interesting twist, responses to Mooney's story on the *Chronicle* website include one person's claim that Stearns himself stole ideas from him.

19. Caplan discusses the authorship question of the *Rhetorica ad Herennium* in the introduction to his Loeb edition.

20. On the relationship between the *Rhetorica ad Herennium* and *De inventione*, see Caplan xxi–xxxiii.

21. For useful discussions of the topics, see Leff, Conley ("Logical"), and Ochs ("Aristotle's" and "Cicero's").

22. Cited in Barnes 27, who provides very useful background.

23. Piltz provides an engaging introduction to the *Organon*. See especially 55–65 and 92–103.

3   ARRANGEMENT

1. Corax also apparently offered advice about using probability in arguments. One might argue, for instance, that a small man is unlikely to attack a larger one, or that a rich man is unlikely to shoplift. See Cole and R. L. Enos, *Greek Rhetoric*.

2. Notice the close similarity of terms: From the *Ad Herennium*: Inventio in sex partes orationis consumitur: in exordium, narrationem, divisionem, confirmationem, confutationem, conclusionem" ("Invention is used for the six parts of a discourse: the Introduction, Statement of Facts, Division, Proof, Refutation, and Conclusion" [8–9]). From *De Inventione*: "Eae partes sex esse omnino nobis videntur: exordium, narratio, partitio, confirmatio, reprehensio, conclusio" ("These seem to me to be just six in number: exordium, narrative, partition, confirmation, refutation, peroration" [40–41]).

3. On the *cursus*, see Lanham, *A Handlist* 43.

4. See Conley, *Rhetoric* 96–7. The standard work on medieval rhetoric is James Murphy's magisterial *Rhetoric in the Middle Ages*.

5. Lucille Vaughan Payne, discussed in a moment, is an influential proponent of this approach.

6. From the website at www.geocities.com/SoHo/Atrium/1437/structure.html.

7. For a discussion of Samuel Johnson's familiarity with the *progymnasmata*, see Lynn, "Rhetoric."

8. The large number of early manuscripts also indicates the popularity of these manuals. See Kennedy, *Progymnasmata*, for the fullest set of translations and commentary. See Rollinson and Geckle for a good background.

9. For a discussion of the use of models in writing instruction, see Donovan and McClelland.

10. See Beaumont (15–16) and Thornburg.
11. Lindemann says that the classical oration originates with Aristotle (134–5). The structure of an exordium, narration, confirmation, refutation, and peroration is apparently a later development.

4 STYLE

1. Milic's terms for the three approaches to style are "rhetorical dualism," "individualist or psychological monism," and "Crocean aesthetic monism" (67–9). I am replacing Milic's terms with my own user-friendlier ones. I disagree with Milic's negative assessment of the potential for teaching style. My own experience, as will be clear in what follows, is that writers can enlarge their stylistic repertoire almost as easily as they can enlarge their wardrobes, given explicit guidance, practice, and encouragement.
2. The story appeared in the "Education" section. The text of the report itself is available at www.nces.ed.gov.
3. In note 7 on page 6.
4. Shiels's response appears in *The English Journal* (May 1977), p. 17.
5. See e.g., William Labov and J. L. Dillard.
6. Gilyard discusses this episode on pages 639–40.
7. See also Kinloch and Yang.
8. See Nelson, Shanahan, Shanahan and Lomax, and Langer.
9. See e.g., Bereiter and Scardamalia, and Charney and Carlson.
10. This exercise is based on a sentence in Seth Schiesel's review of *Spore*, published in the *New York Times*, September 4, 2008 ("Television" section). Here is Schiesel's sentence: "As an intelligent romp through the sometimes contradictory realms of science, mythology, religion and hope about the universe around us, Spore both provokes and amuses."
11. A selection from *Copia: Foundations of the Abundant Style* is conveniently available in Bizzell and Herzberg, *Tradition*, 597–627.
12. Brooks calls this kind of exercise a "persona paraphrase." See Weiss for an annotated bibliography on imitation.

5 MEMORY

1. In addition to the reference in the Wallechinsky's *Book of Lists*, a survey was apparently commissioned by Reasontospeak.com in 2008, and it revealed, according to the *Sydney Morning Herald* of October 22, 2008, that public speaking was number two, behind death (27% to 23%). Reasontospeak.com offers, of course, coaching in public speaking.
2. See Murphy in *Short History* 65–9.

3. See Stump's overview of "Dialectic" in Wagner 125–46.
4. See Botley 169.
5. For an engaging history of language schemes, see Eco; for illuminating essays on efforts to recover or reinvent the perfect language of Adam, see Aarsleff.
6. For a more detailed explanation, see Lynn, "Johnson" 465–6. My understanding of this shift is based primarily on Wilbur Howell's work, *Eighteenth-Century* 259–98, 441–7.

6   DELIVERY

1. Ratliff's review appears in the December 17, 2008 "Music" section of the *New York Times*.
2. Quoted in Fliegelman 106.
3. See Hall for a discussion of Cicero and Quintilian on the use of the hands.
4. See Howell's discussion in *Eighteenth-Century Rhetoric* 221–30.
5. See Mailloux for a penetrating discussion of this disciplinary history.
6. This description is taken from English 101 at the University of South Carolina, which is actually called "Critical Reading and Composition."

Bibliography

Aarsleff, Hans. *From Locke to Saussure: Essays on the Study of Language and Intellectual History.* Minneapolis: University of Minnesota Press, 1982.

Adams, Katherine. *A Group of Their Own: College Writing Courses and American Women Writers, 1880–1940.* Albany: State University of New York Press, 2001.

Albertinti, John. "Teaching of Writing and Diversity: Access, Identity, and Achievement." In Bazerman, *Handbook* 387–97.

Allison, Libby, Lizbeth Bryant, and Maureen Hourigan. *Grading in the Post-Process Classroom: From Theory to Practice.* Portsmouth, NH: Boynton/Cook, 1997.

Anderson, Diane. "Casting and Recasting Gender: Children Constituting Social Identities through Literacy Practices Research in the Teaching of English." *College English* 36 (2002): 391–427.

Anonymous. *Rhetorica ad Herennium.* Ed. Harry Caplan. London: Heinemann, 1954.

Applebee, Arthur. *The Child's Concept of Story: Ages Two to Seventeen.* University of Chicago Press, 1978.

Applebee, Arthur. *Writing in the Secondary School: English in the Content Areas.* Urbana, IL: NCTE, 1981.

Aristotle. *Rhetoric.* Trans. William Robert Rhys. New York: Modern Library, 1954.

Aristotle. *Topics Books I & VIII: With Excerpts from Related Texts.* Oxford University Press, 1997.

Ashley, Hannah. "Playing the Game: Proficient Working-Class Student Writers: Second Voices." *Research in the Teaching of English* 35 (2001): 493–524.

Atwill, Janet. *Rhetoric Reclaimed: Aristotle and the Liberal Arts Tradition.* Ithaca: Cornell University Press, 1998.

Augustine, Saint, Bishop of Hippo. *Confessions.* Oxford University Press, 1991.

Austin, Gilbert. *Chironomia, or a Treatise on Rhetorical Delivery.* (First published London: 1806.) Eds Mary Margaret Robb and Lester Thonssen. Carbondale: Southern Illinois University Press, 1966.

Axelrod, Rise, and Charles Cooper. *The St. Martin's Guide to Writing*. Boston: St. Martin's, 2001.

Bacon, Francis. *Of the Advancement of Learning*. (5th edn.) Ed. W. A. Wright. Oxford: Clarendon, 1957.

Bain, Alexander. *English Composition and Rhetoric: A Manual*. (First published 1866.) Facsimile repr. Delmar, NY: Scholars' Facsimiles, 1996.

Baldwin, Charles Sears. *Ancient Rhetoric and Poetic*. (First published 1924.) Gloucester, MA: Peter Smith, 1959.

Baldwin, Charles Sears. "The Elementary Exercises of Hermogenes." In his *Medieval Rhetoric and Poetic*. New York: Macmillan, 1928. 23–38.

Baldwin, Charles Sears. *Medieval Rhetoric and Poetic*. New York: Macmillan, 1928.

Ballif, Michelle. *Seduction, Sophistry, and the Woman with the Rhetorical Figure*. Carbondale: Southern Illinois University Press, 2000.

Bandura, A. *Self-Efficacy: The Exercise of Control*. New York: Freeman, 1997.

Barnard, H. C. *A History of English Education from 1760*. University of London Press, 1961.

Barnes, Jonathan. *Cambridge Companion to Aristotle*. Cambridge University Press, 1995.

Barrett, Edward, ed. *Text, ConText, and HyperText*. Cambridge, MA: MIT Press, 1988.

Bartholomae, David. "Freshman English, Composition, and CCCC." In *Views from the Center: The CCCC Chairs' Addresses 1977–2005*. Ed. Duane H. Roen. New York: Macmillan, 2006.

Bazerman, Charles. *Handbook of Research on Writing: History, Society, School, Individual, Text*. New York: Erlbaum, 2008.

Bazerman, Charles. *Shaping Written Knowledge: The Genre and Activity of the Experimental Article in Science*. Madison: University of Wisconsin Press, 1988.

Beaumont, Charles Allen. *Swift's Classical Rhetoric*. Athens: University of Georgia Press, 1961.

Belenky, Mary, Blythe Clinchy, Nancy Goldberger, and Jill Tarule. *Women's Ways of Knowing: The Development of Self, Voice, and Mind*. New York: Basic Books, 1987.

Benson, Thomas, and Michael Prosser, eds. *Readings in Classical Rhetoric*. 1969 reprint. Mahwah, NJ: Lawrence Erlbaum, 1995.

Bereiter, Carl, and Marlene Scardamalia. "Learning about Writing from Reading." *Written Communication* 1 (1984): 163–88.

Berlin, James. "Contemporary Composition: The Major Pedagogical Theories." *College English* 44 (1982): 765–77.

Berlin, James. "Rhetoric and Ideology in the Writing Class." *College English* 50 (1988): 477–94.

Berlin, James. *Rhetoric and Reality: Writing Instruction in American Colleges, 1900–1985.* Carbondale: Southern Illinois University Press, 1987.

Bitzer, Lloyd. "The Rhetorical Situation." *Philosophy and Rhetoric* (January, 1968): 1–14.

Bizzell, Patricia. *Academic Discourse and Critical Consciousness.* University of Pittsburgh Press, 1992.

Bizzell, Patricia, and Bruce Herzberg. *The Bedford Bibliography for Teachers of Writing.* Boston: Bedford/St. Martin's, 1984.

Bizzell, Patricia, and Bruce Herzberg. *The Rhetorical Tradition: Readings from Classical Times to the Present.* (2nd edn.) New York: St. Martin's, 2001.

Bizzell, Patricia, Bruce Herzberg and Nedra Reynolds. *The Bedford Bibliography for Teachers of Writing.* (6th edn.) Boston: Bedford/St. Martin's, 2004.

Black, Edwin. *Rhetorical Criticism: A Study in Method.* Madison: University of Wisconsin Press, 1978.

Blair, Hugh. *Lectures on Rhetoric and Belles Lettres.* Eds. Linda Ferreira and S. Michael Halloran. Carbondale: Southern Illinois University Press, 2005.

Blakeslee, A. M. *Interacting with Audiences: Social Influences on the Production of Scientific Writing.* Mahwah, NJ: Erlbaum, 2001.

Bolgar, R. R. *The Classical Heritage and Its Beneficiaries.* Cambridge University Press, 1958.

Bolgar, R. R. "The Teaching of Rhetoric in the Middle Ages." In *Rhetoric Revalued.* Ed. Brian Vickers. Binghamton, NY: Medieval and Renaissance Texts and Studies, 1982. 79–86.

Booth, Wayne. *The Rhetoric of Fiction.* University of Chicago Press, 1961.

Bordelon, S. "Challenging Nineteenth-Century Feminization Narratives: Mary Yost of Vassar College." *Peitho* 6 (2002): 1–5.

Botley, Paul. *Latin Translation in the Renaissance: The Theory and Practice of Leonardo Bruni, Giannozzo Manetti and Desiderius Erasmus.* Cambridge University Press, 2009.

Bowers, W.J. *Student Dishonesty and its Control in a College.* New York: Bureau of Applied Social Research, Columbia University, 1964.

Braddock, Richard, Richard Lloyd-Jones, and Lowell Schoer. *Research in Written Composition.* Urbana, IL: NCTE, 1963.

Brereton, John, ed. *The Origins of Composition Studies in the American College, 1875–1925: A Documentary History.* University of Pittsburgh Press, 1995.

Brereton, John, *Traditions of Inquiry*. New York: Oxford University Press, 1985.

Briscoe, Marianne, *Artes Praedicandi*, published with Barbara Jaye, *Artes Orandi*. Turnhout, Belgium: Brepols, 1992.

Britton, James. *The Development of Writing Abilities, 11–18*. London: Macmillan, 1975.

Britton, James. *Language and Learning*. Harmondsworth: Pelican, 1970.

Brooks, Cleanth, and Austin Warren. *Modern Rhetoric with Readings*. New York: Harcourt, 1949.

Brooks, Phyllis. "Mimesis: Grammar and the Echoing Voice." *College English* 35 (November 1973): 161–76.

Brown, Stuart C., Rebecca Jackson, and Theresa Enos. "The Arrival of Rhetoric in the Twenty-First Century: The 1999 Survey of Doctoral Programs in Rhetoric." *Rhetoric Review* 18 (Spring 2000): 233–42.

Burgh, James. *The Art of Speaking … in which are given Rules for expressing properly the principal passions and Humours, which occur in Reading or Public Speaking*. Philadelphia: Aitken, 1764.

Burke, Kenneth. *Counter-Statement*. (3rd edn.) Berkeley: University of California Press, 1968.

Burke, Kenneth. *A Rhetoric of Motives*. Berkeley: University of California Press, 1950.

Camargo, Martin. *Ars Dictaminis, Ars Dictandi*. Turnhout, Belgium: Brepols, 1991.

Camargo, Martin. "Rhetoric." In *The Liberal Arts in the Middle Ages*. Ed. David Wagner. Bloomington: Indiana University Press, 1983. 96–124.

Cameron, Averil. *Christianity and the Rhetoric of Empire: The Development of Christian Discourse*. Berkeley: University of California Press, 1991.

Campbell, George. *The Philosophy of Rhetoric*. Ed. Lloyd Bitzer. Carbondale: Southern Illinois University Press, 1988.

Campbell, JoAnn. "Freshman (sic) English: A 1901 Wellesley College 'Girl' Negotiates Authority." *Rhetoric Review* 15 (1996): 110–27.

Campbell, JoAnn. "'A Real Vexation': Student Writing in Mount Holyoke's Culture of Service, 1837–1865." *College English* 59 (1997): 767–88.

Canby, Henry Seidel, *et al. English Composition in Theory and Practice*. New York: Macmillan, 1909.

Caplan, Harry. *Of Eloquence: Studies in Ancient and Medieval Rhetoric*. Eds. Anne King and Helen North. Ithaca: Cornell University Press, 1970.

Caplan, Harry. trans. *Rhetorica ad Herennium*. Cambridge, MA: Harvard University Press, 1968.

Cassirer, Ernst. *An Essay on Man: An Introduction to a Philosophy of Human Culture.* New Haven: Yale University Press, 1944.

Charney, Davida. "The Effect of Hypertext on Processes of Reading and Writing." In *Literacy and Computers.* Eds. Cynthia Selfe and Susan Hilligoss. New York: Modern Language Association, 1994. 238–63.

Charney, Davida, and R. Carlson. "Learning to Write in a Genre: What Student Writers Take from Model Texts." *Research in the Teaching of English* 29 (1995): 88–125.

Cicero, Marcus Tullius. *De Inventione, with De Optimo Genere Oratorum and Topica.* Trans. H. M. Hubbell. Cambridge, MA: Harvard University Press, 1968.

Cicero, Marcus Tullius. *Cicero on Oratory and Orators: With His Letters to Quintus and Brutus.* Trans. John Selby Watson. London: George Bell and Sons, 1884.

Clark, Donald Lemen. "The Rise and Fall of Progymnasmata in Sixteenth and Seventeenth Century Grammar Schools." *Speech Monographs* 19 (1952): 259–63.

Clark, Donald Lemen. *Rhetoric in Greco-Roman Education.* New York: Columbia University Press, 1957.

Cole, A. T. *Democritus and the Sources of Greek Anthropology.* Chapel Hill: University of North Carolina Press, 1967.

Cole, Thomas. *The Origins of Rhetoric in Ancient Greece.* Baltimore: Johns Hopkins University Press, 1991.

College Entrance Examination Board. *On Further Examination: Report of the Advisory Panel on the Scholastic Aptitude Test Score Decline.* New York: CEEB, 1977.

Conley, Thomas. *Rhetoric in the European Tradition.* University of Chicago Press, 1990.

Conley, Thomas. "Logical Hylomorphism and Aristotle's Koinoi Topoi." *Central States Speech Journal* 29 (1978): 92–7.

Connors, Robert. "Composition Studies and Science." *College English* 45 (1983): 1–20.

Connors, Robert. *Composition-Rhetoric: Backgrounds, Theory, and Pedagogy.* University of Pittsburgh Press, 1997.

Connors, Robert. Quoted in Octalog, "The Politics of Historiography." *Rhetoric Review.* 7:1 (Autumn, 1988): 30.

Connors, Robert. "Mechanical Correctness as a Focus in Composition Instruction." *College Composition and Communication* 36 (1985): 61–72.

Connors, Robert. *Selected Essays of Robert J. Connors.* Eds. Lisa Ede and Andrea A. Lunsford. Boston: Bedford/St. Martin's, 2003.

Connors, Robert, Lisa Ede, and Andrea A. Lunsford, eds. *Essays on Classical Rhetoric and Modern Discourse*. Carbondale: Southern Illinois University Press, 1984.

Consigny, Scott. *Gorgias: Sophist and Artist*. Columbia: University of South Carolina Press, 2001.

Cope, E. M. *An Introduction to Aristotle's Rhetoric with Analysis, Notes, and Appendices*. London: Macmillan, 1867.

Corbett, William P. J., and Robert Connors. *Classical Rhetoric for the Modern Student*. (4th edn.) New York: Oxford University Press, 1999.

Cowan, Gregory, and Elizabeth Cowan. *Writing*. Glenview, IL: Scott Foresman, 1980.

Crowley, Sharon. *Ancient Rhetorics for Contemporary Students*. New York: Macmillan, 1994.

Crowley, Sharon. *The Methodical Memory: Invention in Current-Traditional Rhetoric*. Carbondale: Southern Illinois University Press, 1990.

Daiker, Donald, Andrew Kerek, and Max Morenberg, eds. *Sentence Combining: A Rhetorical Perspective*. Carbondale: Southern Illinois University Press, 1985.

D'Angelo, Frank. *Composition in the Classical Tradition*. Boston: Allyn and Bacon, 2000.

D'Angelo, Frank. *A Conceptual Theory of Rhetoric*. Cambridge, MA: Winthrop, 1975.

Daniell, Beth. "*Dissoi Logoi*: Women's Rhetoric and Classroom Practice." In *Teaching Rhetorica: Theory, Pedagogy, Practice*. Eds. Kate Ronald and Joy Ritchie. Portsmouth, NH: Boynton/Cook, 2006. 82–92.

Delpit, Lisa. *Other People's Children: Cultural Conflict in the Classroom*. New York: Free Press, 1996.

Dillard, Joe. *Black English: Its History and Usage in the United States*. New York: Vintage, 1973.

Dixon, John. *Growth through English: A Report Based on the Dartmouth Conference 1966*. (2nd edn.) Oxford University Press, 1970.

Dixon, Peter. *Rhetoric*. London: Methuen, 1971.

Donovan, Timothy, and Ben McClelland. *Eight Approaches to Teaching Composition*. Urbana, IL: NCTE, 1980.

Durst, Russell. "Writing at the Postsecondary Level." In Smagorinsky. 78–107.

Eagleton, Terry. *Literary Theory: An Introduction*. Minneapolis: University of Minnesota Press, 1983.

Eco, Umberto. *The Search for the Perfect Language*. Boston: Wiley-Blackwell, 1997.

Edwards, Bruce. *The Tagmemic Contribution to Composition Teaching*. Dept. of English, Kansas State University, 1980.

Elbow, Peter. "Closing My Eyes as I Speak: An Argument for Ignoring Audience." *College English* 49 (January 1987): 50–69.

Elbow, Peter. *Everyone Can Write: Essays Toward a Hopeful Theory of Writing and Teaching Writing.* New York: Oxford University Press, 2000.

Elbow, Peter. *Writing with Power: Techniques for Mastering the Writing Progress.* New York: Oxford University Press, 1981.

Elbow, Peter. *Writing Without Teachers.* New York: Oxford University Press, 1973.

Emig, Janet. *The Composing Processes of Twelfth Graders.* Urbana, IL: NCTE, 1971.

Enders, Jody. *Rhetoric and the Origins of Médieval Drama.* Ithaca: Cornell University Press, 1992.

Enos, Richard Leo. "Ancient Greek Writing Instruction." In Murphy, *A Short History of Writing Instruction.* 9–34.

Enos, Richard Leo. *Greek Rhetoric before Aristotle.* Prospect Heights, IL: Waveland, 1993.

Enos, Theresa, ed. *The Encyclopedia of Rhetoric and Composition: Communication from Ancient Times to the Information Age.* New York: Garland, 1996.

Enos, Theresa, ed. *Learning from the Histories of Rhetoric: Essays in Honor of Winifred Bryan Horner.* Carbondale: Southern Illinois University Press, 1993.

Erasmus, Desiderius. *Collected Works of Erasmus. Literary and Educational Writings 2: De Copia, De Ratione Studii.* Ed. Craig R. Thompson. University of Toronto Press, 1978.

Executive Committee, College Conference on Composition and Communication (CCCC). "Students' Right to Their Own Language." *CCC* 25 (Fall 1974): 1–32.

Faigley, Lester. "Competing Theories of Process: A Critique and a Proposal." *College Composition and Communication* 48 (1986): 527–42.

Faigley, Lester. "Nonacademic Writing: The Social Perspective." In *Writing in Nonacademic Settings.* Eds. Lee Odell and Dixie Goswami. New York: Guilford, 1985. 231–48.

Fantazzi, Charles. *Juan Luis Vives, In Pseudodialecticos: A Critical Edition.* Leiden: Brill, 1979.

Fitts, Karen, and William B. Lalicker. "Invisible Hands: A Manifesto to Resolve Institutional and Curricular Hierarchy in English Studies." *College English* 66 (March 2004): 427–51.

Fliegelman, Jay. *Declaring Independence: Jefferson, Natural Language, and the Culture of Performance.* Stanford University Press, 1993.

Flower, Linda, and John R. Hayes. "Identifying the Organization of Writing Processes." In *Cognitive Processes in Writing.* Eds. L. W. Gregg and E. R. Steinberg. Hillsdale, NJ: Erlbaum, 1980. 3–30.

Flynn, Elizabeth. "Composition Studies from a Feminist Perspective." In *The Politics of Writing Instruction: Postsecondary*. Eds. Richard Bullock and John Trimbur. Portsmouth, NH: Boynton/Cook, 1991. 137–54.

Fox, Margaret. *Women's Speaking Justified, Proved and Allowed by the Scriptures*. London: n.s., 1666.

Franklin, Benjamin. *The Autobiography and Other Writings*. Ed. L. Jesse Lemisch. Afterword Carla Mulford. New York: Signet-Putnam, 2001.

Freire, Paolo. *Pedagogy of the Oppressed*. Trans. Myra Bergman Ramos. New York: Continuum, 1968.

Fries, Charles. *The Structure of English*. New York: Harcourt, 1925.

Gage, John. "On 'Rhetoric' and 'Composition.'" In *An Introduction to Composition Studies*. Eds. Erika Lindemann and Gary Tate. Oxford University Press, 1991. 15–32.

Galbraith, D., and M. Torrance. "Revision in the Context of Different Drafting Strategies." In *Studies in Writing, Vol. IV*. Eds. Torrance and Galbraith. Amsterdam University Press, 2004. 137–57.

Genung, John F. *Outlines of Rhetoric*. Boston: Ginn, 1886.

Genung, John F. *The Practical Elements of Rhetoric*. (2nd edn.) Boston: Ginn and Co., 1886.

Gibson, Walker. *Tough, Sweet and Stuffy: An Essay on Modern American Prose Styles*. Bloomington: Indiana University Press, 1966.

Gillespie, Paula, Alice Gillam, Lady Falls Brown, and Byron Stay. *Writing Center Research: Extending the Conversation*. Hillsdale, NJ: Erlbaum, 2001.

Gilligan, Carol. *In a Different Voice: Psychological Theory and Women's Development*. Cambridge MA: Harvard University Press, 1982.

Gilyard, Keith. "African American Contributions to Composition Studies." *CCC* 50.4 (1999): 626–44.

Glenn, Cheryl. *Making Sense*. Boston: Bedford, 2002.

Glenn, Cheryl. *Rhetoric Retold: Regendering the Tradition from Antiquity through the Renaissance*. Carbondale: Southern Illinois University Press, 1997.

Graff, Gerald. *Professing Literature*. Chicago University Press, 1987.

Grafton, Anthony, **and** Lisa Jardine. *From Humanism to the Humanities: Education and the Liberal Arts in Fifteenth- and Sixteenth-Century Europe*. Cambridge, MA: Harvard University Press, 1986.

Graham, Steve, Charles MacArthur, and Jill Fitzgerald, eds. *Best Practices in Writing Instruction: Solving Problems in the Teaching of Literacy*. New York: Guilford, 2007.

Graves, Donald. *Writing: Teachers and Children at Work*. Exeter, NH: Heinemann, 1983.

Greenblatt, Stephen. *Renaissance Self-Fashioning: From More to Shakespeare.* University of Chicago Press, 2005.

Grimes, Joseph. *The Thread of Discourse.* Berlin: Mouton De Gruyter, 1976.

Haden, Suzette. "Why Newsweek Can't Tell Us Why Johnny Can't Write." *English Journal* 65 (November 1976): 29–35.

Hairston, Maxine. "Diversity, Ideology, and Teaching Writing." *College Composition and Communication* 43 (1992): 179–93.

Hairston, Maxine. "The Winds of Change: Thomas Kuhn and the Revolution in the Teaching of Writing." *College Composition and Communication* 33 (1982): 76–88.

Hake, R. L., and J. M. Williams. "Sentence Expanding: Not Can, or How, But When." In *Sentence Combining and the Teaching of Writing.* Ed. Donald Daiker *et al.* Conway: University of Akron, 1979. 134–46.

Hall, Jon. "Cicero and Quintilian on the Oratorical Use of Hand Gestures." *Classical Quarterly* 54 (2004): 143–60.

Hansen, Mogens Herman. "The Athenian 'Politicians,' 403–322 B.C." In *Greek Literature.* Vol. V: *Greek Literature in the Classical Period: the Prose of Historiography and Oratory.* Ed. Gregory Nagy. New York: Routledge, 2001. 345–67.

Harmon, S. D. "'The voice, pen and influence of our women are abroad in the land': Women and the Illinois State Normal University, 1857–1899." In Hobbs. 84–102.

Harris, Joseph. *A Teaching Subject: Composition Since 1966.* Upper Saddle River, NJ: Prentice-Hall, 1997.

Hartwell, Patrick. "Grammar, Grammars, and the Teaching of Grammar." *College English* 47 (February 1985): 105–27.

Hauser, Gerald. *Introduction to Rhetorical Theory.* (2nd edn.) Long Grove, IL: Waveland, 2002.

Havelock, Erik. *The Muse Learns to Write: Reflections on Orality and Literacy from Antiquity to the Present.* New Haven: Yale University Press, 1986.

Hawk, Byron. *A Counter-History of Composition: Toward Methodologies of Complexity.* University of Pittsburgh Press, 2007.

Hayes, John R. "New Directions in Writing Theory." In MacArthur *et al.* 28–40.

Heath, Shirley Brice. *Ways with Words: Language, Life and Work in Communities and Classrooms.* Cambridge University Press, 1983.

Heinrichs, J. "How Harvard Destroyed Rhetoric." *Harvard Magazine* (July–August 1995): 37–43.

Hill, Adams S. *The Principles of Rhetoric and Their Application.* New York: Harper, 1878.

Hillocks, George, Jr. "Middle and High School Composition." In Smagorinsky. 48–77.

Hillocks, George, Jr. *Research on Written Composition*. Urbana, IL: NCTE, 1986.

Hillocks, George, Jr. "Writing in Secondary Schools." In Bazerman. *Handbook*. 311–29.

Hillocks, George, Jr., and N. Mavrogenes. "Sentence combining." In Hillocks. *Research*. 142–6.

Hirsch, E. D. *Cultural Literacy: What Every American Needs to Know*. New York: Vintage, 1988.

Hirsch, E. D. *The Knowledge Deficit*. Boston: Houghton Mifflin, 2006.

Hirsch, E. D. *Philosophy of Composition*. University of Chicago Press, 1977.

Hobbs, Catherine, ed. *Nineteenth-Century Women Learn to Write*. Charlottesville: University of Virginia Press, 1995.

hooks, bell. *Teaching to Transgress: Education as the Practice of Freedom*. London: Routledge, 1994.

Horner, Bruce. *Terms of Work for Composition: A Materialist Critique*. Foreword John Trimbur. Albany: State University of New York Press, 2000.

Horner, Winifred Bryan. *Nineteenth-Century Scottish Rhetoric: The American Connection*. Carbondale: Southern Illinois University Press, 1992.

Horner, Winifred Bryan, and Kerri Barton. *The Present State of Scholarship in Historical and Contemporary Rhetoric*. (2nd edn.) Columbia: University of Missouri Press, 1990.

Horner, Winifred Bryan. *Rhetoric in the Classical Tradition*. New York: St. Martin's Press, 1988.

Horner, Winifred Bryan, Michael C. Leff, and James Jerome Murphy, eds. *Rhetoric and Pedagogy: Its History, Philosophy, and Practice: Essays in Honor of James J. Murphy*. Mahwah, NJ: Lawrence Erlbaum Associates, 1995.

Howard, Rebecca Moore. "Sexuality, Textuality: The Cultural Work of Plagiarism." *College English* 62 (2000): 473–91.

Howard, Rebecca Moore. *Standing in the Shadow of Giants: Plagiarists, Authors, Collaborators*. Stamford, CT: Ablex, 1999.

Howell, Wilbur S. *Eighteenth-Century British Logic and Rhetoric*. Princeton University Press, 1971.

Howell, Wilbur S. *Logic and Rhetoric in England, 1500–1700*. Princeton University Press, 1956.

Hubbard, Ruth, and Brenda Power. *Living the Questions: A Guide for Teacher Researchers*. York, ME: Stenhouse, 1999.

Hubert, Henry. *Harmonious Perfection: The Development of English Studies in Nineteenth-Century Anglo-Canadian Colleges*. East Lansing, MI: Michigan State University Press, 1994.

Hurlbut, B. S. "College Requirements in English." In *Twenty Years of School and College English*. Eds. Adams Sherman Hill *et al*. Cambridge MA: Harvard University Press, 1896.

Irmscher, William. *Teaching Expository Writing*. New York: Harcourt, 1979.

Jacobi, Martin. "The Canon of Delivery in Rhetorical Theory: Selections, Commentary, and Advice." In *Delivering College Composition: The Fifth Canon*. Ed. Kathleen Blake Yancey. Portsmouth, NH: Boynton/Cook, 2006.

Jarratt, Susan. *Rereading the Sophists: Classical Rhetoric Refigured*. Carbondale: Southern Illinois University Press, 1991.

Jarratt, Susan. "Rhetoric." In *Introduction to Scholarship in Modern Languages and Literatures*. (3rd edn.) Ed. David G. Nicholls. New York: Modern Language Association, 2007. 73–102.

Jensen, L.A., J.J. Arnett, S.S. Feldman, and E. Cauffman "It's Wrong, but Everybody Does it: Academic Dishonesty among High School Students." *Contemporary Educational Psychology (2002)* 27(2): 209–28.

Johnson, Nan. *Nineteenth-Century Rhetoric in North America*. Carbondale: Southern Illinois University Press, 1991.

Joos, Martin. *The Five Clocks: A Linguistic Excursion into the Five Styles of English Usage*. New York: Harcourt, 1961.

Judy, Stephen. "On Second Thought: Reviewing the SAT Decline." *English Journal* (November 1977): 5–7.

Kahn, Victoria. *Machiavellian Rhetoric: From the Counter-Reformation to Milton*. Princeton University Press, 1994.

Katula, Richard. "The Origins of Rhetoric: Literacy and Democracy in Ancient Greece." In Murphy. *Synoptic History*. 3–20.

Kellog, R. T. "Attentional Overload and Writing Performance: Effects of Rough Draft and Outline Strategies." *Journal of Experimental Psychology* 14 (1988): 355–65.

Kellog, R. T. "Effectiveness of Pre-Writing Strategies as a Function of Task Demands." *American Journal of Psychology* 103 (1990): 327–42.

Kelly, Douglas. *The Art of Poetry and Prose*. Turnhout: Brepols, 1989.

Kennedy, George, trans. Aristotle. *On Rhetoric: A Theory of Civic Discourse*. Oxford University Press, 1991.

Kennedy, George. *Classical Rhetoric and Its Christian and Secular Tradition from Ancient to Modern Times*. Chapel Hill: University of North Carolina Press, 1980.

Kennedy, George. *Comparative Rhetoric: An Historical and Cross-Cultural Introduction*. Oxford University Press, 1997.

Kennedy, George. "The Earliest Rhetorical Handbooks." *The American Journal of Philology*, 80:2 (1959): 169–78.

Kennedy, George. "A Hoot in the Dark: The Evolution of General Rhetoric." *Philosophy and Rhetoric* 25 (1992): 1–21.

Kennedy, George. *A New History of Classical Rhetoric*. Princeton University Press, 1994.

Kennedy, George. *Progymnasmata: Greek Textbooks of Prose Composition and Rhetoric (Writings from the Greco-Roman World)*. Society of Biblical Literature, 2003.

Kent, Thomas. *Post-Process Theory: Beyond the Writing Process Paradigm*. Carbondale: Southern Illinois University Press, 1999.

Kimball, Bruce. *Orators and Philosophers: A History of the Idea of Liberal Education*. New York: Teachers College Press, 1986.

King, Margaret. "Thwarted Ambitions: Six Learned Women of the Italian Renaissance." *Soundings* 59 (1976): 280–304.

Kinloch, Valerie Felita. "Revisiting the Promise of Students' Right to Their Own Language." *College Composition and Communication* 9 (September 2005): 83–113.

Kinneavy, James. *Greek Rhetorical Origins of Christian Faith*. New York: Oxford University Press, 1987.

Kinneavy, James. *Theory of Discourse*. New York: Norton, 1971; repr. 1986.

Kitzhaber, Albert. *Rhetoric in American Colleges, 1850–1900*. Dallas: Southern Methodist University Press, 1991.

Kleingünther, A. *Protos Heuretes. Philologus*. Suppl. 26 (1933): 43–65.

Knoblauch, Cyril, and Lil Brannon. *Rhetorical Traditions and the Teaching of Writing*. Portsmouth, NH: Boynton/Cook, 1984.

Kopelson, Karen. "Of Ambiguity and Erasure: The Perils of Performative Pedagogy." In *Relations, Locations, and Positions: Composition Theory for Writing Teachers*. Eds. Peter Vandenberg, Jennifer Clary-Lemon, and Sue Hum. Urbana, IL: NCTE, 2006. 563–71.

Kubota, Ryuko. "New Approaches to Gender, Class, and Race in Second Language Writing." *Journal of Second Language Writing* 12 (February 2003): 31–47.

Kuhn, Thomas. *The Structure of Scientific Revolutions*. University of Chicago Press, 1962.

Kutz, Eleanor, Paolo Freire (adapted), and Hephzibah Roskelly. *An Unquiet Pedagogy: Transforming Practice in the English Classroom*. Portsmouth, NH: Boynton/Cook, 1991.

Labov, William. *Language in the Inner-City: Studies in the Black English Vernacular (Conduct and Communication)*. Philadelphia: University of Pennsylvania Press, 1972.

Lang, James. *On Course: A Week-By-Week Guide to Your First Semester of College Teaching*. Cambridge, MA: Harvard University Press, 2008.

Langer, J. A. *Children Reading and Writing: Structures and Strategies*. Norwood, NJ: Ablex, 1986.

Lanham, Richard. *The Economics of Attention: Style and Substance in the Age of Information*. University of Chicago Press, 2006.

Lanham, Richard. *A Handlist of Rhetorical Terms*. (2nd edn.) Berkeley: University of California Press, 1991.

Lanham, Richard. *Revising Prose*. (4th edn.) New York: Longman, 1999.

Lanham, Richard. *Revising Business Prose*. (4th edn.) New York: Longman, 1999.

Lanham, Richard. *Style: An Anti-Textbook*. New Haven: Yale University Press, 1978.

Lawler, Traugott, ed., trans. *The Parisiana poetria of John of Garland*. New Haven: Yale University Press, 1974.

Lazare, Donald. "Teaching the Conflicts about Wealth and Poverty." In *Left Margins: Cultural Studies and Composition Pedagogy*. Eds. Karen Fitts and Alan France. Albany: State University of New York Press, 1995. 189–205.

Leff, Michael. "The Topics of Argumentative Invention in Latin Rhetorical Theory from Cicero to Boethius." *Rhetorica* 1 (1983): 23–42.

Lindemann, Erika. *A Rhetoric for Writing Teachers*. (4th edn.) New York: Oxford University Press, 2001.

Locke, John. *An Essay Concerning Human Understanding*. Ed. and intro. Peter H. Nidditch. Oxford: Clarendon, 1975.

Locke, John. *An Essay Concerning Human Understanding*. London: W. Tegg, 1849.

Logan, Shirley Wilson. *"We Are Coming": The Persuasive Discourse of Nineteenth-Century Black Women*. Carbondale: Southern Illinois University Press, 1999.

Lunsford, Andrea A., ed. *Reclaiming Rhetorica: Women in the Rhetorical Tradition*. University of Pittsburgh Press, 1995.

Lunsford, Andrea A., Kirt Wilson, and Rosa Eberly, eds. *The Sage Handbook of Rhetorical Studies*. Thousand Oaks, CA: Sage, 2009.

Lunsford, Andrea A., and Lisa Ede. "Audience Addressed/Audience Invoked: The Role of Audience in Composition Theory and Pedagogy." *CCC* 35 (May 1984): 155–71.

Lynn, Steven. *Samuel Johnson after Deconstruction*. Carbondale: Southern Illinois University Press, 1992.

Lynn, Steven. "Johnson's Rambler and Eighteenth-Century Rhetoric." *Eighteenth-Century Studies* 19 (1986): 461–79.

Lynn, Steven. *Texts and Contexts*. (6th edn.) New York: Longman, 2010.

MacArthur, Charles. "The Effects of New Technologies on Writing and Writing Processes." In MacArthur *et al.* 248–62.

MacArthur, Charles, Steve Graham, and Jill Fitzgerald. *Handbook of Writing Research*. New York: Guilford, 2006.

McCroskey, J. C. *An Introduction to Rhetorical Communication*. (7th edn.) Boston: Allyn and Bacon, 1997.

McIntosh, Carey. *The Evolution of English Prose 1700–1800. Style, Politeness, and Print Culture*. Cambridge University Press, 1998.

Mack, Peter. *Renaissance Rhetoric*. New York: Palgrave, 1994.

McKeon, Richard. "Rhetoric in the Middle Ages." *Speculum* 17 (1942): 1–32.

McQuade, Donald. "Composition and Literary Studies." In *Redrawing the Boundaries: The Transformation of English and American Literary Studies*. Eds. Stephen Greenblatt and Giles Gunn. New York: MLA, 1992. 482–519.

Mailloux, Steven. *Disciplinary Identities: Rhetorical Paths of English, Speech, and Composition*. New York: MLA, 2006.

Maimon, Elaine, and Barbara Nodine. "Measuring Syntactic Growth: Errors and Expectations in Sentence-Combining Practice with College Freshmen." *Research in the Teaching of English* 12 (1978): 233–44.

Maimon, Elaine, and Barbara Nodine. "Words Enough and Time: Syntax and Error One Year After." In Daiker, Kerek and Morenberg. 101–8.

Marrou, H. I. *A History of Education in Antiquity*. Trans. George Lamb. London: Sheed and Ward, 1956.

Matsen, Patricia, Philip Rollinson, and Marion Sousa. *Readings from Classical Rhetoric*. Carbondale: Southern Illinois University Press, 1990.

Matsuhashi, Ann. "Pausing and Planning: The Tempo of Written Discourse Production." *Research in the Teaching of English* 15 (1981): 113–34.

Mattingly, Carol. *Well-Tempered Women: Nineteenth-Century Temperance Rhetoric*. Carbondale: Southern Illinois University Press, 1998.

Meade, Richard. "Who Can Learn Grammar?" *English Journal* 50 (February 1961): 87–92.

Mellon, John. *Transformational Sentence Combining*. Research Report No. 10. Urbana, IL: National Council of Teachers of English, 1969.

Michael, Ian. *The Teaching of English: From the Sixteenth Century to 1870*. Cambridge University Press, 1987.

Mihesuah, Devon. "'Let Us Strive Earnestly to Value Education Aright': Cherokee Female Seminarians as Leaders of a Changing Culture." In Hobbs 103–19.

Milic, Louis T. "Theories of Style and Their Implications for the Teaching of Composition." *College Composition and Communication* 16 (1995): 66–9.

Miller, Carolyn. "Genre as Social Action." *Quarterly Journal of Speech* 70 (1984): 151–62.

Miller, Joseph, Michael H. Prosser and Thomas W. Benson, eds. *Readings in Medieval Rhetoric*. Bloomington: Indiana University Press, 1974.

Miller, Richard E. "The Arts of Complicity: Pragmatism and the Culture of Schooling." *College English* 61:1 (September 1998): 10–28.

Miller, Richard E. "Composing English Studies: Towards a Social History of the Discipline." *College Composition and Communication* 45 (May 1994): 164–79.

Miller, Richard E. "A Writing Program's Assets Reconsidered: Getting beyond Impassioned Teachers and Enslaved Workers." *Pedagogy* 1 (2001): 241–9.

Miller, Susan. *Trust in Texts: A Different History of Rhetoric*. Carbondale: Southern Illinois University Press, 2008.

Miller, Thomas. *The Formation of College English: Rhetoric and Belles Lettres in the British Cultural Provinces*. University of Pittsburgh Press, 1997.

Mills, Gordon. *Hamlet's Castle: The Study of Literature As a Social Experience*. Austin: University of Texas Press, 1976.

Mooney, Paul. "Yale Professor at Peking U. Assails Widespread Plagiarism in China." *Chronicle of Higher Education News Blog*. November 21, 2007. http://chronicle.com/news/article/3678/yale-professor-at-peking-u-assails-widespread-plagiarism-in-china.

Moran, Michael G. *Eighteenth-Century British and American Rhetorics and Rhetoricians: Critical Studies and Sources*. Westport, CT: Greenwood, 1994.

Morenberg, Max, Donald Daiker, and Andrew Kerek. "Sentence Combining at the College Level: An Experimental Study." *Research in the Teaching of English* 12 (October 1978): 245–56.

Muckelbauer, John. *The Future of Invention: Rhetoric, Postmodernism, and the Problem of Change*. Albany: State University of New York Press, 2009.

Murphy, James J., ed. *Medieval Eloquence: Studies in the Theory and Practice of Medieval Rhetoric*. Berkeley: University of California Press, 1978.

Murphy, James J. *Medieval Rhetoric: A Select Bibliography*. (2nd edn.) University of Toronto Press, 1989.

Murphy, James J., ed. *Renaissance Eloquence: Studies in the Theory and Practice of Renaissance Rhetoric*. Berkeley: University of California Press, 1983.

Murphy, James J. *Rhetoric in the Middle Ages: A History of Rhetorical Theory from Saint Augustine to the Renaissance*. (First published 1974). Tempe, AZ: Arizona Center for Medieval and Renaissance Studies, 2001.

Murphy, James J., ed. *The Rhetorical Tradition and Modern Writing.* New York: MLA, 1982.

Murphy, James J., ed. *A Short History of Writing Instruction.* (2nd edn.) Davis, California: Hermagoras Press, 2001.

Murphy, James J., ed. *Three Rhetorical Arts.* Berkeley: University of California Press, 1971.

Murphy, James J., and Richard Katula, with Forbes Hill and Donovan Ochs. *A Synoptic History of Classical Rhetoric.* (3rd edn.) Mahwah,NJ: Lawrence Erlbaum, 2003.

Murphy, James J., moderator. "The Politics of Historiography." Octalog. *Rhetoric Review* 7 (Autumn 1988): 5–49.

Murray, Donald. *Learning by Teaching.* Portsmouth, NH: Boynton/Cook, 1982.

Murray, Donald. "Teach Writing as a Process Not Product." *The Leaflet* (November 1972): 11–14. Repr. *Cross-Talk in Comp Theory: A Reader.* Ed. Victor Villanueva. (2nd edn.) Urbana: NCTE, 2003. 3–6.

Murray, Donald. "Write Before Writing." *College Composition and Communication* 29 (December 1978): 375–82.

Murray, Donald. *A Writer Teaches Writing.* (2nd edn.) Boston: Houghton Mifflin, 1985.

Myers, Greg. "From Discovery to Invention: The Writing and Rewriting of Two Patents." *Social Studies of Science* 25 (1995): 57–105.

Nadeau, Ray. "The Progymnasmata of Apthonius in Translation." *Speech Monographs* 19 (1952): 265–85.

Neel, Jasper. *Plato, Derrida, and Writing.* Carbondale: Southern Illinois University Press, 1988.

Nelson, Nancy. "The Reading-Writing Nexus in Discourse Research." In Bazerman *Handbook.* 435–50.

Newkirk, Thomas. *The Performance of Self in Student Writing.* Portsmouth, NH: Heinemann, 1997.

Newlands, Carole, trans. *Peter Ramus's Attack on Cicero: Text and Translation of Ramus's Brutinae Quaestiones.* New York: Routledge, 1995.

Newlands, Carole, and James J. Murphy, ed. *Arguments in Rhetoric Against Quintilian: Translation and Text of Peter Ramus's Rhetoricae Distinctiones in Quintilianum (1549).* Dekalb: Illinois University Press, 1986.

Newsweek Writers. "Why Johnny Can't Write." *Newsweek* 92 (8 December 1975): 58–65.

Nold, Ellen, and S. W. Freeman. "An Analysis of Readers' Responses to Essays." *Research in the Teaching of English* 11 (1977): 164–74.

North, Stephen. *The Making of Knowledge in Composition: Portrait of an Emerging Field.* Portsmouth, NH: Boynton/Cook, 1987.

Nystrand, Martin *et al.* "Rhetoric's Audience and Linguistics Speech Community: Implications for Understanding Writing, Reading, and Text." In Nystrand. *What Writers Know: The Language, Process, and Structure of Written Discourse.* New York: Academic, 1982. 1–28.

Nystrand, Martin. "The Social and Historical Context for Writing Research." In *Handbook of Writing Research.* Eds. Charles MacArthur, Steve Graham, and Jill Fitzgerald. New York: Guilford, 2006.

Nystrand, Martin. "Where Did Composition Studies come From? An Intellectual History." *Written Communication* 10 (1993): 267–333.

Ochs, Donovan. "Aristotle's Concept of Formal Topics." *Speech Monographs* 36 (1969): 419–25.

Ochs, Donovan. "Cicero's *Topica*: A Process View of Invention." In *Explorations in Rhetoric: Studies in Honor of Douglas Ehninger.* Ed. Ray McKerrow. Glenview, IL: Scott, 1983.

O'Hare, Frank. *Sentence Combining: Improving Student Writing without Formal Grammar Instruction.* Research Report No. 15. Urbana, IL: National Council of Teachers of English, 1973.

Ohmann, Richard. *English in America: A Radical View of the Profession.* New York: Oxford University Press, 1976.

Ohmann, Richard. "Professionalizing Politics." In Rosner *et al.* 227–34.

Ohmann, Richard. "Use Definite, Specific, Concrete Language." *College English* 41 (1979): 390–7.

Olmstead, Wendy. *Rhetoric: An Historical Introduction.* Oxford: Blackwell, 2006.

Olson, Gary. "Clichés: Error Recognition or Subjective Reality?" *College English* 44 (February 1982): 190–4.

Ong, Walter J., S.J. "The Writer's Audience Is Always a Fiction." *PMLA* 90 (January 1975): 9–21.

Ong, Walter J., S.J. *Orality and Literacy: The Technologizing of the Word.* (2nd edn.) New York: Routledge, 2002.

Paine, Charles. "Relativism, Racial Pedagogy, and the Ideology of Paralysis." *College English* 51:6 (October 1989): 557–70.

Pajares, Frank, and Gio Valiante. "Influence of Writing Self-Efficacy Beliefs on the Writing Performance of Upper Elementary Students." *Journal of Educational Research* 90 (1997): 353–60.

Parker, William Riley. "Where Do English Departments Come From?" *College English* 28 (1967): 339–51.

Payne, Lucille Vaughan. *The Lively Art of Writing.* New York: Follett, 1965.

Perelman, Chaim and L. Olbrechts-Tyteca. *The New Rhetoric: A Treatise on Argumentation*. University of Notre Dame Press, 1969.

Perl, Sondra. "The Composing Processes of Unskilled College Writers." *Research in the Teaching of English* 13 (December 1978): 317–36.

Phelps, Louise Weatherbee. *Composition as a Human Science: Contributions to the Self-Understanding of a Discipline*. Oxford University Press, 1991.

Pianko, Sharon. "A Description of the Composing Processes of College Freshman Writers." *Research in the Teaching of English* 13 (February 1979): 5–22.

Plato. *Gorgias*. Trans. W. R. M. Lamb. Loeb Classical Library. London: Heinemann, 1925.

Plato. *Phaedrus and Letters VII and VIII*. Trans. Walter Hamilton. Repr. New York: Penguin, 1981.

Poster, Carol. "Aristotle's Rhetoric Against Rhetoric: Unitarian Reading and Esoteric Hermeneutics." *American Journal of Philology* 118 (Summer 1997): 219–49.

Poulakos, John. *Sophistical Rhetoric in Classical Greece*. Columbia: University of South Carolina Press, 1995.

Pressley, Michael, Lindsay Mohan, Lauren Fingeret, Kelly Reffit, and Lisa Raphael-Bogaert. "Writing Instruction in Engaging and Effective Elementary Settings." In Graham *et al.* 13–27.

Price, Margaret. "Beyond 'Gotcha!': Situating Plagiarism in Policy and Pedagogy." *College Composition and Communication* 51 (September 2002): 88–115.

Quintilian. *Institutes. The Institutio Oratoria of Quintilian*. Trans. H. E. Butler. 4 vols. The Loeb Classical Library. Cambridge, MA: Harvard University Press, 1920–22.

Rabil, Albert, Jr., ed. *Renaissance Humanism: Foundations, Forms, and Legacy*. 3 vols. Philadelphia: University of Pennsylvania Press, 1988.

Ramus, Peter. *Arguments in Rhetoric Against Quintilian* [1549]. Trans. Carole Newlands and James J. Murphy. DeKalb: University of Northern Illinois Press, 1983.

Rebhorn, Wayne. "Baldesar Castiglione, Thomas Wilson, and the Courtly Body of Renaissance Rhetoric." *Rhetorica* 11 (1993): 241–73.

Ricks, Vickie. "'In an Atmosphere of Peril': College Women and Their Writing." In Hobbs 59–83.

Rijlaarsdam, Gert, and Huub van den Bergh. "Writing Process Theory: A Functional Dynamic Approach." In MacArthur *et al.* 41–53.

Riley, Kathryn, **and** Frank Parker. *English Grammar: Prescriptive, Descriptive, Generative, Performance*. New York: Pearson, 1998.

Ritchie, Joy, and Kathleen Boardman. "Feminism in Composition: Inclusion, Metonymy, and Disruption." *College Composition and Communication* 50 (1999): 585–606.

Roberts, Rhys. *Greek Rhetoric and Literary Criticism.* New York: Longmans, 1928.

Roberts, Tim S. *Student Plagiarism in an Online World: Problems and Solutions.* Hershey, NY: Idea Group, 2007.

Rohman, Gordon, and Albert Wlecke. "Pre-writing: The Stage of Discovery in the Writing Process." *College Composition and Communication* 16 (1965): 106–12.

Rollinson, Philip, and Richard Geckle. *A Guide to Classical Rhetoric.* Signal Mountain, TN: Summertown, 1998.

Rorty, Richard. *Philosophy and the Mirror of Nature.* Princeton University Press, 1979.

Rose, Mike. *Writer's Block: The Cognitive Dimension.* Carbondale: Southern Illinois University Press, 1983.

Rosner, Mary, Beth Boehm, and Debra Journet. *History, Reflection, and Narrative: The Professionalization of Composition, 1963–1983.* Stamford, CT: Ablex, 1999.

Rosten, Leo. *The Many Worlds of Leo Rosten.* New York: Harper, 1964.

Royster, Jackie Jones, and J. C. Williams. "History in the Spaces Left: African American Presence and Narratives of Composition Studies." *College Composition and Communication* 50 (1999): 563–84.

Rucker, Darnell. "Plato and the Poets." *The Journal of Aesthetics and Art Criticism* 25 (Winter 1966): 167–70.

Russell, David. "Historical Studies of Composition." In Smagorinsky. 243–75.

Russell, David. *Writing in the Academic Disciplines 1870–1990.* (2nd edn.) Carbondale: Southern Illinois University Press, 2002.

Salvatori, Mariolina. *Pedagogy 1819–1929: Disturbing History.* University of Pittsburgh Press, 1996.

Sánchez, Raúl. *The Function of Theory in Composition Studies.* Albany: State University of New York Press, 2005.

Schiappa, Edward. *Landmark Essays on Classical Greek Rhetoric.* Davis, CA: Hermagoras, 1994.

Schiappa, Edward. *Protagoras and Logos: A Study of Greek Philosophy and Rhetoric.* Columbia: University of South Carolina Press, 2003.

Schilb, John. *Writing Theory and Critical Theory.* New York: MLA, 1994.

Schultz, Lucille M. *The Young Composers: Composition's Beginnings in Nineteenth-Century Schools.* Carbondale: Southern Illinois University Press, 1999.

Schwegler, Robert. *Patterns of Exposition*. New York: Longman, 2003.

Scott, Fred Newton, with George Carpenter and Franklin Baker. *The Teaching of English in the Elementary and Secondary Schools*. New York: Longmans, Green, and Co., 1908.

Scott, William. *Lessons in Elocution*. London: Longman, 1779.

Shanahan, Timothy. "Nature of the Reading-Writing Relation: An Exploratory Multivariate Analysis." *Journal of Educational Psychology* 76 (1984): 466–77.

Shanahan, Timothy, and R. G. Lomax. "An Analysis and Comparison of Theoretical Models of the Reading-Writing Relationship." *Journal of Educational Psychology* 78 (1986): 116–23.

Shaughnessy, Mina. *Errors and Expectations: A Guide for the Teacher of Basic Writing*. New York: Oxford University Press, 1977.

Sheridan, Thomas. *British Education*. London: Strahan, 1756.

Sheridan, Thomas. *Lectures on Elocution*. London: Strahan, 1762.

Shor, Ira. *Freire for the Classroom: A Sourcebook for Liberatory Teaching*. Portsmouth, NH: Boynton/Cook, 1987.

Sloane, Thomas. *Donne, Milton, and the End of Humanist Rhetoric*. Berkeley: University of California Press, 1985.

Sloane, Thomas. *On the Contrary: The Protocol of Traditional Rhetoric*. Washington, DC: Catholic University of America Press, 1997.

Sloane, Thomas, ed. *Encyclopedia of Rhetoric*. Oxford University Press, 2001.

Smagorinsky, Peter, ed. *Research on Composition: Multiple Perspectives on Two Decades of Change*. New York: Teachers College, 2006.

Smith, Adam. *Lectures on Rhetoric and Belles Lettres*. Ed. J. C. Bryce. Indianapolis: Liberty Fund, 1985.

Smith, Michael, George Hillocks, and Julie Cheville. "'I Guess I'd Better Watch My English': Grammars and the Teaching of Language Arts." In *Handbook of Writing Research*. Eds. Charles MacArthur, Steve Graham, and Jill Fitzgerald, New York: Guilford, 2006. 263–74.

Smith, Morton. *The Ancient Greeks*. Ithaca: Cornell University Press, 1960.

Smith, Morton, and Warren E. Combs. "The Effects of Overt and Covert Cues on Written Syntax." *Research in the Teaching of English* 14 (1980): 19–38.

Smith, William. *Dictionary of Greek and Roman Biography and Mythology*. Vol. I. Boston: Little, Brown, 1867.

Smitherman, Geneva. *Talkin and Testifyin: The Language of Black America*. Detroit: Wayne State University Press, 1986.

Sommers, Nancy. "Revision Strategies of Student Writers and Adult Experienced Writers." *College Composition and Communication* 31 (1981): 378–88.

Spanos, Margaret. "Thinking about Writing: E. D. Hirsch's *Philosophy of Composition*." *boundary 2* 8:2 (Winter 1980): 349–61.

Sprague, Rosamond Kent. *The Older Sophists: A Complete Translation by Several Hands ...* Columbia: University of South Carolina Press, 1972.

Sprat, Thomas. *History of the Royal Society*. Eds. Jackson Cope and Harold Jones. St. Louis, MO: Washington University Studies, 1958.

Stoehr, Taylor. "Tone and Voice." *College English* 30 (1968): 150–61.

Strong, William. *Sentence-Combining: A Composing Book*. New York: Random, 1973.

Strunk, William, and E. B. White. *Elements of Style*. (4th edn.) New York: Longman, 1999.

Stump, Eleonore, trans., ed., with notes and essays on the text. *Boethius's "De topicis differentiis."* Ithaca: Cornell University Press, 1978.

Stump, Eleonore, trans., with notes and an introduction. *Boethius's "In Ciceronis Topica."* Ithaca: Cornell University Press, 1988.

Sutherland, Christine Mason and Rebecca Sutcliffe, eds. *The Changing Tradition: Women in the History of Rhetoric*. University of Calgary Press, 1999.

Swift, Jonathan. *Proposal for Correcting ... the English Tongue*. London: Tooke, 1712.

Tate, Gary, Amy Rupiper, and Kurt Schick. *A Guide to Composition Pedagogies*. New York: Oxford University Press, 2001.

Tate, Gary, Edward P. J. Corbett, and Nancy Myers. *The Writing Teacher's Sourcebook*. (4th edn.) Oxford University Press, 1999.

Thomas, Joseph, Frederick Manchester and Franklin Scott. *Composition for College Students*. New York: Macmillan, 1925.

Thomas of Salisbury. *Summa de arte praedicandi* ("The Ultimate Guide to the Art of Preaching"). Published as Thomas de Chobham. Ed. F. Morenzoni, *Corpus Christianorum, continuatio medievalis* 82. Turnhout: Brepols, 1988.

Thornburg, Thomas. *Swift and the Ciceronian Tradition*. Muncie: Ball State University, 1980.

Tobin, Lad. "Process Pedagogy." In *A Guide to Composition Pedagogies*. Eds. Gary Tate, Amy Rupiper, and Kurt Schick. New York: Oxford University Press, 2001. 1–18.

Tompkins, Jane. *A Life in School: What the Teacher Learned*. New York: Basic, 1997.

Town, K. "The Process Approach: Early Versions in the *English Journal*, 1912–1960." Unpublished doctoral dissertation, Ohio State University, 1988.

Trimble, John. *Writing with Style.* (2nd edn.) Upper Saddle River, NJ: Prentice-Hall, 2000.

Ulman, H. Lewis. *Things, Thoughts, Words, and Actions: The Problem of Language in Late Eighteenth-Century British Rhetorical Theory.* Carbondale: Southern Illinois University Press, 1994.

Vickers, Brian. *Classical Rhetoric in English Poetry.* London: Macmillan, 1970.

Vickers, Brian. *In Defence of Rhetoric.* Oxford: Clarendon Press, 1988.

Vickers, Brian., ed. *Rhetoric Revalued: Papers from the International Society for the History of Rhetoric.* Binghamton, NY: Center for Medieval & Early Renaissance Studies, 1982.

Wagner, David L. *The Seven Liberal Arts in the Middle Ages.* Bloomington: Indiana University Press, 1983.

Wallechinsky, David. *The New Book of Lists: The Original Compendium of Curious Information.* Edinburgh: Canongate, 2005.

Ward, John O. *Ciceronian Rhetoric in Treatise, Scholion, and Commentary.* Turnhout, Belgium: Brepols, 1995.

Wardy, Robert. *The Birth of Rhetoric: Gorgias, Plato, and Their Successors.* London: Routledge, 1996.

Warnick, Barbara. *The Sixth Canon: Belletristic Rhetorical Theory and Its French Antecedents.* Columbia: University of South Carolina Press, 1993.

Warriner, John. *English Grammar and Composition.* New York: Harcourt, 1963.

Weathers, Winston. "Teaching Style: A Possible Anatomy." *College Composition and Communication* 21 (1970): 144–9.

Weathers, Winston. *An Alternate Style: Options in Composition.* Portsmouth, NH: Boynton/Cook, 1980.

Weidner, Heidemarie. "Silks, Congress Gaiters, and Rhetoric: A Butler University Graduate of 1860 Tells Her Story." In Hobbs 248–63.

Weiss, Robert. "Imitation Theory and Teacher Writing: An Annotated Bibliography." *Rhetoric Society Quarterly* 11:4 (Autumn 1981): 243–52.

Welch, Olga, and Carolyn Hodges. *Standing Outside on the Inside: Black Adolescents and the Construction of Academic Identity.* Albany: State University of New York Press, 1997.

Wendell, Barrett. *English Composition.* New York: Scribner's, 1891.

Wertheimer, Molly Meijer. *Listening to Their Voices: The Rhetorical Activities of Historical Women.* Columbia: University of South Carolina Press, 1997.

Whately, Richard. *Elements of Rhetoric*. London, 1828. Facsimile reproduction, intro. Charlotte Downey and Howard Coughlin. Delmar, NY: Scholars' Facsimiles, 1991.

Williams, James D. *Preparing to Teach Writing: Research, Theory, and Practice.* Mahwah, NJ: Erlbaum, 1998.

Williams, Joseph. *Style: Ten Lessons in Clarity and Grace.* (7th edn.) New York: Longman, 2002.

Wilson, Thomas. *The Arte of Rhetorique* [1560]. Ed. Peter E. Medine. University Park: Penn State University Press, 1994.

Winterowd, Ross. *Rhetoric: A Synthesis*. New York: Holt, 1968.

Winterowd, Ross. *The Contemporary Writer: A Practical Rhetoric.* New York: Harcourt, 1975.

Witherspoon, John. *The Selected Writings of John Witherspoon.* Ed. Thomas Miller. Carbondale: Southern Illinois University Press, 1990.

Wollstonecraft, Mary. *A Vindication of the Rights of Woman with Strictures on Moral and Political Subjects.* London: Joseph Johnson, 1792.

Woods, Marjorie Curry, trans. *An Early Commentary on the Poetria nova of Geoffrey of Vinsauf.* New York: Garland, 1985.

Wooten, Cecil, ed. *Hermogenes' On Types of Style.* Chapel Hill: University of North Carolina Press, 1987.

Worsham, Lynn, Sidney Dobrin, and Gary Olson. *The Kinneavy Papers: Theory and the Study of Discourse.* Albany: State University of New York Press, 2000.

Wright, Elizabethada and S. Michael Halloran. "From Rhetoric to Composition: The Teaching of Writing in America to 1900." In *A Short History of Writing Instruction.* (2nd edn.) Ed. James J. Murphy. Mahwah, NJ: Lawrence Erlbaum Associates, Hermagoras Press, 2001. 213–46.

Yang, Charles. *The Infinite Gift: How Children Learn and Unlearn All the Languages of the World.* New York: Scribner, 2006.

Young, Richard, and Yameng Liu, eds. *Landmark Essays on Rhetorical Invention in Writing.* New York: Routledge, 1995.

Young, Richard, and Yameng Liu, Alton Becker, and Kenneth Pike. *Rhetoric: Discovery and Change.* New York: Harcourt, 1970.

Zaluda, Scott. "Lost Voices of the Harlem Renaissance: Writing Assigned at Howard University, 1919–31." *College Composition and Communication* 50 (1998): 232–57.

Zinsser, William. *On Writing Well.* 25th Anniversary Edn. New York: Collins, 2001.

Index

CPSIA information can be obtained
at www.ICGtesting.com
Printed in the USA
LVHW041029130919
630975LV00002B/63